The Goodkin Guide to Winning in Real Estate

The Goodkin Guide to Winning in Real Estate

SANFORD R. GOODKIN

DAVID McKAY COMPANY, Inc.
NEW YORK

Library of Congress Cataloging in Publication Data

Goodkin, Sanford R
The Goodkin guide to winning in real estate.

1. Real estate investment. 2. Real estate investment—United States. I. Title. II. Title: Guide to winning in real estate.
HD1375.G65 332.6′324′0973 76-57920
ISBN 0-679-50611-X

10 9 8 7 6 5 4 3 2 1

MANUFACTURED IN THE UNITED STATES OF AMERICA

Design by Bob Antler

This book is dedicated to the memory of my father, Robert R. Goodkin, who taught me common sense, a most uncommonly used thinking tool. He gave me my name and my motivation. I share any success with this good kin.

CONTENTS

INTRODUCTION ix

Part One: **HOMEWORK**

1. Why Invest in Real Estate? 3
2. What Kind of Investor Are You? 16
3. Trends 30
4. Location, Timing, Use 49

Part Two: **BEFORE YOU LEAP**

5. Advisors and Dealers 65
6. Joint Ventures and Syndicates 79
7. Financing Your Deal 92
8. Investment Options 117
9. Deals 127
10. Risks 149

Part Three: LOSERS AND WINNERS

11. Some Losers 179
12. Eleven Probable Winners 196
13. Two Probable Long-Term Winners 218
14. A Third Long-Term Winner 233
15. Ten Key Rules to Real-Estate Investing 253

APPENDIXES

Appendix A: Marketing Development Check List 263
Appendix B: Definitions of Market Segments 266
Appendix C: Project Analysis 269
Appendix D: Format of Covering Letter to Lenders 271
Appendix E: Land Purchase and Development Check List 273
Appendix F: Check List for Buying an Office Building 279
Appendix G: Check List for Buying an Apartment Building 285
Appendix H: Glossary of Real-Estate Terms and Phrases 290

INDEX 332

INTRODUCTION

"Have I got a deal for you!"

How many times have we heard comedians use that line? And they get a laugh every time. We all know there are suckers born every minute—even while our birth rate decreases. And we also know that one of life's basic struggles is to avoid being that sucker.

My profession, as Chairman of the Sanford R. Goodkin Research Corporation, is to protect large real-estate investors from being conned. Usually, they get conned by themselves: They hear about a great real-estate deal, and emotions cloud their brains, blot out their eyesight, numb their vital senses, cancel all educational achievements, and make monkeys out of these men—wasting years of evolution.

I am writing this book for them, and for you—the individual investor. This book is meant to keep you out of trouble. I will also make you aware of the vast opportunities—and risks—in the rapidly changing world of real estate.

One thing that I have learned: There is money to be made in real-estate investing. Some of that money will be made by sharpies victimizing amateurs with that old come on, "Have I got a deal for you!"

Nothing inhibits making money in real estate more than advice given to amateurs who think they can "make a killing" in a land or property deal. The killing is soon of their own spirit, as the realities of the marketplace overcome their emotions.

Real estate is a tough place for amateurs. But it can be a fun place, a creative place. Deals are being made every day, even during hard times. (Perhaps that's the best time to make deals.) There are great days coming for people who can see the opportunities in land, in commercial and industrial growth. And each growth statistic is a vitamin for real-estate investment and use.

Land is the one resource that underlies everything—figuratively and literally. It is where we build the places in which we work, live, shop, and play. That gives it power. But it *is* changing. Its uses, design, and productivity are shifting, but not its users. The users are still you and me—the people who buy land, build on it, make money from it, or simply walk on it contemplating their lives and futures.

Real estate is buying land, and putting it to its best use. Real estate is taking old buildings and making condominiums out of them or new offices. Or, real estate is putting together a shopping center, apartment complex, housing project, that bring together the basic principles of this great game: timing, use, location.

Real estate is, as you will learn in this book, many things to many people. It is a tax shelter and an inflation hedge. It will fluctuate, but it will always be in demand—and give you profits—when you follow the advice in this book, and use caution. You won't have to determine whether or not real estate will boom—but *when.* Timing is of the essence. You'll also learn what kind of real estate best suits you and your pocketbook, and *where* it may be found and placed. You'll learn the importance of timing, how to select advisors, get loans, know a good deal (and a bad one), and what to look for in your own area.

What this all comes down to is you. *You* will learn how to be responsible for the success or failure of your real-estate investments. You will learn to understand your own motivations. You must select the real-estate opportunities that fit your interests and means—and watch them like a hawk.

There are great opportunities in real estate. New fortunes will be created from these opportunities. More importantly, many smaller fortunes will be made because the investor understood what he was doing (and why), because he sought advice, knew his marketplace, and carefully watched his investment. He took nothing for granted.

This book will help you develop a knowledge of what real estate is all about. It will help you develop a real-estate strategy, to invest in real estate that is financially and emotionally rewarding to you. If you're already a real-estate investor, this book will help you to expand your knowledge and to grow.

You will find, looking back in a few years, that more important than the land and the properties were the people who helped (and hurt) you. This book will steer you toward the helpers, and away from the others with the quick and easy windfalls and the great deals.

Have I got a deal for you? No. There are rules and cautions in this book, a glossary of terms, helpful charts and check lists. There is also advice: basically, that there is no sure way to make a lot of money *fast* in real estate, but the track is there and the opportunities golden. You're going to deal for yourself and discover the excitement and self-respect of handling real estate. Don't expect miracles or instant riches, but do seek the challenging encounter of making money in creative ways.

Maybe that's the most basic thing I've learned in this

business: You can make money. Winning at real estate is just a matter of knowing how. This book should guide you to that goal.

Sanford R. Goodkin
Del Mar, California

PART ONE
HOMEWORK

1

WHY INVEST IN REAL ESTATE?

You've got some money. It's burning holes in every pocket.

Whether it came from a windfall, an inheritance, or your blazing wizardry in business, you've also got a problem. What should you do with your money? Inflation is stealing the value of your dollars even as you read this book. As you turn the pages, you might as well be tossing dollar bills out the window.

Inflation means that the purchasing power of your money is decreasing. A given amount of money—your dollar—buys less and less. The crisis of the early 1970s was the level of inflation. Double-figure inflation played havoc with the economy. Financial institutions, in their competition for funds to compensate for decreased future purchasing power, raised interest rates to astronomical levels.

What should you do with your money? You can sock it away in a savings account at your local bank (which is slightly better than stuffing it into your mattress). You can roll dice and gamble, or buy stocks and bonds (and nervously follow the market's vagaries every day). Or, you can invest in real estate.

Since the beginning of time, precious gems, metals, and real estate have been prized as things of value. They are all tangible and have a beauty that others admire. There are deep psychological reasons why people value real estate above gold, diamonds, or silver. Real estate has a type of permanency that no other possession has. It endures, it offers its owner a limited degree of immortality. Land—the earth—is also the source of all things man possesses and his final resting place.

Real estate also offers more extensive use than other stores of value. Gold, silver, and diamonds all have limited industrial and aesthetic uses. But real estate contains both intrinsic value, and the opportunity for man's creativity: It can be developed. The quantity of real estate suited for development—naturally and by public policy—is becoming more limited. And the use of that limited real estate is becoming more intensive through man's building vertical communities. This limitation and intensification make real estate increase in value, and that value should rise at a rate faster than inflation.

What, then, are your choices to beat inflation? There are exotic investments like coins, art, and precious metals; tax shelters like cattle, oil, and gas, and mining ventures; corporate stocks and bonds; U.S. Government securities; certificates of deposit, commercial paper, and other monetary securities; and municipal bonds. But some of these, heated by inflation, may take years to stabilize. Moreover, basic investor confidence required for bullishness in the stock market cannot be expected until the end of the decade. Disenchanted with the vicissitudes of the market, many investors have turned to real estate as a solid resting place for their funds in these uncertain times.

Corporate bonds and municipal securities appear to some as good investments because they offer long-term yields. But these yields are vulnerable to inflation. If inflation and interest rates are controlled, corporate bonds and municipal securities will increase somewhat in value. Real estate, however, will increase more because "reasonable rate" money will facilitate the marketing of developed real estate, and the development of land.

U.S. Government and monetary securities have also caught the fancy of the investing public because of their current high yields. But those yields are subject to the same loss of purchasing power due to inflation. Their short-term nature, moreover, will prevent them from enjoying the increase in price which will occur in both long-term securities and real estate. Further, the rate of increase in developable land should rise faster than inflation. For these reasons, real estate may well be an excellent buy for you.

What Are You Looking For?

So you've got some money. Whether you're a surgeon, a successful executive, or the guy who brought Aunt Berthie her Alice B. Toklas brownies every day before she died (remembering you generously in her will), you've decided real estate is the place to put your dollars. I'm glad you made that choice. You'll not only beat inflation, but you'll also have some fun doing it.

Investing in real estate raises two initial questions: What do you want from it and what will it actually give you?

First of all, you must understand your own motivations. Then you can decide which real-estate area is best for you, and what you are seeking. Do you want to make money? Have an ego trip? To be a manager of apartments or condominiums? To retire on income? To gamble with money you can afford to lose?

Before getting into real-estate investments, you should do a little thinking about yourself. Here is how I rate your chances:

- If you upset easily, worry a great deal, have no self-confidence—please keep your money in the bank.
- If you gamble, are up and down, must be able to put your hands on cash fast—stay at the race track.

On the other hand:

• If you like taking chances, can stand some aggravation, get along with people—real estate can be good for you.

• If you like to risk some money, share that risk, and don't expect to get rich overnight—real estate can be fun for you.

• If you are financially creative, like to wheel and deal, can stand the heat in the kitchen, and tolerate stomach pains—get into real estate! You will make money, lose it, and make more.

Real estate appeals to many different people. It can be tumultuous or quiet, depending on who you are and what you want out of it. This is what gives it excitement and uniqueness. Real estate is definitely not plain vanilla.

A real-estate investor does not pick his action, and then sit back quietly and count his money. He must watch the legalities, the environmental reports, the zoning, the strength of the market, the financial obligations. He must follow closely his partners and fellow investors, the shifting markets, the population movements, building and buying trends. He cannot let someone else take the blame, and he alone must accept the responsibility.

Investing in real estate presents two basic options: investing in land or investing in improved real estate.

Land. This is literally the ground you walk on. Hopefully, it is also in a good location in a growing neighborhood. But *it* won't work for you. You must work for *it.* It has to be carried. It may appreciate over a long term, or quite suddenly. You have to watch the zoning, and, perhaps, get it changed. Unless it is agricultural land, it sits there waiting to be used. When it goes into use, it becomes improved real estate.

Improved Real Estate. You can either buy improved real estate, or develop it upon land you've purchased or leased.

Basically, improved real estate means simply that a building is placed upon land. Building is quite different from holding land. A smartly purchased building, well located, can pay off itself *plus* give you profits, or even a tax shelter.

While land has the glamour, improved real estate has the glitter—of gold.

Increasing Real-Estate Demand

The basic economics of our system favor the investor in real estate. Real estate, despite the stagnation of the seventies, remains a sound investment. Why? Largely because there is a limited supply and increasing demand. Traditional economics—of which we should be wary—teaches that limited supply and increasing demand mean higher prices.

Of course, one of the first things you learn in economics is that price is determined by supply and demand. Demand may be a desire for more real-estate products (homes, shopping centers, office buildings) or different real-estate products (more expensive homes or offices), or land. There is a big difference between potential demand (or the desire to buy) and effective demand (or the ability to buy).

That difference is the ability on the part of the buyer to pay for or finance what he would like to buy. As government and business continue to come up with financing techniques to permit buyers to purchase the real-estate products they want, and buyers are confident enough to commit themselves to long-term real-estate obligations, the basic economic laws of the marketplace will pertain. And the real-estate investor will benefit. Demand will continue to increase the value of the limited supply of real estate.

There are clear triggers for increased demand for products in the real-estate field: more households, changes in the ways people earn a living, higher incomes, new products, improved land use, job changes, age preferences, a desire to live in a comfortable climate, and the elimination of substandard housing. Demand feeds on demand, and broadens the opportunities for investment.

First, as a potential investor, you must understand what is happening to people across the United States (there will be much more on this in Chapter Three). Most of the people live in only eight of the fifty states in the U.S.: California, Ohio, Massachusetts, New York, New Jersey, Illinois, Michigan, and Pennsylvania. But that condition is changing. Better than one quarter of the American population now lives in a state different from their place of birth. One in five Americans move every year, yet almost two out of every three do not cross county lines. Still, states like California, Florida, Arizona, and Texas attract out-of-staters at a fast pace.

People are getting married later, divorcing more. New family units are forming quickly, breaking up, re-forming. Women's liberation has brought the females out of the kitchen and into the working places. They earn their own money and upgrade their standard of living. In increasing numbers, married women now work outside the home, and the family, as a result, has more income and can afford better housing. This has led to smaller families, which has created a real-estate paradox: How can the number of housing units increase while the population remains constant, or decreases?

The answer is an increase in households, or headships as the statisticians call them. Every time a family becomes divorced, or newlyweds move out of the family nest, the demand for housing is increased. The key to housing demand, therefore, is the rate of family formations.

This rate, I believe, will generally increase as our population continues to expand. The increasing divorce rate will also contribute to this growing need for housing. Fully 85 percent of young people have formed their own households after marriage. Youngsters between twenty-two and twenty-four move every other year.

Shopping development is tied directly to housing development. People tend to shop near their homes. To convince the supermarkets, drugstores and department stores to locate in a proposed shopping center, the investor and developer must show them the significant buying power—people and their incomes—within the trading area. Homes mean shoppers, and shoppers mean income to these stores.

Changing economic patterns have also created demand for industrial and office facilities. This demand was, in the mid-1970s, more variable and riskier than housing, shopping developments, or land. The best locations for industry had been changing for the two previous decades from the center of the city, where rail terminals and ports were located, to the outskirts of the city, near major highways. Industrial development in the outer city grew because space could not be found in the inner city; rising taxes, crime, poor transportation, and aging facilities also helped push industry outward.

People like to live near their jobs. Not surprisingly, industrial development quickly followed the flight from the inner city to suburban housing. Now, office complexes are sprouting among the trees in suburbia. As our cities topple into deeper debt—and seek remedies by heavily taxing whatever businesses and industry remain—and as energy conservation (and high gasoline prices) takes hold, we will see a continuing industrial and office development in the suburbs, where population is concentrated.

As I will discuss in detail in Part III, it is the home that causes much of this development shift. And more than simply providing beauty or shelter, the home is a status symbol. The really wealthy often spend massive sums in building their personal monument. All families know that others will judge their socioeconomic status by their address. The location of your home determines the way you live, who you know, and the quality of the education your children receive. Location also affects the type and quality of commercial, governmental, and recreational services available to the whole family; it even determines what advertisements (and products) you see and buy.

A combination of desirable location and adequate housing structures creates housing demand. High-rise apartments near cultural and work facilities, new housing developments with special features like pools or Jacuzzi whirlpool baths, bay-front homes with views, all influence the new buyer. Shopping for new housing is a Sunday recreation for some families. When they see something new, better, or different that they want and can afford, they usually buy it. Apartment dwellers are convinced to buy when they see tennis courts or new green space in planned communities, and the economic advantages of owning rather than renting are made clear.

The real-estate business is on the brink of a revolution in land use and building which will stimulate new demand. Mixed-use developments, where people can walk to work, shopping, schools and play, will spring up all over the urban landscape. Modular units whose roofs serve as the patios of the homes above will create attractive gardens in the air. Plastics and other synthetic materials will create practically maintenance-free buildings.

Those who work in center city will want the opportunity to live, shop, go to school, and play near their work. Buildings will become towns, like the Hancock Building in Chicago that contains offices, commercial shops, and residential units. Gerald Hines is a developer with vision: His high-rise "cities within cities" which include the magnificent Galleria complex in Houston, plus numerous other multi-use "vertical villages," will be duplicated in many other areas. The desire of people for a pedestrian, human-scale development, which conserves energy and space, will lead to continued rebuilding of the center city. It will also create opportunities for you.

The outer city, as well, will profit from the advantages of elevator travel in vertical space over horizontal automobile travel. Shopping centers are likely to be redeveloped as complete urban centers for the communities they serve. Residential units may ring them, and the present buildings may be converted into a honeycomb of shopping, office, residential, school, and public facilities with attractive parks and plazas at different levels.

As populations change and expand, housing demands rise and shifts take place in people's concepts of how they live, work, and play, the demand for real estate will also shift and increase. Of course, the supply of land is limited to that which is serviced by roads, sewers, water, and other municipal services. Schools, fire, and police departments play a major role in the value of the land. Before you buy, therefore, be alert and careful.

Unless you can reach your property by car, it is not developable and its use is limited to agricultural or recreational activities. Most communities require (by ordinance) that before you build, your property must be serviced by sewer, water, electrical, and other utility systems.

In some areas, beginning in Puerto Rico in 1962, communities have made approval of building plans contingent upon developers arranging with the local government to provide municipal services for the residents of their projects, including setting land aside to house community facilities. In San Diego, park and school fees must be paid on all new units and developers in certain critical areas have been required to furnish temporary school facilities.

These are some of the "risks" involved in real-estate investing. To avoid them, you must watch the real-estate market carefully and continuously. I will discuss these risks, trends, and markets in detail later. But for now, it is vital, as a first step, that you understand the broad parameters of the real-estate business, and decide for yourself what kind of investor you want to be.

Why Invest in Real Estate?

If you hold cash for investment, you have several real-estate choices before you. The rapid growth era of the 1950s and 1960s is gone, perhaps never to return in our lifetimes. Serious investors must compare real estate with the other most common forms of investment: stocks and bonds. The result of any comparison will show once again that carefully selected income properties, primarily because of the tax advantages in real estate, offer the best bet, even in high-interest periods.

There are three basic ways to invest your money. To illustrate how they work, let's assume that you are an investor in the 50 percent tax bracket and that you have $30,000 in cash to place for the most advantageous return.

Chart 1–1 shows your return, if the money is invested purely for income. The after-tax return to you is just 5 percent.

CHART 1–1 Investing for Income

Dividends on stock Interest on savings Interest on mortgages Land rents	on $30,000 investment	$3,000
Taxes at ordinary income rate of 50%		1,500
Cash flow after taxes		$1,500
Net return on $30,000	5%	

Chart 1–2 illustrates your return if you are able to trade stocks (or possibly real estate) for an annual 10 percent gain. Here, the lower capital-gains tax means an annual after-tax return of 7.5 percent.

CHART 1–2 Investing for Capital Gains

Annual profit on sale of stocks or real estate		$3,000
Taxes at capital gains rate of 25%		750
Cash flow after taxes		$2,250
Net return on $30,000	7.5%	

Chart 1–3 shows the return from an investment in income property. The after-tax cash flow of $3,750 represents a 12.5 percent return on your $30,000, and this yield is achieved without the benefits of leverage. In effect, you are borrowing

$90,000 at 10 percent per year ($9,000) and investing in property which yields exactly the same amount. Chart 1–4 shows the free and clear return. The entire increase in after-tax annual income comes from tax saving.

The tax saving is reached by figuring the difference between the depreciation deduction and the nondeductible mortgage amortization ($5,400 minus $900). The difference of $4,500 not only shelters the entire $3,000 cash flow from tax but also generates an additional tax loss of $1,500 which, when applied to your other income, creates a tax savings of $750.

CHART 1–3 Investing in Income Real Estate

Total investment ($90,000 building, $30,000 land)			$120,000
Gross rental income			18,000
Less:			
Operating expenses		$ 6,000	
Debt service on $90,000 mortgage— 25 yrs. 9% (10.08 constant)		9,000	15,000
Cash flow			$ 3,000
Tax consequence:			
Rent		$18,000	
Expense	$6,000		
Interest (1st yr.)	8,100		
Depr. 25 yrs. 150% (6% 1st yr.)	5,400	19,500	
Tax loss to shelter other income		$ 1,500	
Add: Tax savings @ 50% rate			$ 750
Cash flow after taxes			$ 3,750
Net return on $30,000	12.5%		

Three other factors make this type of real estate advantageous. First, the equity build-up from annual mortgage amortization will be realized in cash, if the property, upon resale, is sold for at least its cost of $120,000. Second, income property with short-term leases provides its own protection against continued inflation. Third, gradually increasing cash flow is reflected in gradual capital appreciation over the years.

CHART 1–4 Free and Clear Return

Rent		$ 18,000
Operating expenses		6,000
Net operating income		$ 12,000
Total investment		$120,000
Free and clear return	10%	

Where are such properties found? They exist in every solid neighborhood, in the inner city and the outer suburbs. During periods of financial pressure, such properties can be purchased at bargain prices. All you have to do is find the property, know it is in a good location, learn how it might be used—and develop it. The coming chapters will help you in this process.

Why invest in real estate?

• History teaches us that whether you prefer land or improved real estate, your investment will appreciate in value. Generally, the value of real property is constantly increasing due to market growth, land scarcity, and inflation itself.

• There is also the attraction of the accrual and expansion of equity investment through retirement of encumbered debt and increase of property value.

• Improved real estate offers income-producing attractions, a continuing annuity of cash flow, and potential profits.

• Real estate offers leverage of equity investment—the ability to purchase real property at a price less than current market value. There is also the attraction of obtaining more value for equity investment and a generally better return on investment than other opportunities, due to equity yield.

• There are tax shelter benefits, depreciation benefits, and other tax advantages.

• Finally—and don't underestimate it—real estate offers the aesthetic satisfaction of having a tangible investment you can walk around, admire, open and close doors in, and actually feel, both in your hands and your senses.

Convinced? Good! Now let's take a look at what kind of investor you want to be (and become), what investments might be best for you, and where you can find them.

2

WHAT KIND OF INVESTOR ARE YOU?

Patience is virtuous on the wine rack—and in the real-estate business.

Like good wines, you should clearly understand where you came from, who you are, and where you're going. Real-estate investment means putting your money and/or credit into a piece of land or a building. In the past, many of these investments were "blind," that is, the investors did not really know whether the deal would make money or not. After all, what was there to know? Everyone we spoke to "made money" in real estate. This friend bought a parcel of land, got it rezoned, and "made a killing." That friend built an apartment and got cash out of it every month, plus the building *appreciated*!

No friend tells you about the money he *lost*. No friend shares the agony of not knowing anything about a deal until it's too late, and his shirt is gone. Land cannot disappear. But the monies invested in a bad real-estate deal can evaporate faster than a promoter can fly to Acapulco.

As a first set of guidelines, remember that real-estate deals are good *only*:

- when the population in that area is going up;
- when your advisor is a professional who examines all the risks before asking for the money;
- when you, the investor, know your motivations for getting into the deal, and match the deal with them.

Before you take the rubber band off your bankroll, you must know what kind of investor you want to be, and what kind of deals you want to invest in.

An investment portfolio must be tailored to meet your risk preferences and investment capabilities. Before putting down a dime, you must know which types of investments are too risky for you. You should avoid investments that will keep you awake at night. You should honestly determine how much you can safely invest. Don't stretch a beer budget to cover champagne tastes.

To help you size yourself up for an investment portfolio, I will describe several broad categories of investors, their investment patterns, and the first step each should take toward being better real-estate investors.

Those who search for future benefits and especially capital appreciation, I will call "Net Worth Builders." Those who seek immediate returns, largely in the form of spendable income, I will label "Income Seekers." Obviously, the Net Worth Builder, who is willing to wait for future rewards, can take more risks than the Income Builder, who is dependent upon immediate income from his investment.

Net Worth Builders

These investors are in the prime of life and earning enough money to meet their present needs. They want to add to their investment capital. Net Worth Builders fall into three groups.

The amount of money the investor has to invest in one year (or at one particular time) decides into which group he belongs:

- The Green Chip Investor, with up to $10,000 to invest.
- The Silver Chip Investor, with more than $10,000 to invest.
- The Gold Chip Investor, with more than $50,000 to invest.

The Green Chip Investor. This is Joe Middle Class. He earns between $15,000 and $30,000 a year. With today's high cost of living, if he's married with two children and making less than $15,000 he's probably borrowing just to hold his head above water. He probably considers himself relatively wealthy with a net worth of $50,000 to $100,000.

The major investment for most Green Chip Investors is their home. Some Green Chippers, however, are plungers who try to make it big on their little bit of capital. They take losses, and feel the pain deeply. Others consider anything beyond a savings account or government securities to be too risky. The Green Chipper invests in what the stock market calls "businessmen's risk stock" with a moderate degree of risk and solid growth potential. Occasionally, the Green Chipper may rent out a home in which he previously lived, or accumulate enough money to buy a small apartment or commercial building.

The Green Chipper follows advice from others—his boss, his wife. His professional advisor is likely to be a stockbroker or real-estate broker. That broker, however, has limited expertise, and may put his clients only into his current merchandise of investments, or into deals he regularly handles. Sometimes, he gets *his* advice from the boys "downtown" or "upstairs."

My advice to the Green Chip Investor is not to be too timid. If you are in this category, you may not trust your own knowledge. You may sometimes be overwhelmed by your advisor. Ask that advisor questions. Push him to get better investments, to broaden himself and his base. (You may be helping him make more money for himself and for you.) Do research yourself, and use your judgment and instincts to tell whether you are getting the right answers. Upward mobility is not a sin, and you are overdue.

The Silver Chip Investors. These are the professionals: doctors, dentists, lawyers, accountants, airline pilots, and executives with earnings between $30,000 and $100,000. The Silver Chipper limits his single investments to $25,000. His net worth may fall between $100,000 and $500,000.

The Silver Chipper has money—and is vulnerable. He is highly respected by others. As a doctor or airline pilot, he holds human life in his hands. His professional training has given him feelings of elitism; he thinks he is smarter, more worthy than the rest of the world. He is at the top of the sucker lists.

Fast-buck artists have no trouble convincing the Silver Chip Investor that he is a member of a select group who can —for a hefty sum—get in on the ground floor of a big operation. The suede-shoe boys stroke Mr. Silver Chip's ego as if it were a concert violin.

Silver Chippers are notorious undertippers. They are also cheap when they should be extravagant: They hate to pay for sound, professional advice. They deal instead with middlemen whose commissions frequently are many times more costly—especially when a deal fails—than sound investment advice. I have heard too many times: "This deal was brought to me by Dr. Smith. He's a damn fine surgeon, and ought to know a good deal when he sees one."

Unfortunately, the Silver Chipper fails to see that cutting through the human skin and dissecting phoney real-estate baloney requires distinctly different skills.

The Silver Chip Investor too often falls into bed with extremely poor managers, who are too busy putting together new deals to operate and manage the old ones. By default, the investor sometimes has to step in as the manager. This becomes the kiss of death. Mr. Doctor decides that he can run his practice and the deal at the same time. He is usually in the middle of surgery when a critical decision must be made.

The Silver Chipper, once burned, may become investment shy, holding out capital when an infusion is needed (and might save the deal). He spends thousands for a fancy piece of medical equipment, and nickels and dimes on investment management.

The Silver Chipper's home usually turns out to be his investment. He can afford to buy a well-built home in a good area. The Silver Chipper likes to be an insider, and is not too keen for public securities. When he does invest in stocks, he tends to look for a killing in speculative issues in glamour industries. An over-the-counter salesman who knows him can usually get him to put a few thousand into a new "hot issue."

Syndicates depend on the Silver Chip Investor. He will swing into both development syndicates and syndicates to operate an income property. Tax shelters offered by the real-estate syndicate and other investments (oil and gas wells, cattle, mines) are distorted out of perspective by the Silver Chip Investor. The tax shelter becomes the primary and not—as it should be—the secondary motivation for investment.

The Silver Chipper also buys income property, and gets himself into trouble. Instead of recognizing that sound diversification spreads risk, he goes for large investments in few properties rather than moderate investments in many properties. His aversion to paying for experienced management complicates this problem: Sound management is crucial to the success of large investments. A study in confusion is the professional building run without experienced property management by the very professionals who own and occupy space in that building.

The Silver Chip Investor may buy into vacation homes and recreational lots. He may also get burned by listening to the salesman's pitch about rental income and future resale profits.

The Silver Chip Investor needs to learn one basic lesson: While he is highly talented in his profession, he should turn his investments over to a professional, well-trained real-estate counselor. The Silver Chipper has much to learn, especially about making his money work for him. He should search out skilled professional advisors, listen to them and pay for them. Above all, the Silver Chip Investor must avoid get-rich-quick merchants, and recognize that the low road of steady gains often passes the high road of quick killings.

The Gold Chip Investor. This is usually a top executive of a public corporation, the owner of his own successful business, or a well-established professional. He earns more than $100,000 a year and has a net worth in excess of $500,000.

The Gold Chip Investor is someone experienced in making good decisions based on right information. That's how he got where he is. He knows how to blend tax accountants with lawyers with brokers to make financial projections. The Gold Chipper searches out appropriate assistants and pays well for them. He also pays more attention than other investors to the dealer, and carefully considers the reputation of the person behind the deal. He can be trapped, however, by the slick "name-dropping" dealer, who convinces the Gold Chip Investor that the dealer has handled the money of other fast-movers.

The Gold Chipper is diversified in his overall investments. He assigns a certain percentage of his capital to low-risk, moderate-risk, and high-risk ventures. Low-risk capital goes into municipals (for tax shelter) and high-grade bonds. Businessmen's risk securities and income properties provide the moderate risk element of the portfolio. Speculative securities and development and tax shelter syndications are his crap shoot.

The Gold Chipper has one major flaw: He likes being identified with his major investments (his business bears his name); he enjoys public adulation for the edifices his money creates. His home, therefore, is likely to be expensive, and suitable to such a limited market that it can only be sold at a loss. If he gets into the design of the apartment and commercial buildings in which he invests, they, too, are likely to be overdone for the markets they serve.

The Gold Chip gentleman sometimes makes the mistake of not diversifying within classes of investments. He is a loner, and doesn't enjoy investing with others. For example, when he invests in oil for tax shelter it may be impossible to convince him that he would be better off buying a piece of a dozen wells rather than the entire interest of two wells. The Gold Chip Investor needs to pause and ask: "Am I doing this for my ego or because the market is good?"

Income Seekers

Income seekers are retired or semiretired people who have worked for their money and now expect their money to work for them. While we are focusing on the needs of individual investors in this book, we must examine pension and profit-sharing trusts for the income seekers. Those trusts are becoming a major means of providing for the retirement needs of investors who are largely Income Seekers.

Traditionally, the primary real-estate investments of individual Income Seekers have been: (a) equity interests in income property, mainly small apartment buildings; (b) second mortgages: The income properties were frequently acquired over a period of time from real-estate brokers. They probably were chosen because they were located near the investor's place of business or home. He could easily keep an eye on them.

The second trust deeds were acquired through the same local real-estate broker, or through mortgage brokers recommended to the investor by mutual acquaintances, the investor's attorney, accountant, or other professional advisors. At retirement age, the Income Seeker might sell his securities and unimproved property and convert them into these income-producing investments.

Income Seekers have, during the mid-1970s, found themselves in some financial trouble. The income properties they acquired over the years have been engulfed by inner-city ghettos, and have become massive liabilities for which the only solution appears to be abandonment. In New York City alone, more than 250,000 housing units have been abandoned. Also, second mortgages, yielding 8 to 10 percent, make little sense with low-risk government and monetary securities bringing higher interest rates, even though these securities have been shown to be highly vulnerable to inflation.

Income Seekers have been desperately searching private syndicates, public syndicates, pension, and profit-sharing trusts, and Real Estate Investment Trusts (REITS). These have been put together in sound portfolios (more on REITS in Chapter Eight), which include professionally managed income properties and inflation-protected ground leases.

Aware of these categories, you, the potential investor, must decide which type of investor you are, and which you wish to be. There are other questions:

• What do you want from real-estate investment? Do you want a piece of land that is lying in the path of growth? You buy it cheap and make money on it as the population expands to reach your property. But where is the population growing, and why?

• Do you want a building with income? There may be many opportunities—but which one? Real estate may be a good hedge against inflation, but not everywhere, and not with every building. If your building is in a good area and already built, it may have great potential for generating monthly income, appreciating in value, being a real property that can be traded for something more valuable, or sold to someone else at a profit.

• Do you want property for little cash so that you can leverage it until it becomes more valuable? Leverage—that's a magic word in real estate. It means that you control something of value with little cash. That property can be sold or traded at a higher price, so that your small cash has earned you a big profit. This Las Vegas mentality is fundamental to real-estate thinking. Why put down a lot of cash to control a deal you are trying to sell (turnover) for capital gains or straight profit? Put in a few dollars so you can get out of it more than you put into it.

• Are you looking for a tax shelter in the coming real-estate boom? You want to take the risk of not having too many tax dollars flowing out of the investment, while you need the tax shelter. You may leverage the tax shelter and make some appreciation on it, at any time you can attract a buyer. Or, you may stay in the deal, getting tax protection, while the deal accumulates appreciation and equity for you, for later years.

Tax shelters do offer flexibility. As long as incomes go up, there will be ready markets for real estate which can shelter taxes. This will always remain a fundamental attraction for making deals, unless Congress passes legislation removing tax shelters.

• Are you looking for a deal which you can share with other investors?

• Are you looking for heavy risk along with great rewards? You might be willing to take a disproportionate gamble on a deal, but if the deal works out the rewards could be large.

• Are you looking for something to manage that will take your personal effort as well as personal money? That is the definition of a nest egg, and you become the hen watching it develop. I like an investor with that personal involvement, as long as he doesn't let it drain off his last dime.

Remember that real estate concerns the presence and movement of people. The marketplace means how many people, in the location surrounding your deal, who may want to buy, sell, lease, shop, rent, or trade what you have for their money. The success of your deal hinges on whether or not there are other opportunities for these people that are better than yours.

The people of your marketplace are not concerned with how much money you have in your deal, how much you have overpaid, how much personal agony you have spent on the deal, who your lawyer or accountant might be. They are interested—if you are buying—in what you can put up. And they are interested—if you are selling—in whether they can afford what you have.

Thinking of yourself as a seller, you will have to look at the interest market: Will a buyer need to refinance your deal when he buys it from you? Why should he want to do this?

A marketplace is created when you have something that somebody else wants. That might be real estate, or money to buy real estate. You reach an agreement based upon how much competition there is for your deal, how much cash you want, whether the deal can be leveraged, and whether they can put their money somewhere else with less risk and with equal return.

As a potential real-estate buyer, you should ask: What exactly are the opportunities? If they are unique, why? Be skeptical. Each deal is different—a different physical site, different property features. Is the real-estate deal really better than government bonds or the stock market?

Learn from every deal you make. There are as many types of deals as there are dreams. Here are a few ideas for your initial investment that appeal to me:

1. a new home
2. a resale home
3. an apartment which you manage
4. an apartment which you invest in and have professionally managed
5. a small shopping center
6. a small office building
7. a medical building
8. a recreational vehicle park
9. a mini warehouse development*
10. a hotel or motel
11. a large shopping center or part of a syndicate
12. a piece of apartment-suitable land, before it is zoned for apartments
13. any kind of raw, unzoned land for speculation

* A small, garage-type structure for small storage needs.

I will discuss many of these choices in detail in Part III. These are good areas of potential growth where you might consider putting your money today. As a guideline, here are some areas preferred by one large investment outfit on the West Coast. Since real-estate interests fluctuate with the changing market, consider that these choices were made in 1976.

Apartments. Invest only in middle-income, semi-luxury, luxury, garden, townhouse, or multistory. The minimum size is 150 units (some funds prefer larger projects). These apartments have to be five years old or more. All must have an occupancy (units rented) in excess of 90 percent of scheduled gross income. (This is the total rental income if all units are rented.) New projects will be considered only if they can reach 90 percent in three months. (I feel that six months is more realistic.) Management is handled privately by the investors.

Shopping Centers. Invest in neighborhood, community, or regional centers. Malls are preferred, with minimum size of 100,000 square feet. No center should be ten years or older. Investors prefer strong local tenants anchored by a large retail store or supermarket and a large drug merchandiser. Leases must contain tax protection. Location must indicate strong demographic trends with increasing retail-marketing potential. Investor manages his own facilities.

Office Buildings. Market unsteady, but will accept both high- or low-rise of 50,000 square feet that is ten years old or less. Should have strong major and minor tenants with 90 percent occupancy. Prefer suburban location with strong demographic trends, or a new downtown location. Investor manages facilities himself.

Mobile Home Parks. Another rapidly changing investment with high risk. Prefer existing year-round permanent residential parks with a minimum of 200 pads. (A "pad" refers to the mobile home site that is rented to the mobile home owner.)

The project must have economic occupancy of 90 percent of scheduled gross income. New projects must be able to reach 90 percent within three months. (Again, I feel that six months is more realistic and still profitable.) All projects must be attractive, well built, and well maintained. Investors prefer to manage project themselves.

Warehouses. A real sleeper in the field. Investors prefer 100,000 square feet or more with strong local and national tenants. Minimum ten-year leases with escalation provisions. Prefer suburban locations, preferably in industrial parks.

Parking Garages. Improved surface parking lots considered, but prefer multistory garages with a 300- to 500- car capacity, located in a central business district.

There are what the pros are looking for and going after. What kind of deals should you, the new real-estate investor, look at? There are as many good deals as there are good ideas. You might consider the following list:

Residential. Rehabilitation: single dwellings, single dwellings into multiple units, multiple units into condominiums, single units into single rentals.

Build: new singles on skipped lots, new singles on small tracts closer in, new singles in small high-priced neighborhoods, turnkey single dwellings for larger company.

Build: condominiums as primary residences, condos as luxury residences, condos for retirees and empty-nesters, condos related to specific sports, convert smaller condos into rentals, condos for secondary residence, condos for time-sharing or condotels (motels that sell rooms and then rent them to produce income for the buyer).

Build: small apartments on skipped land, apartments in neighborhoods with existing singles, apartments for conversion later, apartments in conjunction with commercial properties, apartments for empty-nesters or walk-to-work-ers, mid-rise near population and amenities, high-rise in urban area.

Diversify. Build: apartments in conjunction with hotel/rental pool, apartments as part of a joint venture/turnkey, apartments to sell, apartments to retain.

Commercial. Develop: small retail half acre for convenience shopping, small retail two to four acres for neighborhood shopping, small specialty shopping areas, franchise shopping area (high traffic), rehabilitate existing shopping center for environmental touch, develop small shops in conjunction with recreational or tourist attraction, rehabilitate store fronts as rentals, develop retail with expanding apartment community.

Special. You might also be interested in: office condominiums, professional-office condos, seasonal condos, professional-medical condos, mini-warehousing, speculative warehousing and industrial buildings, industrial park development, combination office and industrial building within an industrial park, parking structure, recreational vehicle structures and parks, mobile home park or service core, government concession land (recreational, residential, commercial uses).

Other possibilities include: student and faculty housing, special government programs for sale, rental or leasing, food-storage buildings, mini-theaters, sports complexes.

No matter what appeals to you, remember that real estate is a local opportunity that depends upon its specific location, your ability to tie up the land, and good timing to make things happen. To accomplish this, you will have to do all of your homework.

The best investment strategy is to be personally involved with your marketplace, monitor the area, watch the growth and change, concentrate on making the best deal you can. Check everything out yourself. Walk the land, tour the building. This is sound, practical strategy. Sure you can get hurt, but bed isn't the safest place either. To make money, you must take risks.

Because real estate changes, every deal is unique. There is plenty of room for ingenuity, but none for dishonesty. The guy who cheats soon finds he has no market. People learn, and don't return.

There is nothing like real estate. People love to own it, touch it, buy and sell it, dream of it. It is where the average person finds loads of legitimate deals to make. It is also where the economy is growing, and where the opportunities are.

Now that you're convinced real estate is for you, and you understand the range of choices you have in putting your money to work, where do you begin to look? In selecting the best investment for you, we need to understand what is happening to your marketplace—America and its people. What are the real-estate trends today, and how do you follow them?

3

TRENDS

You have made some important decisions already. There are more to come. You know that real-estate investment is for you, that you have an amount of money to invest, that there are real-estate deals that attract you for a variety of reasons.

But, still, there are steps to take before getting into the deals. You need to learn to spot trends in real-estate markets, and to do that you must understand what has happened in real estate in the past, and be able to look at the future.

One of the most significant trends taking place is the shift in the American population. After World War II, our metropolitan areas grew rapidly. During the past generation some 30 million people left the countryside and settled in the cities. Already, more than 74 percent of our people live in major metropolitan areas. (See Chart 3–1.) Americans enjoyed unprecedented mobility.

After World War II, in 1945, returning G.I.s found few apartments, fewer new homes, and no luxurious mobile trailers.

CHART 3–1 Population Growth Rates
Top 30 U.S. Metropolitan Areas 1960–1974

Rank	*Population Growth Rate (In %)*	*Population Growth (Millions)*
1	Orange County	Washington/Baltimore (2.13)
2	San Jose	New York (1.50)
3	Tampa/St. Petersburg	Los Angeles (0.96)
4	Washington/Baltimore	Orange County (0.90)
5	Atlanta	Chicago (0.78)
6	Phoenix	Houston (0.78)
7	San Diego	Detroit (0.74)
8	Miami/Ft. Lauderdale	Miami/Ft. Lauderdale (0.73)
9	Houston	Dallas/Ft. Worth (0.71)
10	Riverside/San Bernardino	Atlanta (0.68)
11	Denver	Tampa/St. Petersburg (0.63)
12	Dallas/Ft. Worth	San Diego (0.57)
13	Minneapolis/St. Paul	San Francisco/Oakland (0.55)
14	Indianapolis	San Jose (0.54)
15	New Orleans	Minneapolis/St. Paul (0.52)
16	Newark	Denver (0.47)
17	San Francisco/Oakland	Philadelphia (0.47)
18	Detroit	Phoenix (0.44)
19	Kansas City	Riverside/San Bernardino (0.44)
20	Los Angeles	Newark (0.41)
21	New York	Indianapolis (0.31)
22	St. Louis	St. Louis (0.29)
23	Cincinnati	New Orleans (0.25)
24	Milwaukee	Kansas City (0.21)
25	Boston	Cincinnati (0.18)
26	Chicago	Milwaukee (0.17)
27	Philadelphia	Cleveland (0.09)
28	Cleveland	Buffalo (0.04)
29	Buffalo	Pittsburgh (0.00)
30	Pittsburgh	Boston (0.39)

Source: Prepared from Census Bureau Data by Sanford R. Goodkin Research Corporation

Even as supply began to catch up with demand in the 1950s, the boom continued. Between 1960 and 1970, the country's total population grew by 13 percent. There were 10.4 million households in the 1950s, and another 10.6 million in the 1960s. Compare that with approximately 2.5 million housing starts in 1972 alone, and another 2.1 million in 1973.

The jump during the 1960s was unprecedented. In 1966, there were 1.42 million housing units of all types being built. Six years later, there were 2.9 million. The number of apartments was growing from 350,000 to 940,000 in 1972. Mobile homes went from more than 63,000 in 1950 to 103,000 in 1960, and to almost 600,000 in 1972. There were people, on wheels and of every age, making mobile homes and parks a smart investment.

Change in the 1950s and 1960s spelled growth. The growth gave sustenance to investors and builders and the people who bought homes and trailers. But nothing is more constant than change itself. And the smart real-estate investor now knows that the boom turned very quickly to bust in the mid-1970s. As we will discuss in detail in Part III, the growth in housing, mobile homes and apartments came to a standstill during the double-digit inflation. In the 1980s, we may hit three million housing units. But the message of the seventies was clear: Watch the trends.

Assuming—and I believe it—that the housing/apartment/condominium/mobile home boom is returning, here's a tough question for you: How many of these new residences will have wheels, how many will be rentals, and how many will be single-family homes?

In the mid-1970s, a serious fact of American life became increasingly clear: A new population shift became evident. (See Chart 3–2.) People who had moved to the northern industrial centers were moving out. And they weren't just moving to the suburbs, they were getting out of the region. The country's population, on an increasing scale, was moving into what soon got dubbed the "Sun Belt." Orange County, California, grew by 128 percent in population between 1960 and 1974. San Jose, California, jumped 84 percent, and Tampa/St. Petersburg grew 82 percent. Fort Myers, Florida, went through the roof with almost 200 percent population growth—and dozens of home builders went crazy with work in the middle of our nation's major housing slump.

CHART 3–2 Forces of Change in Number of Households Regional Areas of the U.S. 1970–1980

Regional Area	*Natural Growth*	*Headship Increase*	*Net Migration*	*Total*
NORTHEAST	60%	34%	6%	100%
New England	60%	30%	10%	100%
Middle Atlantic	60%	35%	5%	100%
NORTH CENTRAL	72%	32%	—4%	100%
East North Central	72%	30%	—2%	100%
West North Central	72%	37%	—9%	100%
SOUTH	62%	25%	13%	100%
South Atlantic	54%	22%	24%	100%
East South Central	80%	33%	—13%	100%
West South Central	68%	27%	5%	100%
MOUNTAIN	61%	21%	18%	100%
PACIFIC	57%	23%	20%	100%
TOTAL	63%	28%	9%	100%

Source: "America's Housing Needs," 1970–1980, Joint Center for Urban Studies, MIT and Harvard University, December, 1973

As a real-estate investor, therefore, you need to determine not only *what* people will want to buy (and invest your money in that), but also *where.* The ten largest metropolitan areas of the 1950s and 1960s will not be the ten largest of the 1970s and 1980s. Following that trend is vital to your real-estate success.

Opportunities come in surprising places. People moved from the rural South to the urban North and Midwest; now they are moving back. The investors and builders making money in the mid-1970s were in the Sun Belt. But what areas hold the profits of tomorrow?

To help you answer that question, let's look at America tomorrow. Despite the fact that the nation may gain as many as 50 million new citizens before the year 2000, America may not change much, unless some present trends reverse or shift dramatically.

First, we clearly see a shift in the age grouping of the population.

After World War II, the baby boom began and continued until after the Pill arrived in the early 1960s. That little tablet, Jack Paar, and Johnny Carson changed the evening bedroom behavior of millions of us.

Between 1945 and 1965, the average age of the country dropped sharply. Now, the median age is about 28 years. Further, between 1960 and 1973, the live-birth rates (births per 1,000 people) dropped from 22.4 to 15.3—a dramatic 50 percent!

There were two major causes for this dip. The boom babies of World War II grew up, married, and completed their families. Most importantly, there is an increasing tendency among the present teen-agers to postpone marriage until they reach their late twenties. This delay created the low birth rate of the early and mid-1970s.

Birth expectations of American women are now dropping. In 1967, wives in the 18 to 24 age bracket expected to have an average of 2.9 children each. By 1971, that expectation had dropped to 2.4 children each, and surveys for the mid-1970s showed an expected average of 2.3.

Census officials have indicated that there are strong trends toward a continuing decline of the birth rate; one projection placed the average number of children per wife in 1980 at 1.7. Based on this trend, it is fair to say that the two-child family is the wave of the future. This statistic will have a major impact on real estate for the remainder of the century. It is clearly one of those long-term, slow-moving trends that change America.

With a dip in the birth rate comes a continuing slip in

the death rate. As a result, America is starting to get older. By the year 2000, the median age of our population may rise from its present 28 years to 34 years. This, too, will have a strong impact on real-estate markets.

Secondly, there is a shift, as mentioned, of mobile Americans from cold to warm climates.

Of the 50 million new persons to be added to our population between 1970 and 1990, almost 66 percent of them will live outside the traditional population centers of the Northeast and North Central states. The majority will move into warmer climates, especially in the Southwest and Southeast. The big gains will be in California and Florida, followed by Texas, Colorado, Arizona, Georgia, and the other mild-weather states.

Here's one projection, from the Joint Center Urban Studies at MIT and Harvard, that indicates where most of the new population will settle by 1990, compared with where it is concentrated today.

CHART 3–3

	Today	*New Population Gain 1975–1990*
Northeast and North Central States	51.5%	44.3%
South Central States	15.8%	11.4%
Mountain States	4.3%	4.7%
South Atlantic States	15.3%	16.3%
Pacific States	13.1%	23.3%
	100.0%	100.0%

The shift is more evident as you examine in-migration patterns, and compare the projections for the different regions during the 1970 to 1990 period. (In-migration refers to the number of people coming into an area, as opposed to the number of people in that area leaving it, which equals the net in-migration.)

CHART 3–4

	Natural Growth	*Net In-migration*	*Total*
Northeast States	94%	6	100%
North Central States	104%	—4	100%
South Central States	102%	—2	100%
Mountain States	82%	18	100%
South Atlantic States	76%	24	100%
Pacific States	80%	20	100%
Total United States	91%	9	100%

Third, there is a shift out of the metropolitan areas. One pattern to watch here is the possible movement not only from urban, but also from suburban areas outward into rural and semirural regions. If this is happening, and we won't know really until the 1980 census, it could mean a quickening of the shift to the Sun Belt.

During the period from 1945 to 1965, there appeared to be an irreversible trend *toward* the big cities. People left rural America, fleeing from boredom, unemployment, and racial discrimination. They sought better opportunities. Today, however, that trend has stabilized, and there is a small but growing indication that a sizable share of the population is trying to escape the metropolises.

The MIT-Harvard study shows that nonmetropolitan area growth will make substantial gains before 1980:

CHART 3–5 **Number of Households**

	1970	*1980*	*Comparative Change Between 1970–1980*
Metropolitan areas	69.1%	67.9%	62.4%
Nonmetropolitan areas	30.9%	32.1%	37.6%
TOTAL	100.0%	100.0%	100.0%

In sum, the America of tomorrow is getting older, staying unmarried longer, moving to the South and West, and pushing away from the large (and generally northern) cities. It is also gaining by some 2.25 to 2.5 million people every year.

These statistical facts will shape the future of real-estate growth and investment. The demand for land and housing in the next two decades will shift and come from a variety of changing sources. (See Charts 3–6 and 3–7.) That demand may also reach 2.5 million housing units by 1980. The sources, and their projected housing demands, are:

CHART 3–6 Demand for New Residential Units, by Demand Source Regional Areas of the United States 1970–1980

Regional Areas	*Number of Units* *Demographic Needs*	*Other Needs*	*Total*	*Demographic As % of Total*
NORTHEAST	2,806,709	1,726,043	4,532,749	62%
New England	749,587	405,756	1,155,337	65%
Middle Atlantic	2,057,122	1,320,290	3,377,412	61%
NORTH CENTRAL	3,490,494	2,299,079	5,789,574	60%
East North Central	2,555,985	1,529,164	4,085,150	63%
West North Central	934,509	769,915	1,704,424	55%
SOUTH	4,922,392	3,394,461	8,316,853	59%
South Atlantic	2,744,408	1,623,236	4,367,644	63%
East South Central	746,201	758,228	1,504,429	50%
West South Central	1,431,783	1,012,997	2,444,780	59%
MOUNTAIN	776,972	436,465	1,213,437	64%
PACIFIC	2,349,163	1,143,168	3,492,331	67%
TOTAL	14,345,730	8,999,219	23,344,965	62%

Source: "America's Housing Needs, 1970–1980," Joint Center for Urban Studies, MIT and Harvard University, December, 1973

CHART 3–7 **Estimated Annual Housing Demand by Source**

	Number of Units (000)	*Percent*
Natural growth (more people being born than dying)	900–950	39
Headship increase	425–475	19
Immigration	100–150	5
Additional vacancies	125–175	6
Second homes or vacation	225–275	10
Accidental losses, demolitions and others	475–525	21
	2,250–2,550	100

Let's take a look at each of these categories, and what the opportunities might be.

Natural Growth. This one fact alone will create more than 40 percent of all housing needs. The natural growth of the population will come from the normal pattern of people reaching adulthood, leaving home, getting married, and raising a family. Natural growth may account for some 900,000 to 950,000 housing units a year by the end of the decade.

Headship Increases. This is a new category of housing demand and, along with the second-home market, will be an increasingly strong catalyst to housing growth in the 1980s. Headship increase creates almost 20 percent of the housing demand in America.

Americans, enjoying a fairly steady affluence, continue to be able to select where they live, and how they live. More people also want to live alone—the college student, the divorced, the elderly. Further, more than three-quarters of all widows and widowers form separate households, and most of them live alone. As social security and other benefits climb, this trend will continue.

The increased divorce rate adds to this demand. Recent statistics indicate that the annual number of separations are equal to the annual number of marriages—not a particularly cheery note. More residences will be required by this group. Despite the risks of marriage, however, some 90 percent of our adult population still tries it.

Kids are also leaving home at an earlier age. This creates two demands: housing for the kids and housing for the "empty-nester" parents left behind. They find themselves with a large and empty house, and free of the day-to-day care of their children. They want a different lifestyle, and are rapidly creating—as our nation generally ages—new demands in housing.

So do their children. A recent survey of the San Diego, California, housing market shows that the *average* age of single tenants was under 24 years, a further indication of the trend toward independence of young adults.

Immigration. We may view massive immigration to the United States as a thing of the past. But, in fact, some 100,000 to 150,000 new households are still required each year to provide shelter for these new Americans. The majority of these immigrants are young families from Latin America, Europe, and Canada. Most of them join relatives already here. There are also about 100,000 illegals needing housing!

Additional Vacancies. Very conservatively, some 175,000 units are needed each year to allow movement within the housing market. This vacancy factor—about 6 percent of the total demand—also acts as a rent-and-sale-price stabilizing agent. When the vacancy rate slips below 6 percent, there is a strong tendency for rents and sales prices to rise above normal in the classic pattern of demand outstripping supply.

Second Homes. During the next decade, perhaps 10 percent of all new housing units will be second homes. The second home may be a mobile home, a condominium, a cabin in the mountains, or an investment home in a warm climate. Regardless of shape, price, or location, it is a home that may be unoccupied most of the year.

For many people, this second home may represent the interim step between full-time employment and retirement. The owners may gradually increase their use of the home until they fully commit themselves to year-round retirement.

This second home carries a demand that could reach 275,000 units a year. It was a major factor in the housing boom of the early 1970s, and will be a factor again at the end of the decade and into the 1980s.

Accidental Losses and Demolitions. Fire, urban renewal, highway dislocation, decay, abandonment, and myriad other reasons cause a replacement demand every year for between 475,000 and 525,000 new housing units. This is 20 percent of the total demand during good times.

Many of these units are in the center cities, and occupied by the poor. In some cases, these units will be replaced by middle- and upper-income housing, thereby causing the indigent to scramble for the remaining selection of inner-city housing. Not all of the old housing in America, however, is in the inner cities of metropolitan areas. The 1970 census, for example, showed that 62 percent of our substandard housing is outside these metro areas, and even 16 percent of it is in our suburbs.

There are several observations to be made from this. One important one is that you continue to watch the population shifts taking place and the overall population growth.

Population decline, which began in 1973, could become a set pattern, which would throw off all projections about housing in the real-estate market. For now, however, it may also be a short-term phenomenon. But there is a strong trend away from early marriages and early childbearing. This decrease has also been paralleled by a drop in fertility of young women 18 years old and younger, from 204 per 1,000 women (among those born in 1935 to 1939) to 104 per 1,000 women (those born in 1950 to 1955).

A child born in the mid-1970s will find himself living in a

very changed America by the time he reaches age 20. The median age of the other Americans at that time will be 35 years. The child's family's income may be around $23,000, compared to a 1975 level of $13,000. Further, the chances are good that the child may be living in a giant metropolis that will be housing half of our population. We will be older, more affluent (depending upon the rate of inflation) and living closer together.

We will also see the size of the average household decrease, as it has been doing every decade since World War II. (See Chart 3–8.) In 1950, there were 3.5 people per household; in

CHART 3–8 Changes in Persons Per Household United States 1970–1980

	1970	*Projected 1980*	*Change 1970–1980*
Population (000)	203,000	227,000	24,000
Number of Households (000)	63,445	77,790	14,345
Ratio			
Population:Households	3.2:1	2.9:1	1.7:1

Source: U.S. Census Bureau Series E Projections, May, 1974, and Joint Center for Urban Studies, MIT and Harvard University, December, 1973

1970, 3.2; in 1976, 2.94; and by 1990, perhaps, only 2.5. There will also be a great increase in the numbers of households headed by people aged 35 to 44. This will occur during the 20 years before 1990 as the baby boom gets older and older. There will also be a significant increase in the under-35 households up to 1985. This indicates a great many families moving into the optimum home-buying years in the next decade and a half. There will be a profound increase in the over-65 category, and that increase will continue indefinitely especially among widows. (See Chart 3–9.)

CHART 3–9 Projections of Number of Households, by Age Range United States 1970–1990

Age Range:	*Under 35* *Mil.*	*%*	*35–44* *Mil.*	*%*	*45–64* *Mil.*	*%*	*65 up* *Mil.*	*%*	*Total* *Mil.*	*%*
1970	16.0	25.3	11.8	18.6	23.0	36.3	12.5	19.7	63.4	100
1980	24.3	31.4	13.1	17.0	24.3	31.4	15.6	20.1	77.3	100
1990	26.8	29.8	19.4	21.5	25.1	27.9	18.7	20.8	90.1	100
Change 1970–1990	10.8	40.2	7.6	28.1	2.1	7.9	6.2	23.5	26.7	100

Figures may not column to 100% due to rounding.

Source: Sanford R. Goodkin Research Corporation

These statistics, rather than dismaying you, should entice you to certain real-estate choices. There is a wide variety of options opening before your eyes; you need only be alert and receptive to them. As the population steadies and perhaps decreases, as it shifts from one region to another, these choices will have to be made cautiously and wisely and with help. The day of the developer buying large plots of land in front of the super highway is over. Traditional patterns of real-estate development and investment are changing fast.

Both the cities and the suburbs are showing that change almost daily. During the mid-1970s, we have seen the near-default of our major cities, and the erosion of their financial base. We have also seen growth come to a sharp halt in suburbia as housing costs rose; and we have seen the first threat to suburbia's wall fortress in the Supreme Court decision regarding the construction of low-income housing in previously restricted and high-income areas.

Of the two areas, I'm far more bullish on the cities. They already contain substantially sound housing, some of it renovated, and much of it filled with nineteenth-century (or older) charm. Moreover, I like to look at opportunities where others see only disaster. People who ride through Bedford-Stuyvesant and the South Bronx in New York City, or North Philadelphia, or the Hough area of Detroit or Mission District of San Francisco see only the broken windows, ripped-off doors, demolished interiors, and abandoned housing. The smart investor given the right federal and state incentives, may also see opportunity.

Large parts of urban America are festering sores that must be healed. The nation is not going to abandon its cities. Would we turn our backs on our own people, our culture and arts, our great universities, our vital libraries, our centers of finance and business? They will be brought back to life, and when they are, they will offer far more than suburbia: closeness to the office, great restaurants, theaters, exciting mixtures of people and ideas, and (perhaps best of all) freedom from the automobile. What is needed is a Federal Marshall Plan for our cities, like the 1949 Housing Act which contained the promise of providing Americans with decent homes under an emergency situation.

The alert investor will constantly watch Washington during the late 1970s and early 1980s. Federal legislation to rebuild America's cities could mean investment attractions and profits. Moreover, by the time we make a real dent in the urgent housing problem of the inner city, the serious and growing problems of the "instant slums" built in the suburbs after World War II will be upon us. Within the next decade, many of these family-sized cells will be physically substandard or economically at suboptimum use of the land they occupy. Watch them, too. New York City is a perfect example of how this problem catches up with cities suffering from poor financial planning. Slums are economic as well as social planning failures. As the cities' operating costs continue to grow, they rob Peter to pay Paul. Investors get caught in the middle. Cities, however, will receive great attention by both the federal government and the states during the next decade.

Change in the suburbs could be accelerated by increasingly higher gasoline prices and home-heating fuel prices—the energy crisis. Here, too, may rest clues for the alert and careful real-estate investor.

Watching Demand

If you keep alert to the trends outlined above, you will soon learn one more real-estate lesson: The backbone of real-estate investment—deciding where and in what to invest—is understanding consumer demand, and acting on it. This is not only demand in the usual sense of people insisting upon something, but also demand in the sense of people's ability and desire to buy goods and services.

Real-estate demand depends upon a whole range of factors. Some are out of the control of the real-estate investor, the builder, the marketer. For example, during the 1940s, 1950s, and 1960s demand for housing and shopping centers was so strong that real-estate investors got away with making bad buys, backing ticky-tacky housing, throwing up shopping centers on potato fields. Everything they bought, sold, and built got picked up and rented, resold, rebuilt. Demand was hardly measured at all; supply was so short that demand was constant.

By the 1970s, however, all that changed. Demand became more sophisticated, and people soon wanted variety and more for their buck. They demanded better homes, apartment villages, enclosed shopping, air-conditioned malls. Real-estate investors became more creative. They backed, designed, and built malls like the Galleria in Houston, or Topanga Plaza in the San Fernando Valley of California. Underground malls in Montreal and Los Angeles, converted canneries in Newport Beach and San Francisco, attracted people in droves. Anyone who has been in Ghirardelli Square in San Francisco knows immediately that this is where people and appetites come alive.

Real-estate investors, therefore, must also consider shifting patterns of demand. This is as much *watching* for those demands (and understanding trends) as it is *creating* them. A goodly effort is now going into expanding people's desires for specific real-estate products. The smart real-estate investor, today, creates and makes things happen. Others watch and ask, "How can he do that?"

Here are several examples of creative real-estate deals that have made money for investors. They were put together by bright, alert people who watched the trends and understood the changing patterns of demand.

Something Old

Paul Thoryk is a brilliant architect, crazy as a fox. He likes to option a small building for smaller money, redo the front, clean up the interior, and rent it. The building is a step or two above its surrounding competition, and still offers from 20 to 35 cents a month per square foot better value than anything new. The mechanics of these buildings—elevators, air conditioning—are uncomplicated, and carefully checked out. Paul always checks himself or hires a structural engineer.

Financial help has been easy to get. In one venture, he took an old warehouse in Florida, put some supergraphics (drawings) on the walls, added landscaping *inside*, painted, and repaired the place. It was bright, green, alive. He designed inexpensive but attractive partitions to make offices. The place rented like wildfire. He financed the improvements, and has a healthy cash flow. Now, he has investors waiting for each project he completes. Everybody wants in!

Paul took a vacant building on the beach in Southern California, and made it into his own offices. He painted it white inside, put his business graphics right on the walls, left the outside alone and ended up with an exciting office. Another friend of mine buys old motels. These are still in the mainstream of traffic, but run down. He deals in units of under 30. He converts them into exciting offices for local professionals, or renovates them for small apartments, getting double the rents that the motel ever got, with a minimum of fixing up.

Here, too, he checked his investment carefully, and his check list included:

1. visibility from the road
2. the amount of traffic on the road, obtained from the local highway department
3. the immediate environment on either side. If it is too run down, he stays out.
4. the vacancy factors among larger buildings, which help him determine the need for smaller and cheaper office space
5. structural soundness of the building to avoid expensive repairs.

Something Borrowed

Another friend of mine travels around old neighborhoods in places like Dallas-Fort Worth. He watches for single-family houses that might be "worn-out" and ready for sale.

"I never ask if something is for sale," he told me. "I take it for granted that everything is. It is just a matter of how much and in what mood I can put the person. I listen to tales of woe, hatred for the government and spouse. When I'm accepted as a friend, or at least a good listener, then I deal."

My friend accumulates a number of contiguous single-family homes. He looks for areas he feels can easily be rezoned to apartments. He knows there is a need for apartments in the areas where he looks; he sees offices going up nearby, and has learned that people prefer to walk to work. He looks for an urban area with a good market.

After my friend accumulates enough land for at least 100 apartments (at anywhere from 24 to 50 units per acre), he gets the land zoned for apartments and begins to build. This kind of action is profitable only if you can convert the single-family-zoned land into apartments. There's a large section about rezoning in Chapter 10.

Never Blue

To avoid getting burned while you're putting together these kinds of deals, remember these words of caution:

- Make certain that the word doesn't get around that someone is buying all the land.
- Do not buy in a ghetto. The best place is a neighborhood that is beginning to decay, not one that is putrified.
- Keep looking for new parcels for noncontiguous apartment structures.
- Always look for "walk-to-work" apartments close to everything. You won't need fancy amenities, since people are looking for shelter and convenience. Retirees and widows love these locations because of the conveniences.
- Do your rezoning homework and you will face little opposition. After all, you are moving into a "transitional area" in which multifamily housing or offices make sense. Usually, the zoning boards are tickled you are there.

I have another client who picks up homes and converts them into neighborhood shopping areas. He prefers corners, and usually gets enough sites to make about 20,000 square feet.

Other possibilities include buying small-store operations and running them as a chain, or independently of each other but in a real-estate "package."

Brownstones or rowhouses offer opportunities, if you don't mind doing some of the work yourself. Clean up the insides, decorate, strip wood, add carpeting, convert each floor into separate apartments, co-ops, or condominiums. One friend of mine has a wife who is an interior decorator. They do a building, she fixes up one apartment like it was a showcase in Neiman-Marcus's best window. Buyers come in, fall in love with the place, buy an apartment and ask her to decorate it. Husband and wife both make money on the deal.

If the old and borrowed ideas sound enticing, heed these words of caution:

- Avoid illusions of grandeur. Try small units at first, and work up.
- Check plumbing and wiring in all old units you consider. Pay a structural engineer to do this *before* you buy the place.
- Buy in a good neighborhood that has the right conditions for what you want to do: offices, walk-to-work apartments, brownstone or rowhouse renovation. You can double your money in the right areas.

The measurement of any opportunity is the distance between when the trend was spotted and when the investment was made. Getting on a bandwagon means that the trend has already been observed by a lot of people, and the profit potential has been greatly reduced. It's not easy to measure a trend. I try to do it by reading, by watching who has succeeded and who has failed, and why. I have found that reading biographies has given me insight into human nature and the mistakes of that nature.

There are some hard and fast rules for real-estate investing after watching the trends:

- Don't rush into any business deal.
- Don't ever let anyone name-drop you into a deal.
- Do not invest a nickel you can't afford to lose.
- Move out of your office and onto the ground. Learn what the land is really like.
- Look at everything: apartments, groves, condos, mobile parks, office buildings. Then, look for the deal that's best for you.

4

LOCATION, TIMING, USE

Finding the deal that's best for you will take some hard looking. Now that you are aware of real-estate trends, you must read, watch, and listen, and stay abreast of them. In this chapter, you will add some new skills: finding a good location, understanding timing, putting the project to its best use. For this, you will also need to understand research and market analysis.

Location

There is no more important word than location in real estate. If the location is wrong, then making a good resale will be almost impossible. The best locations for shelters and other improved real estate are:

- in a growing area
- in a growing neighborhood new or up to two years old

• in a stable neighborhood between three and ten years old. The lawns are in. Trees are fully grown or close to it.

• in a neighborhood where resales are hard to find, but there is a demand for that neighborhood

I find these areas by riding around a neighborhood that looks appealing to me, and watching for broker signs.

What's a good neighborhood like? All neighborhoods evolve, and older ones usually go downhill unless they are affluent and retain their sociological characteristics. Younger neighborhoods appreciate very well and quite rapidly in some "hot" areas; that is, where the economy is good, employment high, shopping nearby.

Some questions might be: Who lives in the neighborhood? Are they proud people who keep their investments up? Are there a lot of kids tearing the place down? Are you part of the culture, or a stranger to it?

Location means something different when you are buying land. The rules change slightly. One sharp friend of mine told me: "There's nothing to buying land. You buy it cheap and you sell it higher than you bought it. Then you brag about it."

But smart land buying takes more than that. You may buy the land, and sell to a builder. You may buy it, and go in with the builder; this is called a joint venture. You may buy into a syndicate. But whatever you do, holding that land costs you money, and lots of it. High interest rates may slow development of your land; so may zoning restrictions. We'll discuss all this later, but, for now, it is important to note that careful land selection is vital to real-estate investing. Getting land into profitable use is discouraging. But holding it is more expensive.

Since value is tied to use, location of your land—as in selecting improved real estate—is crucial. Only limited amounts of vacant land in outlying areas (not urbanized and not serviced with utilities and municipal services) will be developed in the short-term future. New areas will not be opened for development because of: (a) concern with preserving the natural environment; (b) concern by municipalities with the high cost of providing streets, utilities, schools, parks, police service, and other facilities and services; (c) concern with energy costs by consumers; (d) possible concern with reinforcing the economic and social significance of the center city and existing urban areas; (e) concern with promoting mixed use; (f) concern by communities and regional planning agencies with restricting growth.

These are major considerations to ponder while looking for your real-estate investment. Where new development does occur, it is likely to be on a large, new-community scale, which would justify rapid transit links to nearby urban areas. It will provide complete residential, commercial, work, and community facilities. The day of the small, scattered subdivisions, where a developer could get the right land buy, are gone for a long time.

So remember in buying land: Location is the most important word. Where you can find what you want in outlying areas, at the right price, and with approval already in pocket for development, purchases could be made with caution. But both developers and lenders have very good memories, and they recall vividly the scare of 1973 to 1974, when gasoline prices rose sharply and the federal government talked of serious conservation measures. This makes land purchases risky. And, if anything, all these forces that undercut the market for outlying land will probably intensify in the near future. Anyone foolish enough to ignore these forces deserves the heavy carrying costs he will undertake.

We have all met someone whose father or grandfather once controlled the corner of Main and Spring Streets. "If only Dad had kept it," goes the timeless lament, "he would have left me a millionaire."

Timing

Timing and location are interlinked. The condition of the location makes timing important. It is not done by guess work, although I cannot rule out intuition or even luck. If you buy a great piece of outlying land where the population is growing, housing and shopping centers will be needed. When they will be needed, when mortgage money will be available, and when the right time to buy and to sell occur will determine your profits. It is timing for the use of the land that allows a real-estate investor to make money.

Timing is also important in buying (or selling) improved real estate. When interest rates begin to cool, good areas will be in demand. Until the early seventies, people were able to get cheaper mortgages on their property; when interest rates went up, they didn't want to sell and then buy again at a substantially higher rate. During tight-money times, potential buyers often can't even qualify for mortgages. This creates a bad time to buy and a bad time to sell.

The only good thing is that inflation makes the higher interest rate on improved property look better as the property appreciates.

Fortunes have been made in both land and improved real estate. But they come, large and small, only when the property is held until it becomes vintage "wine." Timing is everything in land investment. It comes alive when the use is right and the location strong. A good example of the perfect blend of location, timing, and use occurred when suburbia was born. Cheap parcels of land, located in front of the population wave, doubled and tripled in price. Shopping centers were needed on land that farmers thought could only be fertilized for corn. But keen-minded real-estate investors saw the combination: location, timing, use. They made a bundle.

Use

An investor buys land because he expects to put it to a profitable use. He either expects a continuing income from the property or, if he's a developer, he looks for profit from the sale of the property after he's developed it.

The key is use, called "highest and best use" in the business. Profit depends on putting the land to this highest and best use, and the land's price before that use has begun. Usually, what the buyer can afford to pay is determined by the future use of the land, the price the ultimate user will pay—the expected profit and costs.

For example, the price you pay for a piece of land is not the really important cost. Rather it is how much engineering and site preparation has to be done in order for that to become a buildable lot. I have seen land that cost $1,000 an acre cost $100,000 for site preparation because it is hillside. This is particularly true in areas that have water just below the surface, as in Florida, or in low-lying land next to swamps or bodies of water, or on hillsides or rolling land.

The more units developed on a piece of property, the more dense or intense the use, and the higher the price that can be paid for it. However, as Florida's condominium overbuilding orgy proved, there is a limit to how many units you should try to put on an acre. Florida land sales were multiplied by the allowable densities (frequently 40 or more units per acre) multiplied times a low-sounding per unit price, such as $1,500 or $2,500. However, there was no way to sell such high density. Therefore, the builder had to come in with lower densities but having terribly overpaid for the land, he had to fail. Furthermore, commercial users—who generate a profit from land use—can afford to pay more for their real-estate facilities than residential users; store operators can pay more than office occupants, who in turn pay more than industrial users. Thus, the use of land determines the price that can be paid for it. Conversely, the price that is paid for land determines the use to which it must be put in order to justify that price.

The primary determinant of price is location, because location controls use. Industrial firms need to be located near major highways, lawyers prefer to be near the court house, doctors near hospitals. There are a limited number of locations (sites) suitable for a particular use in a given area. Supply and demand dictate that the fewer the available sites for a particular use, the higher the price of these locations.

If the price asked by the owners exceeds that level, the property will not be sold until the price of finished units for that use increases to permit a higher land cost, or changes in circumstances justify a higher (or more intensive) use of the property.

An example of the effect that location and price play in limiting use occurs when land in existing residential neighborhoods is priced too high to allow its development with moderately priced single-family housing. If municipal officials do not permit lower-priced land to be developed for such housing, the lack of available sites will be one of the factors (along with high construction and financing costs) that slows or halts development of middle-income single-family housing.

Use and location, therefore, control land values. Commercial land is worth many times more than residential land. Industrial land runs higher than single-family but lower than apartment and commercial land. It pays for the investor getting the option to buy, also to get the land rezoned.

I'll give you an idea of how the initial low down payment—leverage—can control a piece of land, get it rezoned, and make a profit. For example, agriculturally zoned land sells in some areas for $2,500 an acre. Rezoned to shopping, it's worth $60,000 an acre. Single-family land is $10,000 an acre, but rezoned to apartments its worth is $40,000 an acre. Rezone that apartment acreage to high-rise, and the value per acre jumps to $200,000. But location determines the final value.

The determination of the best use of a piece of property, and the price the ultimate user will pay, are decisions based upon knowledge, experience, and (to some extent) intuition. The soundness of the investor's judgment on use and price will determine how well that investor does in real estate.

But real-estate investors who make these moves are not only intelligent or lucky. They have learned and practiced the rules of location, timing, and use. They also know how to get good information in the field, how to read it and understand it, and how to use it.

Research

Market research and analysis benefit the real-estate investor, developer, buyer, and seller. Unfortunately, too few of them pay any attention to it, even though this new technology could save them thousands of dollars and gallons of antacid tablets. Too many people in the real-estate business like to go by instinct and intuition alone. They let "gut feelings" overrule their intellect and perception.

It's one thing to be at the right place at the right time. But you should also be there with the right product, and having the right product at the right place comes from knowing and listening to a solid market analyst. In the past, the real-estate investor who was not exactly on his market was able to scrape by. Today, however, a near miss may result in slow sales, or no sales at all—a loss.

Today's consumer, from home buyer to investor, is better educated, has more knowledge, and a better idea of what he wants than previous consumers. He's tighter with his money, stretching the dollar and demanding more for it. For some consumers, like the Green Chip Investor, buying a home is the most expensive product they will ever purchase.

Reaching these sophisticated consumers today is an art. Yet few real-estate investors, planning to buy, develop, and then either sell or hold property, take advantage of the people and firms trained to collect and report data about the real-estate market. The last three chapters have detailed the complexities of this business, and the variables of our population. Getting all the help you can before investing a dime seems to me to make terrific sense. Facts gathered by market analysts can help you to buy (or sell) a given property, plan its correct use, determine the site (or method) for a development program, and plan a strategy for the best penetration of a given market. Market research helps take the risk out of pinpointing location, timing, and use.

The name of the game is "proper planning." As a real-estate investor, you must know where you are going, how long it will take you to get there, how much you will need, what moves you should make, and how to make them. The successful real-estate investor moves on facts, experience, intuition, and judgment. Market research will gather all the facts, confirm the wisdom of your experience, and cross-check the certainty of your intuition.

There are many sources of information you can use to check out your real-estate deal. Some of them can be found in libraries and public records, others must be determined by professional market-research companies.

The U.S. census, for example, contains a wealth of information about income levels, race, mobility, birth, the number of people occupying a housing unit, details concerning housing, and other demographic factors.

The decennial census covers a house-to-house report. The Census Bureau also conducts a current population survey based on a monthly sampling of about 35,000 interviewed households. This information is used to keep the decennial census up-to-date.

Public records may also supply information within a given area on real-estate sales, plan developments, transfers, mortgages, foreclosures, building permits, planned roads and highways. Additional data may be obtained from community organizations, including Chambers of Commerce, development corporations and agencies, governmental agencies, political organizations, industrial associations, and others.

These sources of data are open to anyone. Research organizations, because of their experience in the field, are probably able to gather data for you more efficiently and more error-free than an individual or firm approaching the research for the first time.

In addition, a research organization that has been in business for any length of time will have a data bank from which it can draw information for a specific client.

Original Research. After the existing data has been studied, original research may be needed to round out the picture and assure its accuracy. Here, the primary reliance is on personal interviews of the people in the area. The number of people to be interviewed will vary from project to project depending upon, among other things, the size of the area involved.

A research organization will ordinarily draw up one or more interview questionnaires, and either use the employees of an established interviewing organization or its own permanent staff of interviewers.

You can do your own interviewing, if you wish. But having a professional outfit do it—in the cases when your deal warrants such an outlay—is well worth the expense.

The interviews are not necessarily limited to residents of the area or traffic circulating in the area, but may also cover builders, developers, and others. A survey may be made, for example, by interviewers circulating at a competitive subdivision. Such a survey is not undertaken without the permission of the developer whose customers are being surveyed. If permission is not forthcoming, there are various other ways of getting the interviews. You might check the license plates of the cars, and then check the car registrations, which furnish the residences of the traffic. With this information, a telephone interview or mail-out questionnaire can elicit the necessary research information you need to make your real-estate decisions.

As part of the survey of a community, the research team will thoroughly cover the community and note the important characteristics, such as the type of homes, their state of maintenance, the kind of automobiles, road conditions, the location of community facilities, and dozens of other items. This serves as a cross-check on data gathered from other sources, including census figures and interviews.

One of the most difficult, and important, questions asked in your interviews concerns family income. This question is usually saved for the close of the interview, at which point a card containing various family-income categories listed by letter is given to the interviewee. He or she is asked to indicate his or her income by letter category. The fact that the interviewee has been answering questions already, and that he or she is being asked only to indicate a code letter (and not a specific sum), is calculated to produce an accurate response. Cross-checking has borne out the accuracy of information obtained this way.

Research Analysis. One of the chief shortcomings of research companies is their unwillingness to make specific recommendations and sale projections. But they are valuable in recommending the strategy for penetrating a particular market and predicting how the competition may respond to your initial thrust. They may also suggest a counterstrategy to offset the expected move by your competitor.

Good market research should be on a continuing basis where the size of the investment warrants it. On a regular schedule, the economics of the market are examined to determine changes that have taken place or are about to take place. The competition is checked out to determine if they have developed any new models or are planning on doing so. Potential competition is checked out to see what new products may be coming onto the market.

Interviews are conducted to determine any changes in the character of the traffic or changing attitudes about your product.

All of this and other data are then analyzed, and recommendations are made pertaining to the location of your potential investment, the timing, and its use and acceptance by your future customers (whether they are renters or buyers). Continuing research enables you to judge the timing of your next unit or investment in the same area. Continuing audits will allow you to adjust the size of your investment, shift your merchandising strategy, and increase or decrease the amount and price of your product.

For builders, marketing research can help determine the depth of their market and the number of units that can reasonably be expected to sell in a given market area and on a specific parcel of land. Such information is also of value to investors, joint-venturers, and others. Research helps developers determine price range, land costs, plan sizes, layouts, timing and location relationships.

In general, the real-estate investor profits from market research by discovering the following facts:

- The basic demographics of a region—population, housing, income, etc.
- The best locations for specific real-estate projects.
- What's for sale, and what isn't.
- Who will buy and who won't.
- Why some people will buy at one location and not another.
- Where the customer market is.
- Where the potential customers work.
- How much they are willing to pay and what type of financing they prefer.
- Which advertising and promotional media reach them most effectively.
- What new products will be successful, and *why* some new products will be successful (or not).

The Rules of Mini-Monopoly

Let's review for a moment. You've got some money and decided to invest it in real estate. You've discovered what kind of investor you wish to be and why you are investing. You've studied the trends, learned to analyze markets for location, good timing, and ultimate use. Now that you've come this far, here are some rules you should understand and follow. I call them the rules of mini-monopoly, and they should help you to enjoy your investment and make a little money, too.

1. Know What Kind of Real-Estate Investor You Are, and Know What Kind of Real Estate You Want. As you'll discover in this book, there is a variety of real-estate deals. You should be sure to fit any deal to your real-estate budget and your real-estate goals.

2. *See the Property in Person.* Remember that each piece of real estate is a separate business. Walk around your potential investment, slam the doors, feel the soil, watch the traffic.

3. *Check Out the Risks.* Can you afford to lose the money you're investing? Try to stay away from long shots. At the very least, enjoy some tax benefits from the deal if it doesn't work out. Make sure your attorney checks out the entire package.

4. *Buy Quality!* The higher the percentage returns quoted, the higher the risks. It pays to buy prime locations even at high cost (but not high bank prime). Invest in a good dealer and expert advice.

5. *Tax Benefits Are Only Icing.* The deal must be a good one that will earn hard dollars when you need them. You will be better off in the long run if you look at it as a hard-money deal while using any tax shelter it throws off. This means that the deal has a marketplace, so that it sells, leases, or does what it was designed to do.

6. *Too Much Leverage Is Dangerous for the Amateur.* When does the cash have to be in? Be sure to give yourself enough time to bring others into the deal.

If the leverage depends upon getting the land rezoned, you may die before the planning commission comes through.

The leverage is good if it takes what you can afford to pay, holds enough of the land to do something with it, and gives you the time (or the dealer) to make it happen. Anything less is asking for lost money.

7. *Be Patient.* Don't get killed looking for a killing. Build in fail-safes to your deal so that you can leave it without too

much pain. Be prepared to carry your investment, even if it takes more than you think it will. This will happen more often than not. Never enter any deal to get rich quick. If you get richer, be thankful. It will only come after careful work, concentration, timing and, perhaps, luck.

8. *Use the Finest Advisors.* They will earn their fees over and over again. But make sure that your advisor is not too busy a person. Make certain that your deal, and you, are very important to him. If he cannot concentrate on your project, he could get you into trouble.

Use an accountant and an attorney who know real estate. Pay for solid, well-done research that pertains specifically to your deal.

9. *Know the Dealer.* Check him out. Do you know who he is? Get references from him, and don't fall for the old line, "We don't have time to waste. Are you in or out?"

Haste makes aggravation and wastes your money. Be prepared for a solid dealer to drive a hard bargain. He should have a list of people who would recommend him. He is worth the effort. Make sure the dealer has a good track record. You *must* know some trusted person or professional who is familiar with him. Never, *never* buy blind from a dealer you don't know, or who doesn't check out.

10. *Know the Location.* This is the key to real-estate deals: location. Make certain, from your research, advisors, and study, that your deal has good location.

11. *Does the Use Fit the Location?* Be sure that the real estate you are interested in has a use. Don't let it lie there; holding can be expensive for you. Make certain that a qualified engineer checks out the land. Even flat ground can have incredible problems.

For a large deal, hire an unbiased, unconnected, but

trustworthy researcher to check out the deal with the location and use in mind. Give him enough time to do a thorough job.

12. Is the Timing Right for Your Deal? Real estate is a fluid, changing market. Zoning and working out deals take time and cost money. Delays can drain your funds.

Even the costs of money change, and that fluctuation can make your deal a poor risk. Make sure that the timing of your deal is as good as you and your advisors can make it. Remember that timing is tied to location and use.

If you follow these rules of mini-Monopoly, you shouldn't end up like my thirteen-year-old daughter, who once said: "I always wanted to own Park Avenue. Now that I own it, why doesn't anybody land on it?"

PART TWO

BEFORE YOU LEAP

5

ADVISORS AND DEALS

In my work I've met many investors seeking advice. I've also learned that the person the investor asks for advice *before* the deal is made helps or hinders the deal as much as any other factor. But who to ask? There is competition in every aspect of real-estate dealings, and you should get all the help you can to keep your competitive edge.

If your deal is big, or if you are putting together a real-estate portfolio, you should think about getting (and paying for) a solid real-estate advisor. A good one will cost you money, but he will also save you a bundle by keeping you out of bad deals.

There is a new breed of advisors available today, a professional core of creative and exciting people who love to manage money brilliantly. One of the best is a Midwest group, headed by a young, dynamic winner. I sat down with him and got this advice from the advisor:

Q: What do you do for your clients?

A: We analyze their financial goals and put them into a

workable pattern. We get our clients to understand reality and that consistency is needed with planning. Then we can put the numbers together for them.

The carrying out of this plan is critical. The most important thing we accomplish for our client is to make him achieve, through consistent planning and consistent growth, the goals he has in mind. There must be a realistic goal; we must set our sights clearly; we have to map out our plan and someone has to do the work. Every client has different needs and goals. Our older clients, for example, are being moved into a more liquid and secure position than our younger ones.

Our expertise is this planning. We put our clients together with experts from different areas. We know the right people. We are like an architect: We create the real-estate plan, but we don't make the bricks.

We design a plan and all proposed actions to be taken by lawyers, investment counselors, and so forth. We have certain performance requirements. When the client's financial goal is well planned and we meet that goal, then we should be out of the picture.

Q: What advice do you have for the $100,000 a year executive?

A: If he's forty years old, self-employed, making $100,000 a year, then he ought to have a retirement plan or pension plan to shelter 25 percent of his income. Maybe that would be triple A securities or triple A bonds, basically a conservative, fixed-income portfolio right off the top. He now has $75,000 left, and should be able to live on $35,000 a year. That leaves him $40,000 for taxes or investments. I would move $15,000 to $20,000 per year into real estate; that will be aided by at least 50 percent of tax, which means a $20,000 real-estate investment will cost only $10,000. Over ten years, that man will have a $200,000 real-estate portfolio and a $250,000 pension portfolio, not including interest.

The problem with people in this income bracket is that they feel so pressed by taxes and inflation. This cuts their spendable dollars. They feel they have to splash—make fast deals and big money. All they keep saying is that they can't save $8,000 a year. So they feel obligated to go into tax shelters or other high-risk deals because they need so desperately to make that 100 percent return on their money.

They should always put some assets into fixed commitments, some more assets (as they build net worth) into an equity-oriented portfolio. And they should move into real property. That way, with inflation, they will always have an income-producing base even if things go backward.

The best investment any of our clients have made is their home. Nobody can compete with the appreciation and pleasure they have received from their home as compared with any other asset in their portfolio. That home is utilized, the tax deduction for maintenance and interest taken, and it has become more valuable. After serving its primary function for the family, the home still ends up being the best investment.

Q: What do you look for in giving advice to a client?

A: We look for balance. We've seen people risk everything for financial success, and that's wrong. We try to distinguish between need and desire for our clients. He needs to retire with dignity, he needs to have family security if he dies or is disabled. He doesn't need, however, to be a millionaire. He might deserve it, but he doesn't need it. Needs ought to be guaranteed, but desires can be speculated with.

Q: What types of investment make sense today?

A: If the client has a low level of anxiety, then the stock market might suit him. Our investment philosophy is that the investor ought to have: a home, cash in the bank (six months at present living standard), related real estate (that is, a doctor renting his own medical building), a balanced portfolio of income-generating or money-market assets, which could be certificates of deposit, bonds, treasury notes, and so forth. Comparing the stock market and real estate, we favor the latter for our clients. One can take the same risks with real estate, and come out better in the long run. With the tax advantages, if everything comes out equal, he can double his money.

But it is very difficult to find good real-estate deals. We

try to put our clients together with good real-estate opportunities; we're the middle man. Our clients invest and buy real estate through us. We take a position right alongside our clients on a subordinated basis, which says: "After you get your money back, we want to share." If our clients prosper, so do we.

My basic advice is to diversify. Diversified real estate and portfolios are your best bet.

Q: What are your investment criteria?

A: Quality rather than quantity.

If I buy a house, I want it in the right location. If I save money, I want it in a sound institution where it is responsibly managed. If I look for stock, I look for quality. I don't look for a fast profit.

Our criteria in real estate is to go to a developer who can put the deal together and provide equity for deals we find are sound. We accept no liability and want a preference return on our money. We only provide financial help, we don't provide creativity. All we want is a fair shake for our investors.

We manage a philosophy. Once we set the foundation, we have to maintain quality. We actually manage high-caliber people to perform certain functions for our clients. We measure performance.

Q: How can a small investor keep ahead of inflation?

A: Through his investment in his home and a new one. His pension reform plan offers opportunities: He will be able to put money away on a tax-shelter basis. Fine tax-shelter plans coming on the market through the new pension-reform plan are good, consistent investments. And consistency pays off.

Real-Estate Team

As you begin to invest in real estate, you will be putting together—whether you wish to or not—a real-estate team. That team may include your real-estate advisor, your attorney, your accountant, and others who may help you in your choices and transactions. There are some rules to putting together this real-estate team, and you would do well to remember them:

- You need a leg man to gather information. He can be paid by the day, week, or assignment. He lives with the project from the beginning.
- You need a legal entity with which to tie up the land. Nothing beats a dependable attorney.
- You need advice on money control. Your accountant can give you solid advice here, and set up the system for you.
- You need market analysis. An outside professional is best here, unless you have the time or your partner can do it.
- You need someone good with numbers to draw up all the math into *pro forma* so that your overall mathematical plan is excellent.
- You need someone good at estimating costs—past, present, and future.
- You need a builder or a contractor who can be hired on a fee basis (general contractor), or as a partner or joint venturer.
- You need someone, perhaps yourself, who takes the overall picture—the figures and the people—and sells it to the money lenders.

The Fiduciary

There are other advisors of value to you. In today's financial market, one special professional stands out: the fiduciary.

The fiduciary can be a trustee, investment advisor or consultant. He differs from his predecessor, the real-estate broker, in one major way: compensation. The fiduciary is paid a fee, usually a retainer. This fee is his earnings and an indication of net worth, and, therefore, the good fiduciary looks for a lasting relationship or steady growth, not immediate profits, from his business with you.

Brokers are rewarded whether a deal is good or bad. The

broker gets paid for selling a piece of property, risky or secure, and doesn't have to worry about pitfalls. He never worries, either, about follow through, since his payment is one-time and made at the point of sale. For these reasons, the broker is not always a reliable advisor, though there are exceptional ones.

The fiduciary, on the other hand, has a unique relationship with his client. That relationship begins far before the sales pitch, and extends far beyond the completion of the sale. The relationship is guided by strict legal requirements called the prudent man ruling (the section codes and state securities regulations). By law the fiduciary must prepare full disclosure of *all* potential liabilities. He must be prepared to demonstrate to your accountant and attorney why he has made a certain decision. Your attorney and accountant should regard him as an equal, a professional advisor. In fact, the fiduciary himself may be an accountant or an attorney.

Obviously, these are special skills, and special services. A fiduciary is not for Mr. Green Chip, but for Mr. Silver.

The fiduciary must qualify the needs of the investor. He does this by preparing a detailed financial plan. He must determine the investor's salary, his tax deductions and tax liabilities, and conclude what amount of real-estate investment he can safely make. These are tools with which the fiduciary makes crucial decisions.

Some of the questions the fiduciary examines are vital to your financial well-being. They are also excellent questions for you to consider, and to raise with your real-estate advisors.

Do you, the real-estate investor, need liquidity, income, net worth growth through appreciation, or tax shelter? What combination will best suit you? What is the investor's projected earning power? Does the proposed project have future potential liabilities, and can the investor meet these without undue financial hardship? The fiduciary will examine your estate. What happens to your estate if you die or become disabled? Do you have adequate life or disablity insurance? Do you want to pass your assets on to your heirs, or sell them? This might require looking into trusts for the children.

With the complexities of real-estate investment increasing, and the costs of even a small shopping center or office building exceeding $500,000, the real-estate advisor and the fiduciary are becoming ever more important. In fact, the fiduciary is a completely new profession serving this expanding field.

Evaluating the Dealer or Developer

Your advisors will help you to evaluate the deals you may be considering. I will discuss this more fully in Chapter Nine. But before jumping into any real-estate deal, you and your advisors should check out the dealer. There are a number of characteristics to look for: integrity, entrepreneurial ability, track record, land and project inventory, organization, outside talent, financing sources, equity capital, and investor relations. They are all important.

The dealer himself should furnish verbal and written information on these factors, and provide the investor with references for verification of these points. Weighing these, you (the investor) must also determine from your own resources whether or not (a) the dealer is a reputable businessman who will follow the golden rule of investment by treating your investment dollars as he would his own, (b) the dealer has good intentions, but lacks the high-level management ability required in the real estate business, or, (c) the dealer shows signs of wanting to milk his investors dry.

Integrity

You can begin checking out the dealer's integrity by examining the product he produces or intends to produce. What has he dealt in before? If he consistently rapes the public by selling them shoddy merchandise at unfair prices, you should avoid him. Fixing unreasonable prices on good merchandise—even land—is asking to be undercut by competition and, thus, slow sales, which in turn decimate profits through high holding costs. This does not mean that a reasonable premium and above-average return are not justified on a superior product or property. But your judgment will tell you whether or not the dealer is being fair in the marketplace, or cheap.

Another sign of integrity is a good relationship with suppliers. In the building industry with its problems, for example, a history of occasional slow payment to creditors should not be considered damning. But, when a developer is notorious for playing with his suppliers' money, there is little assurance that he will treat your money with any more respect. Moreover, credit manipulation is a sign of a developer's weak underpinnings; of trying to build too much with too little capital. Watch for this weakness and stay away from it.

Playing this kind of credit game has other, often hidden, penalties for you. It may mean that the dealer will be buying his materials at high prices because of his poor credit performance. Or, he may be charged a premium for his known credit game-playing. Whatever, it's your investment monies that will be going to pay for his credit foolishness.

Entrepreneurial Ability

The dealer's entrepreneurial ability is also important. In a literal sense, entrepreneurship means a one-man business. One guy runs the whole show, and takes the whole risk.

Although he may operate as a corporation for tax and other legal reasons, the successful developer is a consummate entrepreneur. John Konweiser, a top-notch developer (and coordinator of seminars on how to become a developer), emphasizes that tight control means that the developer knows "where every cent is spent and his people know he will require them to justify why it should be spent, where it is spent, and that they are getting the best value for it. Not surprisingly, $100 here and $50 there can add up to hundreds of thousands of dollars on a project, and spell the difference between just making wages and making the kind of profit that the risk merits."

Bigness in a developer isn't necessarily an assurance of big profits. The large developers have been having problems; control in the real-estate development industry decreases with size. Responsibility, too, diminshes.

The typical small developer is required by the lending institution to personally sign for the loan he arranges. Unlike other corporate businesses where the corporate structure insulates the developer from liability, the small developer risks his entire net worth on each deal. The executive of a large development corporation who makes a major error stands only to lose his job. The small developer may lose his business, which represents all of his personal financial security.

The small, one-man operator knows every detail of every deal he makes. He understands the multiple ramifications of each decision. (If he doesn't, he isn't in business very long.) He knows whether a particular product improvement will increase sales and profits, or will increase sales at the risk of profits. The executive in the large organization who looks only at the sales end, or the production end, or the financial end loses the essential total perspective of the developer who watches everything from his trailer on the site.

Track Record

Judging the track record of a good developer is difficult. In this business, it is not necessarily a bad sign that he's been broke a couple of times during his business career. In fact, there are people in the field who argue that the ability to bounce back and learn from a failure is essential in developing the guts needed to survive in the risky real-estate game. I would argue that the dealer who hasn't been under, or close to it, probably doesn't know the rules and limits of the game, and may tend to take more chances with your money.

Therefore, a dealer's past track record is important to your understanding of what to expect from him. His reactions to wins and losses tell you about his ability to watch the market and take advantage of it, or to learn from past errors. The more downswings he has weathered, the more likely he is to have learned lessons from earlier problems.

Another very vital part of the developer's track record is the scale of his past operations. How do those projects relate to his present ones? If your man shows consistent growth in the scale of projects he has handled, you've got an ace. On the other hand, if he wants to jump several levels of project magnitude in one step, look out. He may be trying to make a bundle on a really big project, which he can't handle. He could be taking a flier—with your money.

Over-extension and over-expansion are the major causes of failure in the real-estate business. It is one thing for the developer's track record to show that he tried this and learned his lesson, and quite another for it to reveal that he's willing to gamble big with someone else's bankroll.

Land and Project Inventory

Over-extension can mean more than trying to do too large a project. It can also mean trying to carry too heavy a load of raw land and future projects. Annual holding costs of land in the mid-1970s has often reached 20 percent a year. (This is based on interest rates of 10 to 12 percent, real-estate taxes of 2 to 3 percent; plus extra "points" above the "prime lending rate." This insures failure. With holding costs at 20 percent, if a developer makes a 10 percent profit on each dollar of sales, he needs $2 of sales to carry each dollar of land inventory.

The carrying-cost problem increases where the land is partially developed with streets, utilities, and community facilities. In this case, the cost of carrying the property is compounded by additional costs applied both to the land and to the land improvements.

Thus, a large land and project inventory can have an enormous fiscal drag on the developer. A developer with more than three years of advance projects is courting trouble. His only way out is to have a large financial institution as a partner who is willing to warehouse his land inventory by paying the carrying costs and selling it to the developer as he can use it. Or, the developer can find a major private investor, and have him assume the risks.

However, a new industry was spawned during good times, that being people land-banking lots "ready-to-use" for builders who would buy them as they needed them. The builder does not mind this type of dealer or land developer adding a good profit for himself. He would prefer someone else banking the land, using his own resources. This gives him great flexibility.

Organization

A successful developer will avoid maintaining too large an organization. That's a costly ego trip. Money flows into profitable projects in large amounts, and a developer can become trapped into a big organization that is merely a monument to himself.

Equally costly is the wrong type of organization. A weak developer is tempted to hire as employees the attorney and the architect who have been with him in previous deals. In many cases, unfortunately, these specialists lose their creativity when confined to a single organization. Whether it's the security of the weekly paycheck, or the lack of variety of work, they tend to slow down. They get duller, and become luxuries the developer cannot afford to maintain.

The quality and quantity of an effective development organization are interrelated. The solid organization contains front-line people who understand the major segments of the business. It has few, if any, staff specialists who know only limited functional areas. The project superintendent or building manager is a generalist capable of making decisions on marketing and production problems. He is the backbone of the company and the real-estate industry. He often gets a piece of the action (or some form of incentive compensation), and that gives him the same bottom-line awareness as the boss and the investors.

Meet a few project superintendents and the boss's secretary, and you will have a solid idea of what the boss and his company are like.

Outside Talent

The developer or dealer can also be judged by his three "A's": accountant, attorney, architect. Top-level real-estate professionals are so in demand that they can afford to work only for the best firms, and at stiff prices. They have an independence and client respect, and are not tied to any one developer or dealer.

Who they are, what their track record is, and what they tell you (if anything) about the developer or dealer you're checking out, can give you a very solid picture of your man.

Financing Arrangements

Banks and other financial institutions will also give you a great deal of information about developers whom they have financed. They will usually have in-depth knowledge about the developer's integrity, track record, and the other factors we have discussed above. They may not always want to reveal them, but a good contact inside a major lending institution in your area is highly sought and very valuable.

From these institutions you should be able to determine the type and nature of the financing of the developer's recent deals. This will tell you something about his stability and profit-making. If he has the institution involved as a partner, he shows good staying power. (They've checked him out, loaned him their money; they must like him.)

An unsecured line that permits the developer to borrow for general operating capital is an additional sign of good financial relations and strength. On the other hand, a developer who is being charged the top interest rate that financial institutions can charge him is someone to be wary of. Obviously, these lending institutions are concerned about him, and are putting a financial load on his projects that he might not be able to carry.

Financial Stake and Back-Up Capital

The developer's stake can be measured in two ways: how much and for how long.

The dealer should back up his guarantees of performance with hard cash. If he's getting in and out quickly, beware. The best kind of deal is one in which the dealer must continue to work to protect his investors because he is subject to the identical financial risks that they are. So watch what the developer himself commits to the deal.

Further, it is to the investor's advantage to deal with an operator with reserve capital. If problems develop, then it's too late to probe around and find the capital needed to continue. Investors will look upon it as good money being thrown after bad.

The greatest assurance, therefore, that a deal will be pulled out, or at least salvaged, comes from having a developer with a moral and financial commitment to the deal—and the financial ability to act on that commitment.

Investor Relations

The developer should communicate. That is, he must be the kind of businessman who informs his investors in a formal way where they and the deal stand. He must also be reasonably available to the investors for special information and occasional reassurance. The investor should verify from other investors and people who have dealt with the developer before that he is this kind of person.

The sound developer realizes that he owes much more than just money to those who back him. He treats them as partners, and not just money lenders. He is not an alarmist, and appropriately avoids the premature disclosure of problems he expects to resolve. But if his back is against the wall, he should also have the guts to face his investors. In such difficult moments, he must maintain the faith of his investors. If he does, he may be able to draw cash from them, or ideas, or just the inspiration that permits him to save the deal.

Unfortunately, even dealers who are good performers many times do not realize the value of good communications with their investors. A little consideration mixed with foresight could avoid the frustration an investor feels when he does not know where he stands on a deal. A good developer will bring his investors in close to him, and such a skill will make him an even better—and more successful—real-estate developer.

So picking your advisors and screening your developers and dealers is another major step before you enter the real-estate game. There are some variations on this theme of advisors and dealers, and they include schemes we've already briefly discussed: joint ventures and syndicates. The next chapter details them.

6

JOINT VENTURES AND SYNDICATES

I've made good money in real estate. I know one thing for sure: Most of the time I would have been better off as part of a joint venture than on my own. Misery may love company, but happiness deserves it. It is far better to seek deals that are shared by compatible part-time investors, friends, or fellow workers, and put them together with a topnotch pro, than to go it alone.

No matter what type of investor you may be, the selection of your joint venturer will be vital to your mental and financial well-being. Harmony is not unsophisticated or unwanted. It is always exciting when I meet joint venturers who make money and enjoy working together.

My friend Dan Berman, a gifted New York attorney, has compiled a list of investors looking for joint venture deals. A partial rundown includes:

- Mr. High Tax Bracket. He's always looking for some kind of tax shelter.
- Public Corporations. There are always public companies

in real estate or general business that find themselves with excess cash for long-term investment outside their normal business or investment channels.

• Insurance Companies, Banks, Savings and Loan Service Companies. They also have a continuing need to protect themselves against rampaging inflation.

• Pension Funds. The deal needs to be tailored to the fund's tax position. While they are not looking for tax losses and deductions, many pension funds are anxious to break away from complete dependence upon stocks and bonds.

• Foreign Investors. The Arabs, Japanese, Canadians, Germans, and British are investing heavily in the United States. They are driven by fears of inflation, currency devaluations, and political turmoil. The United States offers them financial and political stability.

Foreign accounting practices also drive them here. In Great Britain, for example, property is revalued for accounting purposes every year. The result is that capital appreciation plus a limited income of, say, 7.5 percent looks very good to a British investor.

• Fellow Real-Estate Developers. More and more developers are pooling their monies to get into deals.

If you go into a joint venture, make sure that the "chemistry" is right among all of you. If it isn't, and you still want in, get an attorney who is compatible with the venturers, and stay behind him. Do not let emotions spoil a good working relationship. Some people cannot be good partners, but they are still good people—and better yet, still strong joint venturers. The climate of the deal is made by the participants. So, know who the people are in the deal; if you can't stand them but the deal is attractive, have your attorney act as intermediary.

Joint-venture partners are found everywhere. They may come from financial institutions, be administrators, builder-developers, or marketing-consulting specialists. Private investors, institutions, and public companies may also join as financial partners.

The best place to find investors interested in joint ventures is through a sophisticated mortgage broker in your area. As my friend Berman says, investors are everywhere. But different investors look for different things. The basic range of choice is limited to: ultimate growth, tax losses, and current cash flow.

Why should you join a joint venture? For one thing, it will help you to expand volume and market in your field, if you are a builder or developer. A joint venture also eliminates the need for tying up capital working in equity investments. Joint ventures may assure the continuity of your project's growth, and suffer a minimal effect from the general slowdown in the economy. Further, and this shouldn't be underestimated, joint ventures may open up new banking and financial affiliations that can prove worthwhile in future deals.

How can you attract strong financial partners? Your track record in real estate or other investments should be strong and profitable. You must know your market and project. A strong management team helps, and you should portray it and yourself accurately and honestly, but not too modestly.

Your presentation to potential financial partners must be in a first-class fashion. Admit the risks clearly and honestly, and also show that you have considered them yourself and made appropriate plans for all possibilities and contingencies. Provide answers to all probable questions in a package form. Don't wait for questions to be asked.

You should make this approach to potential financial partners when the market is strongest, and when your track record is proven and well-known. You should appear to need—and, in fact, actually need—additional financial adrenaline in order to continue substantial growth.

When should you make your pitch to financial partners? After your proposed project has been carefully conceived, accurately planned and projected, and *just* before execution. All you need is the financial injection. Financial partners do not want to wait for answers or raise original questions. They want facts, and a project about to take off, a chance to turn a profit. All project and market "homework" must already be done. It should be fully documented and should substantiate the project's merit. It should not have the "smell" of having been pedaled to a mob of other people.

How to Make the Offering

Your prospective joint venturer will want the same information about your deal that the mortgage banker or broker would want.

The prospect will need to know the details of your construction loan financing, planned or existing, and your permanent mortgage financing. Most important, he will want some assurance that you have a lock on construction costs. He'll want to know that you can bring in the job at X dollars, and if you don't, that you will have your hand in your pocket, not his. He'll also want some assurance that when you reach into your pocket, there will be something there.

You could survive without a joint financial partner. You would need money, marketing, and merchandising skills, strong administrative abilities, and solid operational capacity.

The perfect joint financial venture should work well on both sides. The financial impetus given should aid the project in direct and tangible ways: The builder-developer should be free to use his skills to complete the project and perhaps expand his market. By bringing in a financial joint venturer, the builder-developer may sacrifice a piece of his action, but he gains control over his working capital and can spend more time with his business and entrepreneurial skills.

Attracting a financial partner requires several things. You must have a creative management team. To have that, you should do five things:

1. Clearly define and isolate company operating areas.
2. Assign a capable profit-center manager to each of those areas.

3. Give that manager authority and responsibility to perform and produce results.

4. Establish an incentive compensation program for key people. Make them feel part of your investment or development team, and give them a piece of the action.

5. Establish internal management controls and communications that do not dilute or overlap authority and responsibility. But don't lose a constant sense of your business's pulse.

Attracting that financial partner requires that you show him a strong operation. And if you are the investor, the potential financial partner, you should look for that operation. The operation should have a good track record, a well-conceived, planned, and documented project, and its operators must have a strong knowledge of the market and product.

Your Company's Package

If you've formed a company, and you are seeking additional financial backing, you will have to put together a major package. Investors will be looking for that package, and it must include:

- A history of your company, including current involvements.
- A résumé of the principals and key employees.
- The company's last three years of audited financial statements.
- Its current (not more than six months old) financial statement.
- A narrative description of the proposed development, including its present status.
- An independent report on the project's economic feasibility including a market analysis.
- A résumé of development costs with supporting evidence.

• An analysis of the project's financial performance including a cash-flow analysis.

• An independent appraisal. (Financial institutions often insist upon a professional appraiser judging the worth of a piece of property. These appraisers are very important to your final loan commitment. They should be designated as MAI or SREA—which is a professional designation. You should understand that they are always very busy. References are very important in selecting the right company.)

• Architectural and engineering plans with definitive drawings.

• A copy of the recorded or proposed plan or site plan.

• A property-location map.

• Loan commitments, existing mortgages, or evidence of financing availability.

• FHA and VA reports and commitments, if any.

• A property purchase contract or option agreement.

• Leases and tenant information.

• Title policy.

You may wish, of course, to create your own financial package, to joint venture a project and hold all the cards. There are certain "musts" of creating fiscal control, financial stability, and a "profit center" company. Whatever your inclination, there are basic rules in joint venturing and financial control:

1. You must have sufficient working capital to keep pace with your project's development and your market.

2. You must have sufficient cash flow to assure operational continuity—whether of volume, project development, or of market attraction. Market attraction refers to the marketing program that is formulated to merchandise your project to its consumers, including advertising, public relations, and such.

3. If you are a builder-developer, you will need strong subcontractor and material-supplier relationships.

4. If you are building, and your investment is tied to

completion of that building, you will need to renegotiate subcontracts and material-supply unit prices, and to obtain discounts by prompt payment. Strong subs are vital.

5. Internal accounting and financial controls will be vital for accurate reporting. Timing will be everything in getting your investment to work for you. Cost overruns are killing.

6. You will also need to establish and maintain strong banking and mortgage affiliations.

There are changes in the wind. Joint venturing and financial joint partnerships are shifting ground almost daily. Here are some key areas of change:

- Sophistication. In some regions, equity partners and financial institutions are becoming active executors instead of passive equity lenders.
- Competition. Many financial companies are forming money pools and related service groups to plan and execute their own projects. They bid up land costs.
- Total Know-How. Your project will have to be financially stable with dynamic management active in a growth market with a growth product that is in demand. That means staying on top of real estate by reading, listening, talking.
- Develop Loyalties. Financial partners are inclined to prefer to work with capable, known, and skilled partners over and over again. They dislike hit-or-miss deals. If you prove yourself with them, they will return to you time and again.

There are all kinds of venture deals being offered. Many of them are excellent opportunities, and some are outstanding. I happen to think that distress, or foreclosure situations, offer a very tempting attraction.

Today's inflationary climate means that you will have trouble knowing what costs are going to be next month, let alone two or three years down the road. This means that real estate may be a good investment for most folks, but that some may find it disastrous. More and more developers and investors are looking at existing stress deals: the office building only 40 percent rented, the apartment house only 22 percent rented after a decent rent-up period, and so forth. There are lots of these deals around, and many of them have construction already completed except for minor fix-ups.

The smart thinking is, as one wag put it, "Why add your own distress deal to the market when you can buy someone else's?"

No one is going to come to you and say that they have a distress deal they want to unload. But if you check out deals that are slow in renting up, that's how opportunity begats projects and profits. Lots of distress deals surface in prime locations. Some have run into temporary problems that are more than their developers can bear and hold up. The banks aren't anxious to take them back. Most of these projects will come around in time. And there's always the comforting thought that the pendulum of inflation will bail you out of even the dumbest investment over the long haul. Florida condominiums are a good example.

Syndicates

There are real-estate syndicates, and then there are real-estate operations that should be called *sin*dicates! There have been times during my professional life when I didn't trust anything called a syndicate. I've changed—I think.

Just as there are deals and dealers, there are good syndicators and bad. Anyone who can afford a month's rent in a plush office and a month's lease on some good-looking furniture can set up a syndicate. There are always suckers waiting to be conned. I visited one syndicator who had more good-looking chicks in his office than the average college campus. They were all his own cheerleaders. He had one gal pouring tea from his silver service, and when she looked up at you through lush eyelashes and said, "You can trust my boss," you would have needed a heart of brass not to believe her.

One prexy of a dynamic syndicate ran around the West Coast in a maxicoat. He looked like a spaced-out rock star. But the bankers in the East loved him.

The syndicate field was tidied up in the mid-seventies by inflation and reality. The investor lost his naïveté, among other things, and became more cautious. Let us hope it is a lasting characteristic.

Private Syndications

Syndicates are the Silver Chip and Gold Chip investors' method of getting into deals as insiders. The investor deals directly with the dealer, and almost all his money goes into the deal. Very little goes to legal costs, investment commissions, real-estate brokerage fees and management fees that may take 15 to 30 percent of the investor's dollar in a public investment.

A real-estate syndicate is a specific organization formed to invest in (and hopefully profit from) an interest in real estate. Syndication can be in the form of a trust, or a corporate, general, or limited partnership. Investors are offered tax, legal, and practical advantages of real-estate investment, with a comparatively small capital contribution.

A syndicate usually has a specific piece of property to deal, which the investor can see (and should), and evaluate. In a public operation, the properties may be scattered, or not yet chosen. Further, in a public deal, the investor may only meet the salesman, and not the top man himself. Evaluation of the deal is thus clouded, perhaps deliberately.

There are worthwhile brokers and salesmen in the real-estate industry who thoroughly investigate their product and only handle deals they believe in (and sometimes invest in themselves). But it is rare to find the commission salesman with the degree of knowledge and integrity to qualify as an honest-to-goodness investment counselor. Real estate is a big ticket item with big commissions. The sale of real estate and real-estate syndicates has often attracted the fast-buck boys. When approached with a deal, the investor—or preferably a professional hired by him on a fee basis—should check out the salesman's understanding of the deal and his reputation.

You, as the investor, should decide what kind of syndicate you want: a development syndicate or an income-property syndicate. Each has a different way of generating its type of deal.

The investor should earn between 12 and 15 percent on his investment with an income-property syndicate, and between 15 and 25 percent on a development syndicate. But more return also carries with it more risk.

Development Syndicates

The best source of development deals are those professionals who serve the developer. These are attorneys and accountants. You may find a good development deal through your attorney or accountant who knows another professional involved in the deal. A good professional advisor, accountant, or lawyer should know your needs, and put you together with deals he hears about in the course of his business.

There are two other methods for finding development deals. First, the bank or mortgage company providing construction financing to developers should know of them. Interim lenders also know when a developer is stretching his equity cushion too thin. The smart real-estate investor will find out which institutions bankroll developers, and contact a lending officer in one of these institutions. He should ask to be put in touch with developers who might be interested in the investor's action.

This is the acid test of a smart deal: Find someone who's putting money into it. Where the co-investor is a sophisticated institutional lender, the investor can expect that a good job has been done investigating the deal and dealers, and that someone is monitoring performance.

The second method is for the investor to check around with professionals, lending institutions, and construction-material suppliers. They can tell you who are the best small and medium-sized developers in your area even if they are not aware of current deals. Then you might go directly to the developers and make your offer for any worthwhile deals they might have.

This method may take a little time, but it's time well spent. Once the investor finds a solid developer he can bankroll, he is likely to have a long and mutually-beneficial relationship. Many small and medium-sized developers have a group of investors that they carry with them from deal to deal. The projects they handle steadily increase, as do their profits and the investors' net worth.

Income Property Syndicates

Finding good developers is one of the best sources of finding good income-property deals. To keep their operating capital turning, many developers sell out their income-property projects to investor groups after the projects have been completed. That same group of investors may roll over its interest in the development syndicate into an ownership position in the finished project. That offers a likely tax advantage of deferred taxation on their share of the development profits.

To find existing deals, the most typical arrangement is for the investor to establish a working relationship with a real-estate broker who specializes in income properties. Often that relationship is established as a result of the broker's being able to handle a property the investor locates through his own search. These deals can be good if the broker is sound. But the investor should have broker-originated deals checked out thoroughly by an independent professional investment advisor whose fee does not depend upon the deal being made.

The more sophisticated income-property investors have established relationships with thrift institutions and others providing permanent financing for income properties. Through these institutions they learn of deals with financial problems that, as a result, can frequently be bought at a bargain price.

Words of Caution

Beware of anyone who tells you that they have the secret for making money on land deals. Before you put your money into anything, especially syndicates, you should:

- Know exactly what their track record is. Ask for case histories with real names that can be checked out.
- Check with the Better Business Bureau for their background.
- Check with their bank.
- Ask them how they would manage your money, and find out who would manage it.
- Ask how much of the investment would go into land and how much into building; how much would go into miscellaneous items.
- Find out what they know about the property they are selling.
- Ask when they say, "checked by research," who did the research, who owns the research company, and is the research simply composed of boiler-plate statistics or do the statistics have meaning to the investment in question?
- Visit the land and check out the local market.

There are many more investors around than solid syndicates. As a development financing vehicle, syndicates are being forced out of the field by lenders wanting a piece of the action themselves, and by rising costs that place deals beyond the amount of capital that can be raised by the syndicates.

Many investors fail to realize that they can originate syndicates themselves. They can bring together friends and associates into a deal that is too large for them to handle alone.

Consequently, they may miss some good opportunities by not taking a little initiative to become more active and more professional in real estate.

Most states limit the number of people who can be brought into a deal before it must go public with registration. That limitation is often between 10 and 20 people. If there are 35 investors and they live in more than one state, then the Securities and Exchange Commission wants the deal registered in its files. SEC registration costs are about triple that of state registration costs.

In any event, there will be syndicates as long as there are real-estate salesmen who get turned on by the bread to be made in development, or lawyers and real-estate operators out for the action in packaging income-property deals. We began seeing in the mid-1970s the decrease in development syndicates. Since the typical investor can come up with, or only wants to invest, about $25,000 in any one deal, syndicates can handle deals requiring approximately $250,000 of equity capital. Thus, the near future may see syndication limited to income properties. Even in this area inflation and competition by investors for good deals is making syndication more and more difficult.

As far as I am concerned, your own good accountant or tax attorney is the best person to help guide a syndicate of related clients of his. I like working with someone who has been looking over my shoulder prior to the creation of a new deal.

You should always check with a competent professional regarding the ever-changing rules and interpretations of anything that might come under the purview of the Securities and Exchange Commission. Never, never, assume anything about IRS or SEC.

For example, the IRS becomes irritated in a deal that has no probability of producing economic profit as a result of the investment. Also, they do not look with love on a deal where items of credit, gain, loss, or deduction are allocated among the partners in different ratios from the overall percentage of profit and loss.

7

FINANCING YOUR DEAL

There are many kinds of definitions of real-estate deals. One of the best, of course, is mine: "You use somebody else's money to get as deeply in debt as your lender will allow you to get, so that you can tell everybody how rich you are."

Getting your deal off the ground means knowing the financial boys. They can be great friends when they have plenty of money to loan. They are not great friends in times of tight money. The financial boys are primarily concerned about risks. They'll want to know who you are, why they should lend you money, what you are going to spend the money on, how big your overhead is, how much salary you're taking out of the deal, and how well you've studied your market and its potential to sell, lease, or rent what you're putting together.

To get financing, you must develop a financial package. The basic objective of the financial package is to sell the lender (or his representative) on making a loan to you to carry out the project. To do this, you must sell him on the basic facts regarding your project, the borrowers (builder-developer), and the objectives to be accomplished with the financing. And all of this must be done in a way that is easy to understand.

The financial package does not have to be specially created for the lender or beautifully put together. But it must be well-organized and contain a clear and believable analysis that will stand up to careful scrutiny by the lender. To put together such a package, you should try to place yourself in the role of the lender, and ask: "What do I want and need to know about this project to lend it money?"

There are characteristics of your project that will affect the type of financing sought and its source. These are: type of project, purpose of project, and type of financing required.

The lender will want to know what type of project you have in mind: residential, with apartments, condominiums, townhouses, or single-family dwellings; commercial, for single or multitenant; or industrial, for single or multitenant.

Secondly, what is the purpose of the project: Are you building for sale, in order to make a profit on the sale? Or, are you building to own, in order to obtain income?

Thirdly, there are six basic types of financing that should fit your specific type of project: permanent, interim, secondary, land, chattel, and land-sale leaseback.

Package Presentation

Your financial package presentation should contain the basic elements of your project. This contains ten major points. You should prepare:

1. A Description of the Project in Considerable Detail. For an apartment project, the important descriptive items would include the number and size of the units, the number of parking spaces (and the number that will be covered), the proposed rents, the type of construction and the key amenities, like dishwasher, washer/dryer, disposals, and so forth.

For a commercial building, the key descriptive items would include the gross area, the net leasable area, the amount of parking (covered and uncovered), a description of access to the project and the type of construction. You should also discuss the question of whether or not you are delivering finished buildings or a "shell."

2. *A Description of the Owners (the Borrowers).* This would focus on the key principals in the project. It should detail their experience in the business. It must also include financial statements for the principals, and their company if the builder is to be a business firm. There should also be a section on the source of funds available to make the equity investment in the project. Have you done anything like this before?

3. *A Description of the Location of the Project.* This should be a complete description of the location of the project, its size, access, zoning, competition, and other important factors affecting economic and living conditions in the area.

In addition, there should be information on significant building restrictions and proof of the project's compliance with local zoning or expected zoning.

An aerial photograph, a road map, and a large-scale city map would all be useful exhibits in describing the location of your project.

4. *Details of the Purchase of the Project.* If the property is being purchased for the project, a copy of the purchase agreement and an analysis of the method of financing for land purchase should be included.

5. *A Description of All the Consultants on the Project.* This would include the architects, marketing consultants, land

planners, soil engineers, and so forth. Their backgrounds and contributions to the project should be briefly stated.

6. *A Physical Description of the Property Itself.* Such a description should include at least two major items. First, a plot plan with detailed information on the project, its topography, perimeter streets, zoning, and building restrictions. This should show every structure to be included on the site as well as parking spaces and significant parts of the landscaping. If other factors, such as view analyses or sewer and water details, are important to your project, include them, too.

Secondly, there should be elevations and plans for every structure. Typical floor plans should be shown for each type of unit, and plans should also be shown for amenities, or common and utility buildings.

7. *A Copy of Your Construction Contract.* If there is a construction contract, it should be included, and the background of the builders should be provided.

8. *Details of Your Financial Analyses.* These would include a cost analysis, a schedule of the timing of the project, and the specifics of your cash flow.

A cost analysis would show in detail all project costs beginning with land, related fees, and land preparation. Financing for each part of the project would be shown as a separate cost, and the cost of construction would be shown with details of all significant items, both direct and indirect, and with further breakdowns between the material and labor items.

Along with this financial information should be an analysis for the timing of the project. This should detail when the project would begin and the first funds that would be required, how funds will be expanded during the project, and how funds are to be repaid, and when.

It would also be helpful to provide an analysis of cash flow, by month, for any sizable project. This is useful to the builder himself, as well as to the lender. It is also a helpful tool for controlling the project.

9. *A Description of Revenue and Expenses Expected from the Project.* Three major items should be provided:

• Information on revenue should be detailed, including projected leases and other sources of revenue. The rents should be shown on a per-square-foot basis, and the projected terms and types of leases should be indicated. Naturally, if leases are already signed at the time the application for financing is being made, they should be noted. Signed leases are strong indicators of the credibility of the project.

You should also provide details on the key information relating to leases on hand or expected. This would include gross area, guaranteed rent per square foot, terms of lease and renewal clause, percentage rent clauses, and tenant expenses. The information provided will depend on whether or not the project is to be industrial, commercial, or residential. If available, copies of the leases should be attached.

• An income and expense analysis should be included. This should show all income and expense items in detail, and conclude with the net income available for debt service.

• There should be a project evaluation. Beginning with the income available for debt service, one can make an estimate of the value of the entire project, and the amount required to service the loan.

10. *An Analysis of Competition and Market.* A market study would be helpful here. Certainly, an analysis of the competition in the area for the project is needed, and the key features that will act as benefits or hindrances to this project in competition with others in the area should be indicated.

The Loan

Now that you've prepared your financial analysis of your project, with basic data, it is time to talk about the loan itself. There are stacks of factors that affect the negotiating of the loan: the amount sought, interest rate, length, "points" in front, prepayment terms, "kickers" or contingent interests, personal guarantees, tie-ins to construction loans, holdbacks depending upon occupancy or revenue levels, restrictions on junior financing, restrictions on sale of property, closing costs, and other expenses.

In the world of real estate, there are middlemen who are magnificent at getting you the money. They can charm the bored lender, keep up your spirits when the financial world is crumbling. Brokerages like Sonnenblick-Goldman in New York and California are brilliant in their ability to come through. My friend the fiduciary, Larry Robbins, is also a wizard. He has some sage advice about getting financing for income-producing property.

Financing can make or break your investment. Here are some terms and conditions to consider:

The First Trust Deed. Most of the time you will obtain the first from your friendly savings and loan. They are profit oriented, and when dealing with them, stand your ground. Don't let the institution force you into terms and conditions that may jeopardize your investment. Use good business logic.

Always check several institutions for interest rates, amount of loan, and length of loan. This could affect the profitability of your transaction.

Most loans will have an acceleration/alienation clause. This means that if a title is transferred, the loan is due immediately. Sometimes you can avoid paying off the existing loan by using a lease with an option to buy, or an all-inclusive trust deed.

Sometimes there is a prepayment penalty. That is, if you

pay off your loan before it is due, you may pay six months' interest on the original amount or the existing balance. If you refinance through the same savings and loan company, sometimes you can avoid the prepayment penalty.

Financial institutions evaluate each transaction differently, so think and plan your course before you move. The loan you receive today may not be valid tomorrow. Don't be afraid to negotiate with them; they can control the success or failure of your investment.

The Second Trust Deed. This offers you flexibility for creative financing. By adjusting the interest rate, due dates, and monthly payments, you can put together sound underpinnings for your investment.

You should make sure that the time until the due date of the second trust deed is long enough so that the first trust deed is reduced sufficiently to refinance the loan to the original amount, and then use the proceeds to pay off the second trust deed. Don't buy properties with three- to five-year second trust deeds. You cannot build up enough equity on the first trust deed to refinance and pay off the second trust deed in that period of time.

The second trust deed should always be freely transferable. In case of an emergency, you can sell the property and get your cash out. This is your protection or insurance policy. So make sure that the second trust deed is *not* due on sale of the property.

You may want to take a good look at private money seconds (hard money), which normally cost 10 percent and 10 points. You may be able to use the hard-money second when you have a large equity in the property and you only need a small amount of money.

Tight money in the mid-1970s made working with lenders, and especially the savings and loan associations, very difficult. Problems were lack of funds, high rates, and strong demand. In this age of specialization and corporate bigness it is most difficult to find a decision-maker at your savings and loan association. That's not to say you shouldn't try to work with the S & L, however.

There are twelve basic things to consider when dealing with a loan:

1. The existing interest rate.
2. The remaining term.
3. The possibility of refinancing, or sale.
4. The location of the property.
5. The balance of the loan.
6. The amount of a new loan.
7. The prepayment penalty. (What is the amount, and will they waive it?)
8. The cost to assume the existing balance.
9. The interest rate if you assume the balance or increase the amount.
10. Are the payments current?
11. How is the late charge figured?
12. How does the lender enforce the acceleration provision?

Let's say you've found a property that you want to purchase. You have negotiated the price, down payment, and other terms. Now you need your financing. Where do you go and what does it cost?

I think the best way to help you is to put these items in an outline form which you can use as a check list. When obtaining the loan, you must consider the following items:

a. Size of the property.
b. Location of the property.
c. Amount of the loan.
d. Type of property—that is, house, apartment building, shopping center, condominium.
e. Type of loan—that is, short or long term, construction, a combination of construction and permanent.
f. Interest rates and costs.

There are some logical sources for money; two of them—syndicates and joint venturers—have already been discussed. Others include banks, insurance companies, savings and loan associations, real-estate investment trusts (REITS), pension funds, trust funds, private individuals, sellers.

Depending upon the rate of deposits in the various financial institutions, which is another way of saying how much money do they have to loan, various lenders are in the marketplace looking for loans at various times. During periods of money scarcity but still heavy demand, the interest rates go up and financial institutions have little of it; or you shouldn't be bothering them, anyway, because their money is too costly. But, in general, here is how the various institutions work when they have available money.

Banks. They prefer large properties and are not always in the market. The size of the loan depends upon market conditions. They finance about everything and are very strong on your track record. Interest rates are competitive and costs are lower than from Savings & Loans. Mortgage brokers can assist with banks. Don't be afraid of bankers regardless of size. You would be surprised how human and liberal they can be once they believe you.

Insurance Companies. They are also interested in large properties and look at loans of between $750,000 and $1 million or more. They work through mortgage brokers. Any type of project can be financed through them except a single-family house; they prefer apartments, shopping centers, and large office buildings. Interest rates vary depending on how badly the company wants the loan. Costs vary with the company and are very competitive. They prefer shopping and industrial centers, though they come in and out of apartments from time to time.

Savings and Loan Associations. As mentioned above, they are the largest lender in the market financing single-family homes. S&Ls also handle apartments, and like loans in the

$100,000 to $750,000 range. Location is important to them, and they tend to look at the property more than the individual. They will make some loans on commercial, industrial, or shopping centers.

REITs. These are loans for large properties only, and in large sums—usually $1 million or more. REITs have preferred commercial, industrial, and shopping centers, and have had the reputation of making a lot of construction loans. REITs have accepted a higher risk in return for a higher interest rate; and they work only through mortgage brokers.

REITs have undergone several profound changes during the mid-1970s, and should be approached with caution. There are very few that are in good shape.

Pension Funds. This group includes union and retirement funds, and groups like teachers, civil servants, and so forth. They prefer large properties and make loans of $750,000 and over. The rates and costs are higher than from banks or insurance companies, and both property and the individual are considered before making the loan. They make construction and permanent loans, sometimes together. They will also make loans on conventional properties and some vacant land and recreational projects. Pension funds enjoy and exercise more latitude on the types of loans they make, the amounts of the loans, location, and so forth than do regulated institutions.

Trust Funds. These are sometimes controlled by banks, although they can also be set up by individuals and wealthy families. They are usually not in the apartment market and seldom make long-term loans; and they will take 3- to 10-year loans. They usually charge a higher interest rate, but their fees are competitive.

Private Individuals. They may make short term loans at higher rates. They may also loan on vacant land, some will take on apartments; most prefer the single-family market.

They usually work through a mortgage company or loan brokers, real-estate brokers, and so on. Loans may be for 3 to 7 years. These lenders offer the greatest flexibility on fees, terms, and amount of loan.

One should not overlook private lenders from overseas. The Arabs and the Japanese have been especially active in the United States real-estate market during the first half of the 1970s. The prime buys have been small off-shore islands for resorts, forest lands, agricultural areas, hotels, apartments, and condominiums. Typically, Canadians are buying Florida condos, Cubans are buying whole floors and projects for their friends in Florida, and the Germans, Italians and English are moving their funds out of their high-inflation countries.

Both the Arabs and the Japanese like joint ventures with recognizable names that have long track records. This seems to allay their risk-taking. I feel that industrial and financial opportunities are top attractions to foreign investors, although recreation also tempts them.

Sellers. Don't overlook this source of money not only for carrying the second trust deed but also because some will provide great terms on a first trust deed. Be sure you understand the seller's motivation and what he is trying to accomplish by the sale.

Sellers will loan only on property they are selling. There may not be loan fees. The terms and the amount are very flexible, although you might pay a little more in price for better terms. The interest rates are usually lower than the banks, insurance companies, or savings and loans.

The most controversial loan may come from the REITs.

There is much controversy about real-estate-investment trusts and they thoroughly deserve that notoriety. They suffered from over-enthusiasm, poor eyesight, hardening of the common-sense arteries, too much investment money available to them, and a marketplace on fire. This is to say nothing of egocentric management, with presidents falling in love with their own nearsightedness. The end result is that the entire

REIT industry is in disarray, and there is serious doubt whether it will survive. However, it is still important to understand their function, for there are a handful that are excellent financial institutions, which you should get to know.

Every day of the year thousands of airplanes take off safely and land safely, and no one reads about it in the newspaper or hears about it on the radio or television newscasts. It's not news. But, when one crashes, that's a different story. It is news, and it's broadcast immediately and repeatedly by all media.

News media reports about real-estate-investment trusts (REITSs) are somewhat like those concerning airplane accidents. Scores of REITs are operating successfully throughout the country, and no one reads about them in the financial pages or hears about them on financial newscasts. They aren't news. But if one of them takes a nose dive and crashes, like the airplane, it's suddenly news, and the financial media take note and broadcast it for all to see and hear. In fairness, however, a lot of big names have crashed.

But, unfortunately, for the REIT industry and the investing public, which all too often looks only to financial headlines for guidance, the financial writer or commentator isn't always as thorough as his counterpart who writes about airplane crashes. The latter almost always tells the reader or listener what kind of airplane crashed. But, whether through ignorance or some other reason, few financial writers and commentators tell the reader or listener what kind of REIT crashed, nor do they mention that many are still doing well. In this respect, they have distorted the picture. It's a little like implying that because Penn Central, Franklin Bank, and W.T. Grant were all corporations, that form of business structure must be inherently bad.

Not all REITs are alike. There are important differences, about which anyone contemplating a purchase of REIT shares should be aware.

Let's start with the basics:

A real-estate-investment trust is a business trust, managed

by trustees, and qualified under federal tax laws for the benefit of its investor-shareholders. REITs receive special tax treatment, which is a benefit to shareholders. Under the Real Estate Investment Act of 1961, qualified real-estate-investment trusts do not pay any federal income or capital-gains taxes on income or gains which they distribute to their shareholders, provided they distribute annually at least 90 percent of their taxable income and meet other criteria.

The idea behind this special tax treatment is (1) to give comparatively small investors a chance to participate in large, diversified real-estate investments on a scale formerly available only to a relatively few wealthy investors, and (2) to encourage the financing of the large real-estate developments and redevelopments needed in metropolitan areas.

There are two separate and distinct types of REITs, the equity ownership or property trust, and the mortgage trust, with the primary similarities between the two kinds being the name "REIT," and the conduit principle through which double taxation of income or gains distributed to shareholders is avoided. In the simplest of terms: the equity trust is a landlord; the mortgage trust is a lender.

There are also two basic types of trust lenders—short-term or interim-financing lenders (often sponsored by large banks), and long-term or permanent-financing lenders (generally sponsored by insurance companies).

The equity or property trust, in its landlord role as owner of existing income-producing real estate, has the ability to enhance the economic benefit of dividend distribution to its shareholders, since a substantial portion of the distributions made to investors can be tax sheltered by depreciation taken on the properties in the trust. Property trusts also have the additional potential for internal growth because of improved property operations and ultimate appreciation. Gains from the sale of properties may be passed on to the shareholders in the form of capital gains.

Because of loan defaults and major construction cost overruns, many short-term mortgage trusts have had serious difficulties since the early seventies. These difficulties are the ones that, through financial-page headlines, have made REIT an almost profane four-letter word.

On the other hand, the long-term lenders, who take few risks, since they place their loans only after the buildings are completed and substantially occupied, have generally fared much better than the short-term lenders.

Property trusts, which own well-selected and well-managed, income-producing property and which do not commit to purchase a property until it is completed, has permanent financing, and is substantially occupied, have been virtually immune to construction-related problems. This is not to imply that all mortgage trusts engaged in interim financing are failures, nor, on the other hand, that all mortgage trusts involved in long-term financing and all property trusts are successful. For a variety of reasons generally unrelated to the state of the nation's economy and the construction industry's problems (which were the major causes of the disastrous experiences for investors in the short-term-lender REITs), some long-term lenders and some property trusts have also had bad times. Poor or inadequate management headed the list of reasons for poor performance.

Although the property trusts are relatively few in number and new in concept, as an investment opportunity in income real estate they should not be overlooked by investors. They offer the following unique advantages that most people cannot provide for themselves:

1. *Size of Property.* The best combination of a good yield, capital appreciation potential, and ease of management tends to be in the larger-income properties.

2. *Geographic Diversification.* A trust with several properties in separate geographic areas can be a safer entity for an investor than one that owns a single piece of real estate or property in a limited market area.

3. *Functional Diversification.* Most property trusts own more than one type of property, usually including apartment complexes, office buildings, shopping centers, and industrial parks.

4. *Property Selection.* Buying income property is rapidly becoming an area exclusively reserved for the professional with unusual judgment and expertise. A good property trust has or finds management that not only uses sophisticated techniques in the evaluation of and negotiations for improved real estate, but also has extensive engineering, appraising, marketing, legal, and accounting experience to aid in its investment decision.

5. *Property Management.* Probably a major reason most investors don't own improved real estate is that it is difficult to find good managers or to find the time to manage the property oneself. Over the long haul, successful management of income property is even more important than sound property selection.

6. *Liquidity.* The number one reason more people of moderate means don't own real estate, other than their own homes, is the lack of liquidity* provided by most real-estate investments. However, shares of beneficial interests in a property trust are a freely transferable security and, after the offering period, most are listed on a stock exchange or are traded in the over-the-counter market. Clearly, the ability of a property trust to convert its underlying assets of real property into a liquid investment is a valuable benefit.

The above are advantages that every good property trust should offer to the investor who wants the benefits of income-property ownership without the capital outlay required and/or the property selection, management, and maintenance responsibilities that other forms of ownership might entail. Other advantages stem from the fact that shelter-related real estate

* The ability to cash out easily.

(for example, apartments providing residential shelter and commercial/industrial properties housing retail stores and other business and industrial firms) serves basic human needs that must be met regardless of fluctuations in economic, social, or political conditions.

The slowdown in construction, which the nation has experienced since the early seventies, means that the demand for rental apartments in particular, and to a lesser extent retail stores, industrial and office facilities, must be met primarily by existing properties, many of which are currently renting at substantially less than the rates needed to economically justify new construction.

With relatively few new developments coming into the rental market, scarcities have begun to develop, rents are being raised, and yields and property values are increasing. In fact, in some areas of the nation, rental apartments are already in short supply. Thus, one who invests in existing shelter-related real estate through the medium of the property trust gains advantages both from the trust's structure and from the increasing demand for space resulting from construction shortages.

While an investment in real-estate ownership via a property trust appears to offer many more rewards than one in the riskier field of short-term construction financing or the no-growth area of long-term, fixed-income mortgage financing, the prospective investor should get the answers to a lot of important questions before committing his or her money to any given income-property program.

There are four major areas one should examine in selecting the right property trust for his or her investment objective. They are: management, track record, pooling advantages, and service. It goes without saying that some areas are more important than others.

1. Management. An analysis of this important function should be broken down into two broad areas—acquisitions and property management. Innumerable questions about the acquisition function can be asked: How much real estate has been acquired by the deal-makers? . . . What kind? . . . In what areas? . . . What were the prices and terms and timing? . . . What is the experience of the deal-makers? . . . What kinds of checks and balances are deployed in assuring the acquisitions staff and top management that the deal is right?

To give you an idea of how to evaluate these answers, here are some points—supplied by a great winner, Consolidated Capital out of Oakland, California, owners and managers of thousands of units—to keep in mind:

a. Finding the right property in the right place, at the right time, and with the right price and terms requires both the staff and criteria to make the search fruitful.

b. Acquisitions-team members themselves should have special skills, with an emphasis on judgment and an ability to effectively negotiate. They should know real estate and be able to identify desirable areas and properties, and analyze their potential for producing the benefits you're seeking in your particular program. They should be able to anticipate, with some degree of accuracy, the changing markets in income property, and be able to negotiate the right price and terms. They should go at their jobs aggressively, seeking out potential sellers, not waiting for deals to be brought to their desks. Not only should they work closely with real-estate brokers, they should get to know developers, trust and bank managers, and large property owners. They should utilize every tool available to them, including cold calls, referrals, direct mail, and newspaper advertising to identify prospective sellers.

c. Team members also should know what they are looking for. The right property for an equity trust should fall within well-defined parameters. It normally should be considered only in an area that has an existing and relatively large and diversified economic and employment base. Ideally, it should be near other properties already acquired by the investment program or where additional properties might be acquired in the future for maximizing management efficiencies.

In order to reduce the risk to an equity trust investor, the property probably should be constructed already, substantially occupied, have permanent financing, and be producing a cash flow.

d. The property selected should enhance the functional and/or geographic diversification of the program's investment portfolio, thus reducing the risks of economic reversals in any one kind of property and fluctuations of the economy in any one market area.

Properties, such as marinas and golf courses and similar projects, generally would be classified as more risky and probably not suitable for a trust. Restaurants, hotels, fast-food operations, and other similar investments, which are more dependent upon special business expertise than on the inherent value of the real estate itself, also would be classified as a relatively high-risk investment for a property trust.

e. Any property being seriously considered by an equity-trust-investment program should be subjected to in-depth analysis including such factors as: rental income, lease terms, financial strength and mix of tenants, operating expenses, fixed charges, land values, physical conditions, population, area trends, competition, title, zoning, taxes, utility costs and trends, and maintenance and management considerations.

f. Pro-forma statements also should be analyzed, rental surveys taken, the market shopped, and deferred maintenance evaluated. If the transaction is approved following such analyses, the acquisitions committee should be able to take immediate action, which is often necessary to compete successfully for major real-estate developments. Too much haste is bad, but undue delays can also result in lost opportunities.

Property management is more easily measured by the results. You should ask the following questions: Have the cash flows been increasing or decreasing? What is the trend? Is the property being maintained? Is good judgment being utilized on capital expenditures? (Both overspending and underspending can result in lower long-term cash flows.) Who is going to be responsible for property management? Is real-estate management the prime business of the property manager? Examine individuals and their respective credentials, not firms and their reputations. There are many financial institutions with fine reputations of integrity and competency in other areas, but with limited real-estate experience. The property trust that farms out its property management to a nonaffiliated, independent contractor may well lose control of this all-important function, which can make or break the trust.

Property management is ultimately the key to successful income-property ownership, and any owner who neglects it is headed for trouble.

Professional property management is a relatively new profession. It is a far cry from the mama-papa custodial approach of the days, not too long ago, wherein a couple, usually retired, took on the clean-up, paint-up, and collect-the-rent type of chores in exchange for an apartment and a small salary . . . or the selling broker of a shopping center or office building who, as a matter of convenience or necessity, took over the responsibility for running a multimillion-dollar project for the buyer.

The modern property management needed for large real-estate projects is a highly specialized and competitive discipline requiring specially trained and experienced business managers, administrative personnel, professional gardening and maintenance crews, computerized record keeping and, of major importance, innovative marketing techniques, and a proprietary attitude and performance on the part of each on-site property manager.

It requires the customary tools of the trade, such as marketing scripts, rental guides, discount purchasing agreements, maintenance manuals, accounting guidelines, computer reports, and, of major importance, a positive and enthusiastic approach with an attitude of property marketing rather than just property management. Also, the ability to respond to stress situations is a mark of good management. Some of the most successful property-management firms in the country have met stress situations with remarkable creativity.

2. *Track Record.* This is the "report card" of management. Study it carefully. There are some well-educated and experienced people in the real-estate business who have not performed. Conversely, there are people who lack talent but have good track records, because they had adequate performance during good economic times. So it's a good idea to look at the sponsor's track record in both good times and bad. Make sure the track record and apparent management talent go hand in hand.

3. *Advantages of Pooling.* Look at the number and average size of properties in the trust's portfolio. Obviously too many small properties can create property-management problems. Conversely, having just a few large properties tends to limit diversification both functionally and geographically. The biggest property trust may not be the safest, and the smallest does not always have the most risk. Look for a good combination of both size and diversification.

4. *Service to Investors.* While not as important as other areas, this still merits attention. Some property trusts have unique features—monthly dividends, dividend-reinvestment programs, voluntary cash-add-on plans, good communications, and computerized accounting reports. If a trust offers everything else you're seeking, such options and services can be meaningful. On the other hand, they also can be meaningless. For example, using a property trust just because it has a dividend-reinvestment program and detailed reports can backfire if bad management creates a situation where there is no dividend income for a shareholder to reinvest.

These are broad areas for evaluation. To check into the many facets of each is a time consuming yet necessary bit of homework, if you want to maximize the upside potential, while minimizing the downside risk when you put your hard-earned savings into the hands of a stranger.

There are several good property trusts in the United States that would pass such an inspection with flying colors. There are a few that would do even better, for the simple reason that they not only meet the basic criteria described earlier—they exceed it. Of the numerous equity REITs in the United States, I've chosen one, Consolidated Capital Realty Investors, to illustrate the philosophy and operating techniques of a property trust that has survived and, thus far, prospered during a very rough period in the history of the real-estate industry.

Consolidated Capital Realty Investors, or CCRI, as it is referred to in the financial press, is a California-based property trust sponsored by Consolidated Capital Equities Corporation, one of a group of affiliated companies headquartered in Oakland.

The Consolidated Capital companies are income–real-estate-investment specialists. Everything they do is real-estate related. They form and administer investment programs for multiple investors, and then they acquire and manage a diversified portfolio of income properties for each of these programs.

The Consolidated Capital group is one of the nation's largest privately owned real-estate fiduciaries. It has more than 17,000 investors participating in 6 public real-estate investment programs, including CCRI. Don W. Carlson, chairman of the board and chief executive officer of Consolidated Capital, attributes the success to date to four major factors:

1. The skills and attitudes of its key people . . . "real estate professionals with extensive backgrounds and expertise in property acquisitions and property management," as well as strong backup personnel in the fields of finance, law, accounting, marketing, communications, and administration. He says they have demonstrated a unique ability to anticipate trends and adapt to change, and a willingness to roll up their sleeves and go to work to solve problems whenever and wherever they occur.
2. A philosophy of fiscal conservatism.
3. Strict acquisition concepts and criteria.
4. A property management approach that combines pru-

dent business practices and creative and aggressive marketing techniques.

Obviously, Consolidated Capital didn't start with all this expertise. Over the years, Carlson admits, it hasn't batted 100 percent in its acquisition and management of real estate, but it seems to have learned important lessons from its early programs. Because of its experience, it has developed a philosophy that favors:

1. Maintenance of high cash reserves by investor programs.
2. Use of relatively low leverage, and in some cases all cash, in acquiring properties.
3. Acquisition of "bread and butter" rather than what Consolidated considers "fad" properties.
4. Large economically diversified areas such as Los Angeles, Orange and Santa Clara Counties in California, and metropolitan areas like Seattle, Houston, Dallas, Tulsa, and Atlanta.
5. Properties that already have permanent financing and positive initial cash flows at the time of acquisition.
6. Properties with "old" rents that have been established and "flat" for sometime, which, Carlson says, "give downside protection against future overbuilding and also offer the possibility of relatively rapid increases in rents and bottom line yields."
7. Avoiding business-related real-estate investments, which depend more on specialized business expertise than on the underlying value of the real estate involved.

Consolidated Capital's property-management approach is based on the recognition that even a well-located and well-priced property purchased on the best of terms will not produce the yield that it should if the anticipated rents are not collected and/or the expenses exceed expectations.

"Poor property management has caused more failures of

income real estate in the seventies than any other single factor," Marvin T. Levin, president of Consolidated Capital, claims.

"Many owners of unsuccessful properties like to use rent controls, escalating utility costs, overbuilding, the declining economy, and a host of other 'beyond my control' excuses when, in fact, inadequate property management is often the real villain," Levin says.

Properties in CCRI and Consolidated Capital's other investment programs generally are managed by Johnstown Properties, Consolidated Capital's property-management affiliate. Johnstown, which has a staff of more than 500 people, provides full management services for business, industrial, retail, and multifamily residential properties, and supervises over $300 million worth of diversified income-producing properties in more than 50 U.S. cities.

Levin attributes Johnstown's success in the property-management field to a combination of traditional and unusual techniques. In addition to the usual scripts, manuals, guides, agreements, and other rather standard forms and procedures that most large property-management firms utilize, Levin says that Johnstown has developed some approaches and programs that are innovative for the industry.

The Johnstown approach, he notes, starts with thinking in terms of property marketing, which is a much more exciting and challenging concept than that of property management alone. It stimulates enthusiasm and a positive attitude, two very valuable tools in dealing with the public and in solving any problems that might arise. It also helps expand rental and leasing activities away from the property site and out into the areas where prospective residents of multifamily properties and tenants of business and industrial complexes might be found.

The marketing concept led to the development of several innovative promotional programs, which Johnstown uses effectively, Levin says. These include an industrial-sales program for residential properties under Johnstown's management. Under the plan, a member of Johnstown's staff calls on local industries to offer special housing "packages" for employees whom the firms bring in for new assignments, training programs, or interim duties. The package includes a furnished apartment, complete with dishes, linens, and other essential housekeeping items, for a special daily rate. While these programs are not great money-makers in themselves, they do help rent up a complex because, through employee handbooks and other media, the participating firm makes its people aware of a Johnstown-managed apartment community. As a result, many of the new visitors become permanent residents.

Johnstown's innovative programs take many forms. I was particularly impressed by its creative approaches to stress situations. For example, during the oil embargo and the resultant gasoline shortage that the nation experienced in 1974, a Johnstown apartment-complex manager dressed up like a gasoline pump, and posted himself at the nearby intersection of a heavily traveled commuter route, with a large sign carrying this get-the-point message: "If you lived at XYZ Apartments, you'd be home now."

Johnstown also makes extensive use of referrals to generate rental leads for the properties under its management, Levin points out. Satisfied residents of Johnstown-managed apartments are prime sources of such leads. However, residents aren't the only ones who refer prospects to Johnstown's properties. Service-station attendants, motel managers, even managers of other apartment complexes, merchants, real-estate brokers, and taxi-cab drivers, for whom Johnstown hosted a party to introduce the idea, also are among those who participate in and benefit from Johnstown's referral program.

Since Johnstown shares Consolidated Capital's views about the importance of hiring the best available people for every job, Levin says it engages in extensive recruitment activities. Those selected to join the Johnstown organization receive their initial training at Johnstown's own property-management school, which is approved by the Veterans Administration for veteran training. Thereafter, periodic training programs are conducted to keep rental consultants, leasing agents, property managers, marketing consultants, and the other specialists within the Johnstown organization up to date on new programs and approaches to effective property marketing.

When one reviews the Johnstown activities and realizes all that professional property management entails, it's easy to understand why relatively few investors want to personally assume the responsibility for managing their own income properties. As we said before, good property management can make the difference between success and failure in income-property ownership.

It's a point to remember and to investigate, no matter which kind of real-estate-investment program attracts your discretionary dollars.

8

INVESTMENT OPTIONS

This chapter would be like the 15th week of a 16-week-long college course. It is not meant either for easy reading or the rank amateur. I will try to explain things that are very complicated in terms of the various options that investors should be aware of. I passionately believe that the great change in real-estate investing, which differentiates it from the post-WW II era of easy-come-easy-go, is that it takes time to analyze and understand an increasingly complicated, but rewarding, opportunity.

It should be clear by now that an investor can tailor his real-estate deals to give him what he wants in return for his money. By selecting the particular interest and the type of real estate, and by using the leverage of borrowed funds, the investor can obtain the desired amounts of recurring income, capital appreciation, and tax benefits he wishes. He can also control the amount of risk he wishes to undertake. The investor can determine the probable variance in the return from his investment, the possibility of losing the capital investment, and the probability of converting to cash when desired.

This is real-estate investment realism. It means that you, the investor, have studied the market, know yourself and your financial limitations, and understand the risks. You have studied the risks of a certain investment, the return associated with that risk, and you have decided that the risk is worth the expected returns.

Real-Estate Interests

Real estate is divided into two broad classifications depending upon the type of return sought by the investor. These are, broadly, recurring income and sales gains.

The equity interest in "income property" is purchased primarily for recurring income in the form of rentals. Equity ownership of "property held for sale" is acquired because of the profit expected to be realized on resale. Sales gains can be further divided into: investment gains, which qualify for capital-gains treatment because the seller engages in limited activity; and development gains, where the seller creates value through subdividing or improving the property, and the gains are considered ordinary income.

The value of your equity interest in real estate, therefore, varies in accordance with the economic return available from the property. Recurring income is generated only while the property is held. Sales income obviously comes from that event.

Recurring Income. Net rental income, or net return, is determined after deducting from gross rental income an estimated allowance for vacancies, operating expenses, and debt service.

Investors in income property were one of the first groups to equate return with net cash in the investor's pocket and to consider, only for the purpose of determining the income-tax reduction of the gross yield, the accounting profits based upon depreciation. Instead of depreciation, which is not an out-of-pocket expense, rental investors deducted their gross income from the cash out-flow represented by the amortization of indebtedness.

"Cash on cash" has become more universally adopted. At first only popular among rental investors, it is now part of the corporate finance community. In addition to the pragmatic consideration that you can't spend what you don't have, today's sophisticated finance men and women realize that you cannot invest what you don't have. Worse, you are losing the income you might otherwise earn if you had the money. Thus, the loss of a dollar for three years is more than the loss of a dollar. It is the loss of $1.33, or more!

This loss return is called "opportunity return," or "opportunity cost." It represents the income lost because you did not have the opportunity to invest the sum elsewhere for better return.

There are a number of ways to overcome this loss. One way is to pass along more costs to the tenant. More and more leases are being written with cost-of-living adjustments in them; they increase automatically every year, three years, or five years, on the basis of an appropriate price index. Tenants can also be required to pay maintenance costs, insurance premiums, and taxes on a "triple net" lease. Or, when paid by the landlord, the tenants can be required to pay any increase in those operating costs over a specified base-year cost. Finally, fixed increments in rent may be stipulated at given times.

One more word should be made about what to look for, and avoid, in seeking recurring income. Depreciation tax shelter should not be considered in determining whether or not a particular rental property is a good investment. The availability of accelerated depreciation to shelter the yield, and other considerations, should be thought of as "sweeteners" in the deal. There is such a wide variation in taxes paid by possible investors (and also by the same investor in different years) that no uniform assumption can be made about the dollar value of the depreciation allowance. In evaluating the yield from your prospective investment, therefore, depreciation shelter should not be considered at all. If it's there, enjoy it, of course.

Property Held for Sale. Equity investors in capital-gains property usually determine the gain on the sale of the property by deducting its cost from the net proceeds. The total gain is then converted to an average return on investment, which is done by dividing the total gain by the holding period, and then relating the average annual gain to the amount invested. Indebtedness related to the property, real-estate taxes on it, and other holding costs were deducted against the ordinary income during the holding period.

In the case of a capital-gains sale, such costs have occurred at different times. Gains have been realized only over a several-year holding period, and the Internal Rate of Return (IRR) approach may be the best means of determining the return represented by those gains. IRR also allows the investor to evaluate whether or not that return is fair compensation for the risk involved in the investment. By discounting both cash outlays and inflows to present value at an appropriate compound-interest rate, the IRR recognizes the opportunity cost of committing dollars to an investment that will produce a single-shot economic gain at the end of a number of years. In terms of cash outlays, the discount rate recognizes that to accumulate a specified future cash outlay, less than that outlay must be invested now. The return on the initial investment can be reinvested until that initial investment plus the compound return on it equals the required amount.

Similarly, future cash inflows should be discounted because their present value is the sum which must be invested at a compound-interest rate (determined by the risk inherent in the investment) in order to produce these expected cash inflows at the time they will be received.

Development Gains. The determination of the gains and the rate of return on investment from development of real estate is also important to the investor. It involves a somewhat more complex application of the IRR approach used for the sale of investment property. The greater complexity comes from the need to charge against revenues the more extensive set of costs associated with development, and the greater number of cash outlays and inflows involved in a development project.

Operating capital normally is injected into a development project as it is needed when the developer uses his own capital or banking lines. Cash inflows also occur as the escrows for the sales of individual units are closed. When the project is developed in a series of distinct phases, the "front money" frequently must remain in the project until all the phases are completed.

Development probably is the most risky form of real-estate investment. A project may never get off the ground, or, during the two or three years usually required to start up a project, conditions may change—for instance, interest rates may increase. Costs of construction have also skyrocketed: In the early 1970s, the "brick-and-mortar" costs in building jumped in some areas from $15 to $20 per square foot, in a single year. Builders began having to allow more than the typical 50 percent of total unit price for construction costs.

Sales Price and Investment Properties

A logical question an investor should ask before he leaps into a deal is: How is the market value (or sales price) arrived at for investment and development properties? There are three approaches in answering this question.

The Income Approach. The income approach to market value holds that an investor purchases a property for the income flow it will generate. Based upon the return available on competitive investments and the risk involved in this particular property, the investor determines the rate of return which he feels the income flow should represent on his investment.

How much cash should you invest? Find the capitalization

rate (the inverse of the desired rate of return) and multiply it by the income flow.

The Cost Approach. The replacement-cost approach to market value asserts that the sales price of a property is equal to the cost of replacing it, less an allowance for depreciation to adjust for the age and condition of the property. Obviously, on a new property no depreciation allowance is appropriate, and the costs alone determine value.

The Comparable Sales Approach. The comparable sales approach to market value is determined by prices actually paid for comparable property, with adjustments for any advantages or disadvantages of your property vis-à-vis those other properties.

Clearly, the first condition of comparability is that the best use of the properties being compared be the same. Also, the market price paid in the recent sales of properties suitable for that use (which might be a future as well as present use) should be related to the raw land cost that can be budgeted for that use. In cases where the best use will occur in the future, the present value of the property will be derived by appropriately discounting for time and risk to the property's value for its estimated future use.

All three approaches to market value may be applied in determining the value of any one property. But each of the three approaches tends to best determine the value of property for particular uses.

The income approach, for example, is the primary means of valuing improved properties purchased principally for the recurring rental income they will generate.

The cost approach tends to fix value in the case of improved properties purchased by an ultimate user, such as homes purchased as residences and industrial buildings purchased as a plant site by their users.

The comparable sales approach is the major tool for determining the value of unimproved property.

Sometimes a difference in the value of the property under the three approaches creates an investment opportunity. For example, apartment buildings and other income properties may be purchased at a price based upon the income approach and resold at a higher price based upon replacement cost when converted into condominiums.

Use

Use also determines the return on investment. The ownership of personal residences is one of the principal forms of wealth in this country. Although personal residences appreciate in value the same as any other real estate, and can turn out to be an excellent investment, they are still purchased by their owners primarily for their use as a home.

Few owners select homes on the basis of their investment features. Owners are largely influenced in their decisions by how well a home will satisfy the space and locational needs and accords with the taste of the purchasing family.

From the standpoint of use, business ownership of real estate is more limited than home ownership. Most businesses make a greater return on operating capital than they can make from owning their own real estate. By leasing, rather than owning, their real estate, businesses maximize their operating capital and hence their profits. Businesses only own property with specialized uses. These properties, because of that use, are generally difficult to sell or rent except to such businesses.

Tax Goodies

There are two important tax goodies from real-estate investment that you, the investor, should keep in mind. These two are the depreciation shelter of recurring income and the lower capital-gains tax rates applicable on the investment sale of property.

Taxation upon the disposition of the property can be completely deferred if it is exchanged for similar property. It also is possible to make part of an investment with "soft" (tax deductible) dollars by applying part of the purchase price of the property to repay interest and other deductible expenses.

Taxation favors home ownership. The family that owns rather than rents its home gets to deduct interest and real-estate taxes. Homeowners who trade up, by reinvesting in a new home all of the gain realized on the sale of their old home, are able to defer taxation on that gain.

The depreciation deduction (when it is accelerated depreciation) can be diminshed each year and the principal amortization element of debt service increased each year. This inverse relationship between these two variables has a significant tax effect. The investor receives a tax shelter from the depreciation allowance so long as the depreciation deduction is equal to the amortization of the principal on the indebtedness against the property. That is, the depreciation shelters the nondeductible cash outlay represented by principal amortization.

When principal amortization is less than the depreciation deduction (which occurs in approximately the seventh to twelfth year after investment, depending upon the terms of the indebtedness and the economic life of the property), the investor is paying taxes on cash which he does not have.

Two methods have been used to prevent the loss of tax shelters: the refinancing of indebtedness against the property and the sale or exchange of the property. Refinancing restores tax shelter by increasing the interest element and by reducing the amortization portion of debt service. It also frees funds to invest elsewhere and thus increases the return derived from overall investment.

The sale or exchange of property also permits the investor to start a new ball game with another piece of property or investment. Sale has the disadvantage that, depending upon how long the property had been held, the accelerated depreciation will be subject to recapture. That is, ordinary income tax will be paid on the portion of the gain represented by accelerated depreciation. The balance of the gain would be subject to capital-gains tax.

Still, provided that the investor can find a desirable trade property, exchange offers a number of advantages over sale. First, the investor's capital has not been diminished by taxation and the full capital is kept working for him in the new property. Secondly, the investor can realize an economic benefit from his appreciated equity (which usually resulted from both a reduction of indebtedness and appreciation in the value of the property) by acquiring ownership of a property with a higher fair-market value than his original investment. Finally, the interest element of the indebtedness on the trade property can restore his tax shelter.

Nonequity Investments

These investments are less important than equity investments. The nonequity investor has a fixed interest in the property and does not participate in the increases in income and the value of the property that make real estate such an attractive investment.

This difference, however, is breaking down. Lending institutions are realizing that they should get a greater return for the substantial risks they take. They also see that a fixed-interest rate leaves them vulnerable to inflation. Consequently, during the tight money markets of the seventies, lenders established the precedent of sharing in the bottom line, as well as taking from the top. That precedent is likely to endure and even expand into an institutional arrangement where the lender almost always has a substantial equity interest in the projects he finances.

In the past, the two basic nonequity investments for private investors have been:

A Loan. This might be a second mortgage at the maximum interest rate permitted by the usury law, for a 3- to 5-year period, and with as little amortization as the law will permit.

A Long-Term Lease of Real Estate. Little equity is created under the short-term leases that are the primary vehicle through which a user interest—rather than an investment interest—in real estate is acquired.

In the future, ground leases could become more important nonequity investment for private investors. Ground leases have the built-in possibility of sharing with the equity-interest appreciation of the property as a result of both inflation and economic forces. By providing for separate ownership of the nondepreciable land and depreciable improvements, a ground lease can also maximize the tax shelter benefits to the owner of the improvements.

Now that you've learned about the complexities of making an investment, we shall examine some possible deals, and how to evaluate them.

9

DEALERS

After that pause about money, let's refresh our memories about the object of your money: the deals. You've decided to go into a deal. Everything has been checked out, or is being checked out, and it all looks sweet. You may make enough money to get a sports car with a sunroof like your neighbor's. But wait: This is not fun and games. Your pocketbook may start leaking like your neighbor's sunroof if you're not careful.

There is one basic rule that applies here: If you cannot afford to lose your investment, don't make it!

There are no exceptions to this rule. If you have to make a second mortgage on your home to get into the deal, don't do it. Making a deal is not survival. If it is, there is something basically wrong with your business life.

Before you leap, try Sandy Goodkin's reliable check list. Here it is:

First, you must identify your own motivations for getting into real-estate investment. What kind of deals are you looking for? Do you want to remain a real-estate investor, or also become a developer? Do you want to be a real-estate investor full time, or part time? How much time can you give it, and do you have sufficient management to be both an investor and a developer? They are very different worlds.

Second, you must study and know the real-estate-development world before you get into it. The investment world, like any other in business, will ask you for personal financial risk and personal involvement. You will spend a lot of your time trying to control it, but you never can. You'll need staying power when adversity strikes; you'll have to expect the unexpected.

Finally, you should now know, and have begun to gather around you, trustworthy and expert associates and partners.

Clearly, real-estate investment offers a variety of opportunities: housing, large and small commercial buildings, offices, rehabilitation of older buildings, recreational facilities, and urban opportunities of all kinds. But it also offers risks. You must be prepared for crises like:

- Pumping into the deal more monies and credit.
- Becoming personally liable.
- Tight money.
- The deal taking longer than anticipated.
- Zoning or rezoning slowing the deal and causing holding costs and delays.
- Busy partners with a different order of priorities.

These are some guidelines to remember as you enter into your deal. Here is another: Before you sign, be sure you've looked into the best places for the deal that's right for you. What you should have looked at includes:

- One deal at a time.
- Deals in your own backyard.
- Deals within easy traveling distance so that you can look at them.
- Opportunities with a broad market appeal.

• Opportunities with demand in that area.

• Skipped pieces of land in population areas.

• Deals that match your level of investment, time available, and control abilities.

• Deals that can be financed through the standard financial institutions. These include (as mentioned in Chapter Eight) savings and loans, local banks, insurance companies, mortgage brokers, and brokers who are well-known to you or someone you trust.

Now that you've checked my long list (twice, I hope), and if the deal still smells sweet, here is an order of events to follow, and a system for evaluating your deal.

After you've looked around for real-estate opportunities and think you've found a good one:

• Speak to someone you can trust who has good, sound real-estate knowledge.

Has the land been zoned for the use you want? Is it the type of development use that interests you, and one you would want to be involved in?

• Ride the area. Drive up and down each block for a one-mile radius. Plot on a map all the competing factors (or have someone do this for you).

Plot all empty pieces of land for signs announcing competition to your project. Look also for pieces zoned the way your piece is zoned. Have someone then plot visually existing, potential, and under-construction uses on all major roads within one mile of your site. If your plans are commercial and will cover more than 10 acres, go out 2 miles; if commercial and more than 25 acres, go out 5 miles and include only large shopping centers and/or free-standing big-draw centers, a chain department store like Sears, Roebuck, for example.

If your project is offices and less than 20,000 square feet, plot all existing and new offices within 3 miles. If it is offices of more than 20,000 square feet, plot all office complexes within the city market in which your land is located.

If you are redoing an older building into something new, seek out similar unique environments, anywhere, to use as concept proof and comparison as an example for a lender.

• Get demographic data. This simply means find out what the people in your market area earn, where they work, how they live, what their homes cost, and so on.

Check the population growth over the last 15 years in the specific census area of your deal. Then, check the population in the entire Standard Metropolitan Sales Area.

Check the number of households in the same area. Get figures for the number of families in your area and break that down by income. You should also get the number of people per occupied dwelling unit.

Plot all of this on a map according to your census district.

• Locate on that map all roads that will bring traffic to your deal.

Take these roads to the Highway Department, and get the traffic-growth count over the last 5 years. Also get the highway engineers' projections.

• Show on your map all new streets and highways that are planned.

Make certain that you know this. Highway departments and outdoor advertising companies have this information. Make sure you do, too. You can be detoured out of business no matter how well the site is doing now. Cars redirected to new roads always means less business.

• Do an audit on all competition. Have someone take the competition plot, and make an inventory of it.

If the competition is commercial, plot each shopping center by store location, square footage, and dollar volume. Plot also the center's accessibility, visibility upon approach, parking facilities, and convenience of entering and exiting. I, frankly, believe that this requires a professional research company or appraiser, but information can be gained from the Shopping Center Institute and the Urban Land Institute.

Then, plot each competitor's less tangible assets (or liabilities). List its merchandising sophistication (how well its goods are displayed and advertised), its age, its architectural appearance (aesthetic impact on the customer). Finally, determine if each competitor could expand if its owners wanted to.

If your competition is residential, your job is similar. Audit each tract, condominium, and apartment building. List its location, square footage, number of units (and type), and dollar volume (rental income). List its aesthetics and its assets (or liabilities) in terms of customer (renter) amenities.

Talk with real-estate brokers who are important in your area to see what they think of the residential market. Try to determine from them and all other available sources how your competition is doing right now—before you invest. Learn also why they are (or are not) doing well.

If you plan office space, and your competition is offices, also do an audit. This should include: each office building by number of stories, number of offices, age, appearance, parking location, access, cleanliness, cost per square foot, cost for parking, no parking on surface streets, visitor parking and costs, elevator (fast/slow), management (regional or local on-site), private tenant, and vacancies. Also check any amenities.

Now you should have a better picture of what is happening around your property. This should tell you whether the marketplace is doing well or poorly, and what the trend is. It should also enable you to project about whether or not that trend is upward—making it a good place to invest—level, or downward.

It is vital that you uncover whether or not good existing projects are doing poorly. Overall vacancy statistics in apartments, offices, and housing, for example, may look bad but merely reflect a scattering of buildings that are pulling down the market strength. When a deal is going badly, it does not necessarily mean that your proposed deal will suffer the same. You must take great care to examine the whole marketing package.

For frosting on your investment cake, you should also have someone interview prospects—these may be present renters in the area. Your purpose is to see what they like (or do not like), and to determine what improvements or amenities might appeal to them. Just a few good interviews can help give you insights which will be of great benefit to your project. (If you plan to build on vacant land, interview people at your competitor's location.) You should also interview other tenants and bankers in your neighborhood.

If you are buying land, or converting existing old structures, you should, now, begin drawing up ideas for the property's use. These ideas should be based upon what you plan to do in your market. Factors to consider are:

- The size of the building to be constructed or converted.
- The type of building.
- The concept of your building.
- The number of units.
- The sales or rental ranges per square foot.
- The parking requirements (pay great attention to planning these).
- Hallway space (covered or not; air-conditioned or not).
- The security of the tenants.
- Utilities.
- Amenities.
- Landscaping.
- Management costs.

These factors will themselves outline the kind of building or buildings you will construct. They will also help you to assign costs. Adding these costs to the raw-land costs, improvement costs, maintenance costs, marketing costs and management costs will tell you whether or not you are coming into the area at the right competitive moment. They will help you with that elusive commodity: timing.

If your costs come out too high, you have several choices: (1) drop the project, (2) recompute the numbers and cut some costs, (3) design a better mousetrap so that, even at the higher costs, your project will attract the market you seek.

When you are done, you should know how much your

project will cost, how occupied or busy it will be, what its break-even level is, and what its profitability is likely to be. You should also know how much financing you will need, and over what time period. Or, bad news, you will understand that the cash you've put in is inadequate, and you will have to go out and seek partners, form a syndicate or joint venture, or find new financing elsewhere.

Evaluating Your Deal

Maybe you've done all your homework, but there is a nagging doubt: How do you know you've got a good deal? The evaluation of your deal involves answering 3 basic questions:

1. Marketability: Can the product of the deal be marketed?
2. Feasibility: Can the product be produced or operated at an appropriate cost, which allows profit?
3. Financeability: Can the project to produce the product be financed?

Marketability. A deal can be begun in two basic ways. One, a dealer determines that a particular market is being underserved and looks for a product to serve that market. Or, two, the dealer is offered a piece of property in a desirable location and at a good price.

In the second case, the dealer usually determines the potential uses of the property and then the market and profitability of those uses. If one use meets his subjective criteria of a good deal, he buys the property. This property-first (as opposed to market-first) path occurs on both existing and development properties. On an existing property, the price may be right in terms of the cash flow generated by its present use. Better yet, the operator may be able to buy the property at a bargain price because it is being poorly run.

Making the right decision on marketability is one of the most important choices an investor faces. In the first case, measuring the market, coming in at the right spot with the right product (apartments, shopping center, single-family homes, and so forth) takes magnificent research, luck, skill, location, and timing.

Anticipating the economic factors that will make either choice one or choice two prosper, is beyond the ability of most investors. Further, even the best experts and research are thrown off by a prolonged development on any project. The 4- to 5-year lead time of high-rise office buildings, for example, makes them extremely vulnerable to market softness because of overbuilding. Residential projects with a 2-year lead time are less vulnerable. But which is right for your location and market?

As already stated, the best means the investor has to reduce this risk is to select a dealer with a demonstrated feel for the market he serves. Also, as mentioned, formal market studies and data cut risk and help the investor and dealer make their decision. Generally, the larger the project and the longer its development time, the more data the good decision-maker will seek in making his decision. Comparative shopping of competitive projects is called for, and for the large subdivision or new community project it is essential to project local economic patterns (particularly employment) and population growth.

In evaluating your deal, you (the investor) should thoroughly question the dealer about how he reached his decision that there is a market for the product. Does the dealer know what he is talking about? One thing you as investor should not do (unless you are qualified by education and experience) is to take on by yourself the evaluation of the underlying data. But you should use this data, and other market-profile materials, to question strongly the deal you are looking at, and its dealer.

Feasibility. The average investor is usually out over his head in trying to determine project feasibility. It is extremely complex for the layman to know and understand such things as whether or not the operator intends to use the most efficient construction techniques (steel versus reinforced concrete) or operating methods (off-site versus on-site management) and the cost implications of these methods.

The main thing the investor can do is to determine whether or not the operator has been conservative. He should watch operators who make statements like: "While our estimates show we should be able to build this project for so much in dollars and within so many months, we increased both dollar and time cost estimates by so much." In other words, what I am saying here is I tend to trust a conservative developer who tells you right in front that there may be some cost overruns. It is a fact that most nonresidential projects (but including large apartment and condominium projects) do suffer from cost overruns.

All projects cost more than they at first appear to cost. The wise investor has an expert (or two) who is qualified to give strong cost estimates, and then factors in another 10 percent. This is why I urge caution in investing, and repeatedly lecture the investor not to put into a project more than he can afford to lose.

Financeability. Perhaps the best check for the investor on the cost and time estimates of a project is the analysis made by the financial institution backing the deal. These institutions, especially banks, usually have experienced staffs that check out every detail in the paperwork submitted by the developer. And they make sure that these details are in order before committing their institution to the financing.

The financial backing of a deal is its acid test. Since leverage is required in real-estate projects, without financing even the best project is only a pipe dream. The investor should be aware that the following forms of financing are required, and he should be sure that the financing is in order before he shows his money.

1. Front Money. This financing is required in both development and operating deals and is usually furnished by the developer. This is the money spent to gain control of the site—

usually on an option or by a contract with a small down payment and subject to determining the feasibility and economics of the project. Front money further includes obtaining preliminary plans, engineering, and legal studies to develop a package that fully presents the project to those financially involved in it.

2. *Equity Funds.* These are the funds put up by the investors to cover the difference between the overall requirements of the project and the funds to be loaned to the project.

3. *Interim or Construction Loan.* This is the short-term loan made primarily in development projects to convert the property from its present physical form into the product that ultimately will be marketed. Interim loans are usually made by commercial banks and REIT short-term lenders for 90 percent of the permanent loan.

Construction lenders generally require permanent loan commitments, or takeouts* of their position, prior to committing themselves.

4. *Permanent Loans.* These loans, made by thrift institutions, insurance companies, and pension funds in both development and operating projects, are the ultimate lever in the real-estate industry. Permanent loans are the long-term (20 to 40 years) financing that covers between 75 and 95 percent of the ultimate cost of real-estate projects. The shortage of these funds during the mid-1970s caused massive chaos in the real-estate industry. The availability of these funds, therefore, should be watched closely by real-estate investors.

Evaluating Commercial Property

Adversity often creates opportunities. In the mid-1970s' marketplace, many small retail and service businesses were

* See Glossary.

being forced to fold because of the high cost of money and slack consumer demand. The owner of commercial real estate had higher than normal vacancies. Alert real-estate investors were looking for bargains, and they were aware of the fact that vacancies do not always mean a bad property. At the right price, and with reasonable prospects for rerenting, many properties on the block represent good buying opportunities. Again, it's a matter of knowing what you want, what the market is, the location and timing and other factors.

Evaluating Rental Income. First, the investor should evaluate the income he might anticipate from the property. He should be able to distinguish between:

• Scheduled Income: the gross rental income of a property fully rented at prevailing rates.

• Current Income: the gross rental income currently being yielded by the property.

• Projected Income: the gross rental income the investor feels he can reach within the near future (this should be less than scheduled income, but more than the current income).

• Net Operating Income: gross rental income minus all operating expenses.

Analyzing Operating Expenses. The second step is to determine the operating expenses currently being paid and project these expenses into the future. Important expenses for a commercial property are:

• Real estate taxes: The owner's tax bill or the local tax office will indicate the current taxes. It is wise to assume that these taxes will increase.

• Payroll: In a commercial building, this should be a low figure. In an apartment house, with a doorman, elevator operators, maintenance men, and so on, the figure is higher. Examine the owner's payroll figures including taxes and, again, expect payroll increases to keep pace with inflation.

• Insurance premiums: Fire and extended coverage and

owner's liability are the two principal types of insurance held by the owner of a commercial building. Your insurance broker can tell you about these costs.

• Maintenance contracts: These are normally carried for the elevators and heating and central air-conditioning systems; they may also include trash pickup, although tenants are sometimes responsible for that.

• Utilities: Frequently, the tenant pays electricity, gas, water, and sewer charges, but not always. A careful reading of the leases will indicate who bears the burden of these costs. Watch these . . . costs will rush upward!

• Parking-lot maintenance: The owner generally carries this responsibility, which includes cleaning, maintenance, and repair of the blacktop, and painting of the white lines. One rule of thumb estimates the cost at either 5¢ per square foot per year, or $4 per car space per year.

• Maintenance and repair: This includes exterior painting and maintenance, and upkeep of the heating, lighting and plumbing equipment. These costs, normally the owner's, run at least 3 percent of the scheduled gross income per year.

• Replacement reserves: Certain parts of the building will wear out and need replacing. These include the roof, air-conditioning system, elevators, floor coverings, water heaters, and storefronts. An engineer can give you a replacement schedule.

• Lease commissions: This is paid to brokers and is an expense item.

All these costs do represent an annual bookkeeping cost that should be reflected in the expense statement before arriving at net operating income.

Evaluating an Apartment Project

First, look at the square feet of land and the cost per square foot of land; then figure the building cost per square foot of land and net rentable cost per square foot. In any building you have gross building square footage and rentable square footage. These figures will help you determine what the rent should be, and what the value of the property is.

It is important that someone knowledgeable about apartments or a professional appraiser look over expense figures for an inexperienced apartment investor. In furnished apartments, your expenses might be as much as 10 percent higher than in unfurnished ones. Older units, pools, heavy landscaping, are items that add to that expense. In larger apartment complexes you usually have a manager plus an assistant manager, with offices and phones. This is an additional expense. A salaried manager is usually the norm, and in smaller apartments the manager might live rent free.

To determine the expenses of an apartment you might be considering, here are some rules of thumb:

• In a new apartment building (unfurnished) units account for 35 percent of expenses in relation to gross income.

• Furnished apartments run 45 percent of expenses to gross income and I have seen 50 percent.

• Older units depend on construction, condition, type of carpets, and so on. Each of these items must be weighed.

• Apartments built on speculation have a 2 to 4 percent higher expense factor than those built for an owner to own and operate. The plumbing, stoves, drapes, drywall, are of better quality. Inquire about how and why the building was built.

• If you are an investor, you must seriously consider who is going to manage your property. This must be computed as an expense, and it sometimes makes the difference between a "posible" buy or no buy at all.

• Your first-year vacancy factor will depend upon how well you did your homework: location, demand, time of year you open, competition. Know them well.

• If there is no competition in the area, be careful to determine if a need for your apartment exists. In commercial property you can determine it by going to manufacturers and asking what their need is. In apartments, however, it is much more difficult. A good market-research firm can save you plenty here. You must know your market and its future.

Is new employment coming into the area? Are big lay-offs ahead that will affect your tenants? Is a new apartment planned that will compete with you? How would you survive a transition period? There is no way to answer these questions without strong market research. Be sure to get it.

Evaluating a Home

For most investors, this will be their best investment. It should not be made in a hurry, or in the dark. First, go to the assessor's office and check the neighborhood, or hire a college kid to do it for you for $25. Find out the prices and taxes on other, comparable houses. Also, check out the broker; get references. Finally, don't be impatient or let emotion shove you into a deal. Sit back, be cool, and go through Sandy Goodkin's house list:

• Check the Floor Plan. Is it functional? Does it have the space you and your family need?

• Check Each Room. *The kitchen*: Functional, built-ins, appliances in good order (warranties left?), eating area for family meals?

The walls: Clean, even, any sign of rot or mildew or serious cracking?

The floor: What kind of material? Covered? With what and in what condition?

Ceilings: Cracks, breaks, even, any wet spots?

Dining areas: Place for company, large enough for dining table?

Bedrooms: Enough and large enough second bedrooms for furniture the way you wish to use them, or just closets?

Master bedroom: Separate from kids' rooms, private and big enough for furniture?

Bathrooms: Wear, tiles even and in good condition, grouting around tub and shower good (examine carefully)? Are there enough bathrooms for your size family? Try out faucet and toilet, is pressure sufficient? Shower pressure? Sufficient hot water?

Closet space: Enough closets and large enough for your things? Dead storage areas?

Basement: Dry, unfinished or used as a room? Pipe insulated and room well ventilated?

• Check for Insulation. Visit the house on a colder or warmer day. The cost of heating and/or cooling a home is rising, and will not halt until some form of cheaper energy is mass produced, like solar energy panels.

• Check Attic or Attic Space. Can the attic be used for storage? Is it clean and insulated? Are there any wet spots?

• Check the House for Termites. Make sure the deal is contingent on an inspection for termites, which seller pays for.

• Check Fireplace. Does it draw? Is the design and position of it in room attractive? Is the room so small that furniture must be too close to it for actual use?

In many cities you can hire a special inspection service to review the home you are considering. A structural engineer can save you plenty. Call your local Building Industries Association (BIA), Associated General Contractor, or local appraisers association for names of ethical ones. He should check, and so should you, such things as the heating plant, insulated glass, and 125 amp electrical panel.

For a new house, you should determine:

• What in the model home is not included in the package, and what is.

• In what ways would your home differ from what you are being shown?

• What walkways, patio slabs, and so forth are included?

• Is there a garage or carport? An oversize garage is a good resale feature in these days of storage problems.

• Is there a warranty on the home? Do they have the

National Association of Home Builder's warranty, or something just as reliable?

· Are the appliances warranteed? They should be.

· Walk outside the model home (or the one you are considering). Privacy is vital. Can you see into the bedrooms easily? Is there really any outdoor privacy? Will fencing be provided, and how high?

· Are the streets regulated for low-speed traffic or do cars race through the neighborhood?

· You should also check out the builder. Who is he and what has he done before? If you have a banker, ask him. Get the name of the builder's head man, and write him and ask him about his track record.

· Can you get your deposit back? In many places you must be able to get it back.

· Does the builder handle his own financing or must you get it? If you have to get financing, make the deal contingent upon your getting a loan.

· If the home is on uneven ground where there could be slippage or mudslides during bad weather, ask about it. Have an engineer look at the site. Knock on a few doors in the area and ask about the builder and any problems with the houses during inclement weather.

· Does the builder offer a post-sale person to call?

There is also a final, interior check list to go over before signing for the deal. Try these:

· Is the sound muffling from room to room adequate?

· Will you get storm windows and doors and screens?

· Are there dead bolts on the doors, and if not, will you get them with the house?

· Ask your local police about crime in the neighborhood.

· Are there vents in the garage and under gables and eaves?

· Check to see that large mechanical equipment such as air conditioners are on their own electrical circuits.

• Is the house on a sewer or septic tank? If a tank, what is the capacity? Will sewers be coming through, and if so, when and how much will that cost?

• Are you close to land that might be bought by the city and then you and all your neighbors charged for it? (San Diego and other municipalities have started buying open space to preserve it. While this is an excellent idea, it will cost you and your neighbors money.)

There are a lot of things to look for. You should also check schools, and routes to and from them, playgrounds, summer and winter recreation, and so forth. It is worthwhile to slow down and carefully contemplate this immense investment. If you spent as much time as I suggest on all your real-estate investments, you would be sure to make money.

Diversification

Let's say you've already made your choices and you're ready to invest. Let's even say that you've already invested some more, and are ready to invest again, or to move into a better deal. Maybe you've been stopped by inflation, financing problems, operating expenses that don't pencil out, or restrictive local growth policies. Keep the faith. Diversification can permit you to survive and profit from your hard-earned skills in real estate.

Whatever your investment status, there are eight basic rules you should follow to minimize your problems and maximize your profit potential.

Rule One: Look Before You Leap

Diversification for the sake of diversifying may mean zero profits, and capital losses as well. In terms of products and geographical areas, each real-estate market is a separate business. You should stay in the geographical area where you've been operating and where you know the lay of the land. Essentially, stay in the business and area you know.

Remember: The tract-house builder who jumps into high-rise construction is likely to get clobbered.

Rule Two: Stay Away from Known Losers

Learn to recognize what projects are doing poorly, and where they are located. Use your research, intuition, advisors, reading. Office space in the mid-1970s, both in downtown and neighborhoods, was off sharply. So were many vacation condominiums, except those in special markets with outstanding features.

Large-scale projects requiring heavy land-carrying costs make no sense when viewed from the perspective of high-interest charges. The second-home market in the mid-1970s came to a standstill. So did subsidized housing, with its massive maintenance costs and huge cash outlays to comply with bureaucratic red tape.

The skill here is to be up-to-date with the real-estate market in your area, and not get caught in last year's boom and this year's bust. Caution, good advice, excellent contacts, and perception will help avoid losses.

Rule Three: Closely Examine the Winners

I will discuss winners in detail in Part III (along with some losers). For now, small middle-income ($45,000 to $60,000 range) tracts that are not out in the boonies are worth checking out.

Lower middle-income condominium conversions may work out well because capitalized income determines the price you pay and that price is more likely to be less than replacement cost.

Residential condos have been depressed, but the condo

concept has always been a good vehicle for giving doctors and other commercial-space users an inflation hedge.

Look carefully as well at warehouses and other older buildings that are priced below replacement cost and can be economically converted to exciting office or commercial projects. Miniwarehouses for space-short apartment and condo dwellers took off during the early 1970s in the West. They are still worth examining.

There is a market in many areas for small neighborhood convenience-shopping centers if they are anchored by a solid fast-food or minimarket operator.

Industrial projects can also be a good thing if your area is not overbuilt.

Look for the mixed-use condo projects of apartments, stores, and offices in some development areas.

Rule Four: Land Is Cheap

The sharply rising costs of construction materials and financing make the cost of raw land a less critical element in the price of the finished real-estate product. The smart investor-developer today will make his deal contingent upon financing and other prerequisites; better yet, he'll get the landowner to joint venture with him.

Buying land is still a tricky business, but always a wise investment. Remember the basic rules of land buying:

- Make sure the land is not environmentally sensitive, so it *can* be used.
- See it.
- Walk it.
- Find out what is planned for the land. Exactly what has been built, promised, bonded to do?
- Make certain that the developer is using his own name in any land project, not a contrived name for that specific deal.
- Check that there is a good supply of proven water.

• Find out how many lots are being developed. If there are many, what chance will yours have to appreciate?

• If you plan to put in commercial, apartment, or industrial projects, will there ever be enough residents to provide a marketplace?

• Be sure that the land's price is its value. You should be getting a price proportionate to the distance of the land from proven marketplaces.

• Don't say "yes" on the first visit. Think about it and walk around it several times. Remember: Land is cheap—unless you buy a bad deal in it. The true price of land is what it costs to improve it plus the raw cost to you.

Rule Five: Follow the Lender

Many deals fail because they can't be financed at any price. Permanent financing is essential (and you should be for an *equity stomp** to get it).

A lender included in the deal for a piece of the action is a blessing in disguise. To protect his investment, the lender-investor will carry you if things get rough; he'll carry you much further than the lender with a top-end interest only.

Even the pros look for a sophisticated mortgage broker to help them mold deals during times of chaotic money markets like the 1970s, rather than trying to deal directly with money sources. Limit your risk and front money and get the blessing of a permanent lender.

Rule Six: Travel Light

Lighten your overhead load, and play things close to the vest. Have those with bottom-line participation run things. Doing and not directing is the best way to learn. Buy the best

* Lender may wish some equity for himself.

outside services you can get, as you need them. They should help you with design, marketing, and finance areas.

Rule Seven: Two Is a Crowd

There is usually room for only one developer per deal. A partnership between two strong entrepreneurs is like a ship with two captains. It may never leave the dock. Again, buying solid expertise can help you to avoid quarrelsome partners.

Rule Eight: Who Are You?

What is your motivation? What do you want to be? Can you concentrate on getting into and out of your next deal?

Get into deals that turn you on, that motivate you. Never do something solely for the money. Still, do not emotionalize the opportunity. Step back and examine it practically. Ask yourself some questions:

- Is it a good deal?
- Will it retain my interest?
- What kind of money will it take?
- Must it be managed after completion, sale, or rental?
- Who will manage it?
- How much management time do you have to give and how much of that time will the new deal take?
- How much of a front-end (cash) load is needed?
- Is it a single-purpose deal with the consequent difficulty of getting a lender?
- Are you up against very experienced pros who might devour you?
- Is the zoning good, or will it take time?
- If you get sick or otherwise must halt your involvement, who will handle the deal?

- Is the area evolving for the better or worse?
- If the deal clicks, is there room for expansion?

You'll want to answer these questions—and probably think of many more—before you step into any deal.

10

RISKS

Avoiding risks is the name of the game. But sometimes it also pays to take risks—the greater the risk may mean the greater the profits. Actually, risks are being taken at every stage: to loan money, pick a location, decide between apartment projects, offices, or condominiums. Even deciding to go into real estate in the first place was a risky act.

There are other risks that must be met after the basic decisions have been made. These include avoiding recapture of your funds, avoiding moratoria, getting your investment rezoned the way you want; this chapter will teach you some steps to overcome those risks. Finally, there are deals themselves that carry risk, some good and some bad, and I'll give you a list of some examples and how much risk each involves.

Recapture

This is one of the biggest and most dangerous pitfalls for today's investor, and one that he or she probably understands the least. Recapture is actually the tax means for taking a portion of your profits above a fixed amount.

Let's examine a typical two-for-one tax deduction deal:

Sale price:	$4,000,000
To pay off mortgage:	$2,650,000
Net proceeds:	$1,350,000

Step One

	$1,345,000 Taken
Depreciation recapture:	$1,000,000 = S.C. = capital gains 25%
	$345,000 = ACC = ordinary income 50%
Tax liability:	$250,000 (25% of $1,000,000)
	$172,500 (50% of $345,000)
	$422,500

Step Two

Retire nonrecourse debt:	$2,900,000 mortgage
	$250,000 principal paid down
	$2,650,000 balance

When this mortgage is paid off, the IRS views it as a distribution of cash to the partners. Therefore, it is taxed at the capital-gains rate of 25 percent. The tax liability of 25 percent of $2,650,000 is $662,500.

Step Three

Actual distribution of cash:	$4,000,000 sale
	$2,650,000 to pay off mortgage
	$1,350,000 cash proceeds

This is also taxed at the capital-gains rate of 25 percent. But the tax liability, 25 percent of $1,350,000, is just $372,500.

Total proceeds of cash:	$1,350,000
Minus tax liability #1	$422,500
Minus tax liability #2	$622,500
Minus tax liability #3	$372,500
	$(67,500)

In this example, the partners would have to come up with $67,500 to complete the sale of their property. This would be quite a shock to an investor seeing a $1,350,000 profit of sale.

There are ways of avoiding such recapture—not all of them pleasant. You can hold the property for 16 years, then there is no depreciation recapture due to a 1969 IRS ruling. Or, you could refinance. Or, more drastically, you could die.

You should be aware that tax shelter in real estate is not a permanent tax loss. It merely pushes your liability back several years. Uncle Sam is patient, and always tries to collect his tax bills. Therefore, it is additionally important to carefully select your real-estate advisor. His fiduciary duties include understanding this highly complex situation, and planning your best approach to avoid pitfalls, such as recapture.

Moratoria

This may be the biggest initial risk of all. Many communities, seeing prosperity and control in no-growth policies, have put moratoriums on housing construction, sewer lines, school development, and other means of expanding their population. This, of course, has hurt the real-estate investor and developer deeply.

During the spring of 1973, before there was much of a housing slow-down, the International City Management Association (ICMA) mailed a questionnaire to 2,282 cities and 639 counties across the country. The cities had populations of 10,000 or more, and the counties had populations of at least 50,000. Returns were received from 1,115 cities (49 percent) and 177 counties (28 percent).

The results were discouraging to developers. Some 19 percent of the cities and 21 percent of the counties replied that they had moratoria, either on building permits, requests for re-zoning, water or sewer connections or "other" items. Of those cities, almost 64 percent were suburban, and the greatest number with moratoria were in the West; 60 percent of the counties were in the South and West. (See Chart 10–1.)

CHART 10–1 Geographic Distribution of Moratoria (ICMA survey)

Region	*Number Cities Responding*	*Number with Moratoria*	*Percent*	*Number Counties Responding*	*Number with Moratoria*	*Percent*
Northeast	243	46	19	34	5	15
North Central	309	48	16	44	4	9
South	265	43	16	48	13	27
West	253	66	26	33	11	33

CHART 10–2 Impact of Moratoria (ICMA survey)

Jurisdictions Reporting Moratoria	*Delay Building Permits*		*Delay Rezonings*		*Delay Water and Sewer Connections*		*Other*	
	Number	*Percent*	*Number*	*Percent*	*Number*	*Percent*	*Number*	*Percent*
236	142	60	84	36	99	42	30	13

Most of the delays were for building permits (60 percent) and/or water and sewer connections (42 percent). The total number of actions (355) exceeded the number of communities with moratoria (236), which indicates that some communities and counties have put delays or halts on several development actions. (See Chart 10–2.)

During this same period of 1973, the Housing and Urban Development Agency also circulated a questionnaire to all its area offices asking for information on sewer moratoria, and their impact. Of the 76 HUD offices responding, 34 reported sewer moratoria in their districts. Only Region VIII (See Chart 10–3) reported no moratoria within its entire region.

In all, some 226 HUD jurisdictions had some form of sewer moratoria. The highest number was found in one of the busiest development regions: South Florida (Miami, Tampa-St. Petersburg) had 127 sewer moratoria; Cleveland and northern New Jersey also had high moratoria.

Such moratoria, characteristic of the first half of the 1970s, may have a long-range effect and be of indefinite duration. Some 149 cases—by far the majority—were listed as expected to last for an unknown period. (See Charts 10–3 and 10–4.) The types of delays, moreover, were identical to those on the ICMA survey, and indicate a nationwide movement by towns and counties to block real-estate development by similar methods. (See Chart 10–5.)

HUD went back to its area offices to check on the potential sprawl effect of the moratoria. Its offices were asked whether or not housing starts were shifting "to other jurisdictions without moratoria." More than 30 percent of the respondents answered affirmatively, a moderate to major shift was taking place. The importance of this cannot be overstated: As one county or town slows or halts development, that development is moving to another location. More than ever, your use (as an investor) of market research, careful location selection, and timing becomes vital.

My observations of regions on the East and West coasts indicate that moratoria push development into distant fringe

CHART 10–3 **Location and Duration of Sewer Moratoria (HUD survey)**

Region	*Number with Moratoria*	*Less than 6 Months*	*6 to 12 Months*	*12 to 24 Months*	*Over 24 Months*	*Unknown or NA*
I: Maine, N. Hampshire, Vermont, Massachusetts, Connecticut, Rhode Island	5	3		1	1	
II: New York, New Jersey, Puerto Rico	27	24		1		2
III: Pennsylvania, Delaware, Maryland, Virginia, W. Virginia, District of Columbia	15	6		3	6	
IV: N. Carolina, S. Carolina, Georgia, Kentucky, Tennessee, Alabama, Mississippi, Florida	88	4	71	2		11
V: Ohio, Michigan, Indiana, Illinois, Wisconsin, Minnesota	40	1	12	10	17	
VI: Louisiana, Arkansas, Oklahoma, New Mexico, Texas	5	2	1	2		
VII: Missouri, Kansas, Iowa, Nebraska	24	19	2	2	1	
VIII: Montana, Wyoming, Colorado, Utah, N. Dakota, S. Dakota	0					
IX: California, Nevada, Hawaii, Arizona	16	3	4	3	6	
X: Idaho, Oregon, Washington, Alaska	6	1	1	1	3	
TOTAL	226	63	91	25	34	13
Percent responses		28	40	12	15	6

CHART 10–4 Duration Estimates (HUD survey)

Number Cases	*Less than 1 Year*	*1–2 Years*	*3–4 Years*	*Unknown*
226	20	40	17	149

communities outside the moratorium area but within driving distances of major employment centers. People are still obtaining houses, office space, shopping centers or apartments, but at the expense of longer driving times.

Worse still, moratoria, rather than giving impetus to reconcentration in central communities, appears to be encouraging further sprawl—out to where towns are not so strict and land is cheap. This is adding to an even more inefficient pattern of urban and suburban growth—hardly what the advocates of moratoria anticipated. But this will stop in major "hot housing" areas.

Still, these HUD and ICMA observations were taken before the energy crisis. Indications are that moratoria have not diminished, but the reaction to them has changed. Shortages and high costs of gasoline may have a long-term negative-growth impact on fringe areas. The energy crisis and the moratoria hardly inspired confidence in the government's ability to resolve problems of urban growth. The two together have seriously (but, let's hope, temporarily) hurt the needed housing supply.

CHART 10–5 Delays Due to Sewer Moratoria (HUD survey)

Category	*Number*
Building permits	135
Rezonings	10
Water and sewer connections	178
Other (including mortgage insurance, septic tanks, subdivisions, and commercial use)	42

Keep track of moratoria, and the patterns of issuance. You are likely to encounter no-growth policies at some point during your real-estate investing. No growth will kill your investment, but it may also make opportunities sprout not far away. "Managed growth" is different from "no growth" in that it allows a certain number of parcels of real estate to be used within a period of time. Through this process the municipality comprehends that it will continue and, in fact, desires to grow further. The impetus here is to manage that growth so that it is not sporadic, jumping over existing land that hardly has utilities available to it. This is what I call "the New York Syndrome," which points to the fact that cities will simply not stand for the megalopolis or forever-growing patterns of the post-WW II era.

Certain provocative planners have had a strong influence in alerting the public to the fact that undeveloped land has an important public value in general as open space, for outdoor recreation, agriculture, or as sources of water, soil, vegetation, and animal-conservation areas. A developer now must show that the benefit to the general public from his proposed development outweighs its value as open space. His proposed development must also harmonize to the greatest extent possible with the area's ecological systems.

Environmentalism and fiscal restraints can lead to a slow-growth policy. The next step is managed growth: population controls, development prohibitions, and the like. Some of the no-growth opposition to development is based upon the fallacious assumption that development attracts people. In fact, growth areas like California are likely to offer less for the housing dollar than the Midwest or East from which many Californians have moved because it forces buildable land prices up. Worse, no-growth attitudes are limiting the supply of developable land and that will continue in California, Washington, and Oregon, especially.

Zoning

One obvious device widely used to restrict growth, and to preserve the future goal of limited physical and social-economic homogeneity in certain enclaves, is zoning. Here you, the investor-developer, may have a better chance to engage the no-growth people, and to persuade them of the value of your position. But it will take perception, brains, and patience.

The problem of rezoning is not an easily solved one. Zoning is a license for a municipality which allows for only certain uses such as residential, apartment, shopping center, and so on. The benefit of getting an area rezoned is that it can make the piece of land more valuable.

Zoning is deeply mixed up with a community's emotions. It is often wrapped in arguments about ecology, or no growth, or other forms of restriction. There is little effort made in many cases to understand the true nature of the developer's business, either by the community or by many professional planners in these communities. The builder-developer is seen as greedy, rich, and a corruptor of politicians.

Because he changes the land, the developer enrages the neighbors. He may have bought a piece of land in good faith. Hopefully, he has not paid off anyone. He wishes to plan and use the land to build and receive cash flow from his investment. Today, many municipalities are using police powers to halt real-estate investors and developers from using land as it is zoned.

If you buy land, and it is not zoned for the use you eventually wish to see it used for, you have a major problem. If you are a small operator, you can be put out of business before the issue is decided. Remember, holding costs on your investment are going through the roof, just like everything else.

The real-estate investor's problem is composed of the following trouble spots:

a.) He is highly visible. Everyone knows the piece of land, and that he is trying to change it.

b.) What he does to the land then creates a new environment for an entire area. Only where the land was previously ugly (as in strip mining) is such change going to be viewed as totally beneficial.

c.) This new environment will attract "new people," who will be renting or buying and living in this area. The "old people" who are already living there worry that these newcomers will be transient, lower income, bigger families with more cars (and noise), and who will not care for their property as well as the old timers do.

d.) Aroused neighbors can become a political force and intimidate politicians. (So can developers.) And politicians react to political muscle.

If you have bought a piece of land and now find yourself in the position of having to get it rezoned, here are my suggestions. First, you must consider yourself not only a developer, but an educator. You must become a communicator. You must work on your presentation to the zoning board and the public almost as hard as you worked on your deal. Your request for rezoning will die if your presentation is incomplete, too technical, arrogant, or divides you from the people of this municipality.

In putting together your arguments, you must remember Sanford Goodkin's law of the 4 P's:

1. *Presentation.* It should clearly (and with some humility) answer the following questions:

Who are you?
What do you do?
What do you own?
What do you want to do with it?
What makes you think it will work (research)?
How will it benefit the community?
How will it benefit the neighborhood?

To make this kind of presentation, you should have an easily understood map. Pictures of your land also help. You might add pictures of the surrounding land uses, especially if they show poor land use, design, construction. Don't rap another guy (at least not too hard), but take poor uses as a way of saying this is not what you're planning.

You should also consider having your land-use plan presented by a professional planner. Show the land uses in circles on your map after the planner finishes—or while he's talking. Coordinate your circling and his points. Use bold colors for outlining open space circles; that attracts the no-growth advocates.

Have renderings made of your project that show community design and street scenes. This avoids one guy shooting you down because he doesn't like an individual home design.

Show slides of your previous best project. If you don't have any (slides, that is, not well-done projects), show slides of projects that others have done that may be close to what you're planning.

2. *Politics.* You, as the principal investor/developer, should open the presentation and end it.

You should also research the zoning board before your presentation. Where does each live? In which kind of housing (or apartment) design? In the city or out? What is his or her real business? Does he or she have an axe to grind?

Introduce yourself to each member of the board before the presentation so that each feels you are three-dimensional and human. People do not fight friends.

Use a local planner and attorney to supplement your own staff. Show specific knowledge of the community to overcome any taint of being a carpetbagger.

Give them a little more than they expect: more facts, more photos, more understanding of their special community problems (if any) or advantages.

Get to know the politicians' deputies.

Never give your presentation—if you can help it—around

election time. You may unwittingly step into a sensitive issue, or get caught between the press and the polls.

Do not discuss politics on the telephone with anyone.

3. *Be Pragmatic.* This means, to me, being skilled in the matters of business, and practical.

Your presentation must be orderly and well rehearsed (even the jokes). It should be slow, so that your thoughts are clearly heard and understood.

You should show market support for your project. Your slides of other projects should reveal your business side: how successful these projects were, how the traffic was, the parking, how neat the lawns are kept, and so on.

You should present statistics of the smallness of families buying condominiums, apartments, townhouses. Show how the environment is better maintained for these type of units than for single family.

Show how schools have empty seats (you hope), how big lots are wasted space (and sometimes garbage dumps), what alternative uses could be made of these spaces and how they might be wrong for the community—bringing a heavier tax burden, more on-street parking, poor land use.

Show uses for parks and open spaces.

Show yourself as a pro who is believable, knowledgeable, successful, reasonable, proud. Also, you should be someone who wishes to benefit the community, as well as benefit from the area.

4. *Be Pleasing.* Hold your temper. Go in expecting to be attacked, if not by the board then by the audience. Expect the worst. Prepare brief answers to hostile questions, hopefully with some humor. Steal a few jokes from *Reader's Digest* or some other magazine, preferably jokes about builders or people or arguments. Use one—only one—in a tight situation. Humor will crack anger every time.

Listen to questions patiently. Avoid the temptation to

"play" to one side of your audience when there is a hostile or long-winded or ambiguous question. If a questioner catches you flat-footed (you either didn't hear him or can't think of an appropriate response), politely ask to have the question repeated. You can do this by saying that you didn't hear, please repeat the question. Or, of you want to rattle the questioner, pretend momentary confusion over the clarity of the question, and ask if he might rephrase it so that you can understand it. It will seldom be rephrased as harshly as the first time.

Plan your presentation from top to bottom. Begin with the statement—true or not—that you are happy to be there. Introduce your staff and your professionals and give a short description of each one's work. Turn the presentation over to them, and emcee the show. Make sure that you end it, and end it by thanking the board and the audience.

It will also help you if you understand larger issues well in advance. This is part of your keeping abreast of the real-estate business. Understand that some communities do not wish to grow. Understand, too, that local homeowners really believe that apartments and condos are bad. They can be changed only with facts and content.

Cultivate, before your meeting, the planners in your area. Even planners are sometimes unaware of the success and beauty of new ideas and densities. Planners are afraid of what they do not know.

Some Final Thoughts on Zoning. Even if you have the rezoning meeting locked up, make an excellent presentation. Don't make them think that this is an in-and-out deal. Remember, you may be coming back to this same board in a few years for some other rezoning issue. Treat them with intelligence and style. Go first class.

Take planners to facsimile projects. This is an excellent communication.

Finally, give yourself time so that zoning delays do not anger or kill you (literally or financially).

Minimizing Real-Estate Risk

As mentioned, there is an infinite variety of real-estate deals. And there are as many risks. To diminish the risks, here are 4 basic rules you should follow at this stage of your real-estate investment game:

1. Your market-research analysis of the area in which you wish to invest should show it as growing, well-suited to the particular real-estate project you have in mind.
2. Your project should make sound business sense. It must be timely, well-conceived, well-planned, well-executed. Its location—because of the rise in moratoria—must be well-researched and well-placed.
3. You must know experienced professionals: architect, attorney, developer, contractor, managers, advisors, and so on. Is each doing his or her best job, and will the project prosper with them aboard?
4. Your project must be soundly and intelligently financed. It must provide what you are seeking, and allow you financial flexibility.

There is, of course, no way to eliminate risk. Real estate by nature is a risky business, and there are additional risks presenting themselves almost daily: no-growth sensitivities, shortage of utility hookups, selectivity of lender funds, zoning and moratoria delays. What real-estate ventures carry the greatest, or lowest, risks? What are the risk factors in specific deals and tax shelters? Let's examine these questions and help you work toward the deal that's best for you.

Direct and Indirect Investment Risks

Investors can invest directly in real estate, or they can invest indirectly by purchasing the securities of a private or public entity involved in the real-estate industry. I have already detailed this in Chapter Eight. Here, I want to tell you about the risks inherent in direct equity investment and in indirect investments, and the benefits sought from those investments.

Direct Investment. To be sure we know what we are talking about, let's list the direct investments: homes (primary, secondary, and vacation residences), vacant land, improved property (apartments, condos, mobile-home parks), offices, shopping and industrial facilities, hotel and motel buildings, miniwarehouses, recreational developments, agricultural operations, and mixed-use developments. That's a long list, and a lot of opportunities. There are inherent risks in all of them.

The tourist industry, with its wide upswings and downswings, gives hotels and motels and recreational developments substantial fluctuations in income. Because of this, these investments tend to be the most risky form of direct investment. The margin of error in the tourist industry is much slimmer than in other real-estate operations.

Second homes and vacation residences are risky because they are the first to go when things get tough financially. They are also difficult to sell when everyone else has the same idea.

Agricultural operations are risky because they depend upon uncontrollable conditions like the weather. They also need strong management.

The long lead time required to develop and market high-rise office and apartment buildings and large-scale residential and mixed-use projects (especially in the luxury range) makes them risky, too. Changes in the general economic picture and in the specific real-estate markets to which these investments belong add to their shakiness during times of financial strain.

One of the least risky direct investments is a well-located single-family home. Older homes in good condition often command premium prices because they provide significant space and amenities for the housing dollar.

Neighborhood (minimarket) and community (supermarket) shopping centers in established middle and upper income neighborhoods generally show continuous appreciation in value.

The low development and operating costs and rent structures of industrial facilities for small and medium-sized users make them a bread-and-butter investment.

Vacant land within already urbanized areas rarely drops in price.

Expected Benefits. Residences are purchased primarily for use and tax benefits, and secondarily for gain on potential sale. Occasionally, a rental portfolio is established by renting instead of selling previous residences. Rental income as an offset against holding costs also is a partial motivation for purchasing vacation and second homes.

Vacant land offers investment gain, while single-family homes, condominiums, recreational and mixed-use developments are invested in largely for the developmental gains.

Recurring-rental income is obtained from apartments, mobile-home parks, offices, shopping and industrial facilities, and miniwarehouses. That income is sheltered from taxation by the depreciation deduction, with apartment projects being especially favored. A capital gain may "sweeten" these deals, and that gain is often "rolled over" into a more valuable property via an exchange.

The greatest overall return is expected from the risky front runners of a good economy. Hotel and resort properties must throw off an expected cash flow in excess of 15 percent, while shopping centers and office projects leased to financially strong tenants must give 8 to 10 percent of spendable income.

Indirect Investment. These include: private syndicates, public securities (REITs, mortgage, equity and mixed), limited partnerships (single property and blind pool), homebuilders, diversified real-estate operations, and real-estate subsidiaries.

While some of these have been discussed at length before, I wish, to present here, their risks together.

While major office buildings in New York City and other major cities have long been financed by limited partnerships, the widespread marketing of real-estate securities is relatively recent. REITs did not come into their own until 1969, and fell out by 1973. Public homebuilders, diversified real-estate firms and companies with real-estate operations were also an offshoot of the real-estate development boom of the late 1960s and early 1970s.

All these securities enjoyed a bull market reinforced by the real-estate-development boom, and fell hardest when the stock market deflated in 1973 to 1974 and cost overruns hit the industry. The lack of sufficient experience with these securities over several economic cycles makes it difficult to evaluate their relative risk.

REITs and limited partnerships, with the sound management and public understanding that they are more real estate than stock, should be less subject to downside fluctuations than other real-estate securities. Through the use of leverage, they both should be capable of turning in a better upside performance than no real-estate securities. In other words, by reducing borrowing and leverage when the economy swings down, and by increasing them on upswings, skilled management could improve these securities.

Private syndicates have turned out to be the least risky indirect investment. And syndicates formed to operate sound income property are less risky than development syndicates. An existing property with known costs and financing has a lower inherent risk than one subject to the risk of development.

Expected Benefits. Under the mutual-fund principle, REITs can pass on their income to investors as ordinary income or capital gain. Instead of looking for recurring income and gains distributed by REITs, investors looked for gains from the sale of REITs shares. Share-trading expectations resulted.

Private syndications (which are almost always limited partnerships) or public limited partnerships are the only vehicles that can pass tax shelters on to their investors. Obtaining tax shelter from these entities takes the from of arranging tax deductible "soft dollars" in practically all syndicates, and of passing through to the investors the depreciation of income properties. Congress is always reassessing this.

Private development syndicates generate mainly development gains for their investors, and tax sheltered recurring income is the motivating force behind investment in both private and public operating syndicates.

Investors who purchase stock in home builders, diversified real-estate operations, and companies with real-estate subsidiaries expect to be compensated through capital gains for the risk they take. Recurring income in the form of dividends is highly unlikely in real-estate industry corporations.

Various Real-Estate Deals

These are direct-investment deals, and in Chart 10–6, below, I've evaluated them 1 through 10. The larger the number, the greater the need for big money and high risk. Likewise, these would be the deals I would recommend that small investors either stay away from or join a syndication or fund created for the purpose of dealing in the specific project.

There are four categories in the chart; some listings are followed by one asterisk (*), which indicates high risk, or two asterisks (**), which indicates greatest risk, or a dagger (†), which means have experience and staying power. The deal is identified, the type of investor listed, and numerical evaluation of 1 through 10 is given. The type of management called for—professional, personal, or both—is shown, followed by the type of location best suited to the deal's success. Chart 10–7 should be used as a warning rather than as a list of opportunities.

The above is a capsule survey of some tax-shelter investments. This, too, includes their risk to you, the investor.*

* Always check with tax counsel, as Congress and IRS interpretation are constantly revising tax information.

CHART 10–6

Type of Deal	*Type of Investor*	*Deal Evaluated*	*Professional Management*	*Suburban Urban*
Regional Center	Rich/Institutional	10	Top	Both
Convenience	Rich/Institutional	7	Top	Both
Neighborhood	Small/Medium Private	2	Need	Excellent in Both
Speculating Industrial	Private/Institutional	6	Need	Suburban*
Warehousing	Private/Institutional	6	Personal/ Professional	Suburban*
Miniwarehousing	Small/Medium	2	Personal/ Professional	Both
Minitheatre	Small/Group Any Size	4	Personal/ Professional	Both*
Freeway Surplus Land	Private	2	Personal	Both
Store Front Rehab	Small	1	Personal	Both
Apartment Conversion	Any Size	4	Personal/ Professional	Both**

CHART 10–6 (continued)

Type of Deal	*Type of Investor*	*Deal Evaluated*	*Professional Management*	*Suburban Urban*
Hotel Conversion	Medium/Institutional	6	Professional	Urban†
Mobile Home Park	Medium/Large	6	Personal/ Professional	Suburban**
Recreational Vehicle Park	Medium/Large	5	Personal/ Professional	Both/Special* Suburban
Medical Building	Small/Institutional	5	Professional	Suburban**
Small Apartment	Small	4	Personal/ Professional	Anywhere
Over 100 Units	Small/Medium	7	Personal/ Professional	Anywhere
Over 300 Units	Medium/Institutional	8	Professional	Anywhere**
Small Office	Small/Medium	4	Personal	Anywhere
Large Office	Large/Institutional	7	Professional	Anywhere**
Combo Office/ Warehousing	Any Size	7	Professional	Suburban

New Town	Giant	10	Professional	Suburban†
Urban Renewal	Large/Institutional	10	Professional	Urban†
Government Recreational Lease	Any Size	3	Personal/ Professional	Suburban
Farm Land	Any Size	1	Professional	Suburban
Golf Course	Large/Institutional	10	Professional	Suburban**
Motel	Medium/Institutional	7	Personal/ Professional	Suburban**
Hotel	Large/Institutional	10	Professional	Both†
Hospital	All Sizes	7	Professional	Suburban*
Land Spectulation	All Sizes	1	Professional	Both*

* High risk
** Greatest type risk
† Have experience and staying power

CHART 10–7 Survey of Tax-Shelter Investments**

Tax Shelter	*Tax Advantages*	*Tax Risks*	*Other Factors*
Oil and Gas	Drilling, exploration, and development expenses (*intangible drilling and development costs*) are deductible currently as ordinary deduction. Interest on funds borrowed is ordinary deduction. Income from production is ordinary income, but *percentage depletion deduction* (22%) can generally exempt 22% of gross income from tax. Profit on sale of investor's interest held more than six months results in capital gain. Unsuccessful venture—abandonment of investment in dry hole—is ordinary deduction.	See Rev. Rul. 72-135, undermining use of nonrecourse loans from general partner to limited partner. Minimum tax risk on percentage depletion. Minimum tax risk on capital gains. Excess investment interest deduction is limited.	Very high risk. Many dry holes. Limited liquidity. Promoters—know them and obtain references about them.

Equipment Leasing	Accelerated depreciation is available. Investment credit available to noncorporate lessors only in limited situations. Capital gains potential.	Determination of whether transaction is lease or sale. (See Rev. Rul. 55-540 for guidelines.) Minimum tax risk because of accelerated depreciation. Excess investment interest deduction is limited. Depreciation recapture rules may result in realization of some ordinary income instead of all capital gain upon sale.	Limited liquidity.
Cattle Breeding Herds	Depreciation is allowed on purchased breeding cattle. Investment credit is allowed on purchased breeding cattle. Interest on funds borrowed is ordinary deduction. Operation and maintenance expenses (feed and management of purchased breeding animals as well as of animals born to herd) are ordinary deductions.	Excess investment interest deduction is limited. Risk that capital gain on sale may be converted to ordinary income under depreciation recapture rules. Risk of investment credit recapture. Minimum tax risk on capital gains.	Promoters—know them and obtain references about them. Liquidity. High risk based upon past experience.

** From *The Mortgage and Real-Estate Report*; Warren, Gorham, & Lamont, Inc.

CHART 10–7 (continued)

Tax Shelter	*Tax Advantages*	*Tax Risks*	*Other Factors*
	Profits on sale of herd are capital gain if held over two years. Proceeds of animals born to herd but culled as unfit are ordinary income. Proceeds of animals born to herd and held as breeders more than two years are capital gain.	Capital-gain limitation where farming losses exceed $25,000.	
Cattle-Feeding Programs	Operation and maintenance expenses are ordinary deductions. Interest on funds borrowed is ordinary deduction. Profit on sale is ordinary income. Loss is ordinary loss.	Deduction for prepaid feed expenses may be limited to those incurred for business purpose.	Climate and Boycotts affect marketplace
Rental Real Estate	Carrying charges (taxes, insurance premiums, etc.) can be deductible during construction.	Depreciation recapture provisions may result in ordinary income upon sale at gain.	Limited liquidity. Management fees—be alert to amounts charged.

	Operating and maintenance expenses are ordinary deductions. Interest on funds borrowed is an ordinary deduction. Accelerated depreciation may be permitted. Capital-gain potential. Opportunity for tax-free exchanges. Depreciation is allowed on entire investment, cash outlay, including borrowings.	Minimum tax risk because of accelerated depreciation.	
Land	Real-estate taxes deductible. Capital-gain potential.	Minimum tax risk on capital gains.	Lack of liquidity. Long-term holding generally required for large sheltered yield. Generally good inflation hedge. Realty taxes are on the increase.
Municipal Bonds	Tax-free interest. Capital-gain potential.	Interest on loans to buy or carry tax-exempts is not deductible. Minimum tax risk on capital gains.	Stable conservative investment. May yield more after taxes than other investments in same class.

CHART 10–7 (continued)

Tax Shelter	*Tax Advantages*	*Tax Risks*	*Other Factors*
Citrus Groves	Planting, cultivating, and development costs still deductible for old groves—costs for groves planted after December 30, 1969, must be capitalized. Soil and water conservation expenses are deductible. Capital-gain potential.	Minimum tax risk on capital gains.	Attractive economic investment—fewer groves planted because of changes in tax incentives.
Timber	Costs of growing timber are currently deductible. Interest on funds borrowed is ordinary deduction. Capital-gain potential.	Excess investment interest deduction is limited. Minimum tax risk on capital gains.	Economic risk—danger of loss of investment due to natural causes (fire, lightning, windstorms).
Corporate Bonds and Stocks	Capital-gain potential.	Excess investment interest deduction is limited. Minimum tax risk on capital gains.	Market fluctuations.

The Bad Deal

It happens to all of us. You get into a deal, after doing your homework very carefully, and you suspect that all is not going well. You are in it up to your neck. Here are my suggestions:

- Have a face-to-face meeting with the deal-maker. Bring all the agreements along, and make certain that your accountant or attorney is there; make sure that he or she knows the deal and real estate.
- Do not go to the meeting for a confrontation. Think of it as information gathering. Let the dealer show guilt; don't you be the one to create a bad scene.
- Look at the project in person, with an expert, so that you know what it looks like, what is around it, and how far it has progressed.
- Ask the dealer for regular written reports on the deal, and send a copy to your expert advisor. Don't let communication slip until the deal is dead.
- If a licking must be taken, take it. Do not spend good money after bad.
- Remember that deal-makers are usually not good managers. Their creativity is in finding and making the deal. They can be a genius at this phase and an utter washout in making the deal actually happen. Sometimes the deal is really good and valid, but is suffering from the dealer's inabilities. Let an expert look at it. Perhaps it can be rescued. The rescuer can then take a piece of the action for his time.

To avoid bad deals in the future, there are some simple rules to follow. Remember, there are good deals and bad deals, and I can distinguish one from the other in terms of predicting which will work and which will not.

- There is an honest relationship between dealer and investor.

• The deal is fully understood by all parties.
• The parties are all emotionally mature.
• There is an arbitrator available, whom all parties respect.
• All provisions have been well thought out before the deal is made.

This includes answering the questions:

Who is going to put in what money? If the joint venturer is putting up the land, describe it completely and all monies due.

When are all monies due?

Will there be general as well as limited partners?

Will the limited partners be expected to put up additional monies or loans?

When does the capital contribution return to the partners?

Where does cash flow go? And what are the plans for cash flow? What about cash reserves?

Where will profits and losses go? What about special tax-shelter benefits?

Who will manage the deal and what powers will he or she have? What recourse will limited partners have?

What if a partner wishes to sell? Who can sell, to whom, and under what terms?

What if someone dies? What if the partners wish to dissolve?

Thinking about these and other common-sense matters will make for a much more harmonious environment. No matter how big the deal or the dealers, harmony is vital to the success of any project.

PART THREE
LOSERS AND WINNERS

11
SOME LOSERS

The ups and downs of the money market make predictions a source of embarrassment to the best professionals around. I write this book within the context of a very high prime rate and an equally high mortgage-lending rate.

What I would recommend during low-rate periods would be different from what I will recommend here. In this chapter, I shall caution against new apartments because of high-interest rates. But in the next chapter, I shall turn around and point out the many good reasons for apartment investments as the interest rates go down. Please keep this in mind as you read the sections about apartments.

Direct Investment: Areas of Caution

Crystal-ball gazing at the immediate future is difficult enough. Developing a lens that can focus on the distant future is really speculative. In this chapter, dealing with likely losers, and the next—about probable winners—my conclusions are based upon a 2- or 3-year time frame, which I foresee is needed to correct the combination of recession and inflation and to overcome the problems of the particular real-estate markets we will discuss. This discussion is predicated on the belief that the Federal government will prevent general economic conditions from getting any worse. If we blunder into another depression, all bets are off.

The real-estate areas to avoid entirely, or to enter only with extreme caution in the near future, are: (a) new apartment construction where there are rent controls; (b) any investment in office space; (c) the speculative purchase of outlying land; (d) owning or developing subsidized housing; (e) the development of regional and other large shopping centers; (f) buying into the resort and second-home industry; (g) real-estate-investment trusts.

Middle-Income Apartments

Whenever interest rates are high (over 9 percent), most new middle-income apartments won't pencil out. (There are a few developers who have such discipline and experience that they can make money (Fredericks, Mayer—both of California.)

Most middle Americans live in homes; the exceptions are the aged, newlyweds, and empty-nesters. A condominium qualifies as a home, rather than an apartment, because it often has a more attractive exterior, better-finished interior space, a more desirable location and less density (fewer units per acre with more open space). Homes, including condominiums, cost more than apartments. They provide the amount and type of space desired for raising children. When homes sell from $35 to $40 per square foot, including land, apartments cost $25 to $30 per square foot to develop.

The aged and newlyweds are renters because they cannot afford homes. They have an extremely limited amount to budget for housing and represent the lower end and also the bulk of the middle-income rental market.

The empty-nesters choose luxury apartments located near oceans and lakes, center city and parks. They also like the flexibility and convenience of not being tied down by ownership so that they can do the frequent traveling that has become part of their life-style. Usually empty-nesters have lived in several homes and know housing values. If they feel that rental units are overpriced, they will not rent them, and might stay where they are or purchase a well-located condominium apartment. They reason (correctly) that if they must pay that much for housing, they might as well own it and get the benefits of capital appreciation and tax deductions.

The easy money of the late 1960s and early 1970s, and the large numbers of new-family formations and higher mobility, led to a tremendous splurge of apartment construction. Much of it occurred in the suburbs, where land was available and where consumers had moved looking for housing close to shopping and work. Builders, as usual, rushed to get in on a good thing and committed themselves to projects that soon turned out to be losers because of oversupply. In many areas, apartment-vacancy rates shot up and the sales of overvalued condominium units dropped.

Inflation also played a major role in shutting off the splurge of apartment construction. Increases in 3 main categories—construction, interest and operating costs—required rents above what the low-end and newlyweds could afford; empty-nesters passed them by.

Existing apartments are not subject to the construction and interest costs of the inflationary spiral in the apartment-construction business. Still, all apartments have been hurt by massive jumps in utility and maintenance costs, property taxes, and other operating expenses. They are living with rent structures based upon lower operating costs, and it is hurting them.

Apartments could become attractive again if the Federal government provided some relief for the lower middle-income renters. I'm still not convinced that even that measure would get them out of the woods. Owners now holding the rent line to prevent vacancies would increase rents to the level of a satisfactory return on investment. The only way new apartment projects would pencil out would be for the Federal government to put an effective control on inflation, for private owners to eliminate current vacancies, or for the Federal government to press for housing allowance, rent subsidy, income-tax deductions, and other assistance to renters.

If the Federal government cannot (or, worse, will not) relieve with conventional medicines the problem of decreasing real-estate income, the uproar from the unhoused and the poorly housed may force such radical solutions as a national rent control, which would lock present owners into a no-return-on-investment operation, or the public ownership of more low-income apartments. Despite the known horrors of public housing, a continuation of present trends may make it the only solution for all but those people with substantial incomes.

Because of declining vacancy rates in apartments in major American cities, there is a growing need for middle-income and semiluxury rentals, which can have positive cash flow even with as high as 10 percent interest. Location is vital as rentals go up.

Office Space

Offices are highly susceptible to inflation and vulnerable to hyper-saturation. Why?

- There are many older offices available in the form of buildings, homes, industrial areas, converted homes, and mixed-use garden-type buildings.
- The judgment to build large office complexes is often an ego trip. "My building will be better" was the idea. The developer or investor must have financial staying power to survive the dog days.

• Many occupancy rates are exaggerated in order to get rental rolls up, when actually special leases are made at bargain rates, improvements thrown in, and so on.

• The need for office space has not grown as dramatically as in the housing and commercial areas. The marketplace was overbuilt very quickly.

Thus, future office buildings don't pencil out. It is hard to find an existing office building that is a good investment. Office buildings, especially prestige, downtown high-rise towers, often have a negative cash flow. The oversupply is so great, and the narrowing of the market so drastic, that operators are cutting rents or keeping them stable despite cost increases. They hope to get some contribution toward fixed costs, including debt service that often accounts for over 50 percent of total costs. For example, during 1975 an executive interviewed in Century City of Los Angeles underscored the problems of that project by stating that his firm had been paying the same rent for 5 years and the rent was a steal even when they first took occupancy.

There will be good office markets again, as Houston is today, but they will have to be imaginative and well located. Small office buildings, offices combined with warehousing, environmental offices (rehabilitated from older structures), are all opportunities. The big investor will always take his chances in most metropolitan markets even during the ups and downs of the mid-1970s.

The oversupply of office space resulted from a number of factors. The boom of the 1960s had a heavy white-collar orientation and created a heavy demand for office space. Urban-renewal activities in many cities also tended to spawn a rebirth of center city. Prospects for a continuation of that trend looked excellent, and with money readily available too many office projects went up, just as too many apartment projects were undertaken during the same period.

The office glut, however, is far more severe than the apartment market softness. The long lead time and the high front-end investment for office project development make it even harder to lower supply when demand softens. Once several millions of dollars have been sunk into acquiring a site and preparing plans for a high-rise office tower, it is difficult to scrap that investment. Like the gambler who keeps doubling his stakes to try and get even, the developers of massive projects continue to try to solve their problems by putting up new buildings even though all the completed ones are vacant.

Another problem with the office market is the wide range of choice that customers have. Those looking for residential space usually have a limited number of facilities suited to their preferences and income. Service firms (attorneys, accountants, financial institutions, insurance companies, and brokers) and the executive staffs of manufacturing companies, who represent the bulk of the office-space market, can locate in anything from 40¢ per square foot (per month) to $1 per square foot (per month).

Moreover, from an interior standpoint, space is space; low- and high-priced space can be decorated to look the same inside. The recent mushrooming of low-rent industrial developments in the outer city is viciously undercutting the market of the inner-city high-rent districts. Why pay more to travel and hassle with inner-city parking and traffic?

The mid-1970s' recession increased the edge of cheaper outer-city office space over expansion of inner-city space. Prestige is one of the main advantages offered by an inner-city location. Firms quickly decided to forsake prestige when faced with inflation, diminishing profits and tight budgets.

The key to absorbing presently vacant downtown space and creating a demand for more space will be the creation of attractive and affordable residences in center city, as San Diego is planning. Walking to work is highly prized in our society. But the problem of making downtown residential facilities pencil out for anyone but high-income executives has not yet been solved, even with significant governmental underwriting of renewal costs.

If you insist on getting into the office-space investment area, Cross and Brown of New York City have prepared a comprehensive check list of major considerations before buying. It can be found in Appendix F.

Subsidized Housing

There is a department of the government called Housing and Urban Development (HUD). It used to be called just plain old Federal Housing Administration (FHA) until the Great Uncle in Washington decided that housing was also needed in the crowded cities as well as in the suburbs.

FHA performed some great functions, and it had a head man who knew housing, was dedicated, and understood that his department was, in fact, a partner of the shelter industry. FHA's job was to insure mortgages in order to keep the dollars flowing to lower- and middle-income projects. FHA also inspected homes, so that buyers knew that construction was sound and functional. The agency was interested in "lasting marketability"; that is, the product could sell and resell.

As FHA grew bigger, it became HUD. It also became a mouth instead of an arm. It told everyone what was needed in America's housing sector, but it did little. Various government study groups called for more supply of housing for the poor, as well as the middle class. The cry for 26 million homes in the 1970s rang with the fervor of a crusade. But after a great beginning, the department hit a slump. It substituted "wait-a-minute" for action, words for progress. And yet nothing is more important to the shelter industry than this cabinet post.

The introduction in 1961 of the 221 D 3 housing program made possible subsidized financing for private developers (as contrasted with the subsidies since 1937 for public housing). Uncle Sam further held out the significance of tax shelter (already provided by accelerated depreciation) as an incentive for the well-heeled to invest in relieving the housing problems of the disadvantaged.

This linking of subsidized financing and tax shelter aimed to bring down the housing costs to affordable levels through the interest subsidy and to reward investors in this broad market with the taxes saved by applying depreciation tax losses against their other income.

But this apparently excellent recipe for social progress produced an unpalatable mess for two reasons: (1) the massive social problems of the tenants and (2) the stupidities of the bureaucratic administrators. The projects produced astronomical maintenance costs. Cash flow was hurt by the high cost of collecting rents from families with a history of fighting the landlord, and with widely fluctuating incomes and high expenses. Special social services were required which were not contemplated when rents were determined. Municipal tax assessors contributed by assessing projects way above original estimates, partially because of increased development costs.

HUD officials have threatened foreclosures of mortgages on such properties. Foreclosure would mean that the investor would pay massive taxes because of the ordinary income recapture of accelerated depreciation upon the early sale of the project.

HUD also considered rent increases only on an annual basis to adjust for cost increases, rather than when the cost increases actually occurred.

Local administrators with social service orientation, and not business orientation, viewed the developers and investors as profit gougers, exploiters of the poor, and money grubbers. Requests for even small changes in operating procedures were resisted.

The Outlook. Subsidized housing will continue to be a no-no for private investment unless the appropriate action is taken to make sense out of those programs. Local program administrators should be given substantial leeway to make changes in procedures. Local agencies should be required to select as administrators those with a solid background in business and management, preferably in the real-estate field. One of the most successful operations is being run in San Diego by Bill Menegus, a man with service first in banking and then in the finance branch of the U.S. Army. Bill also has a great deal of empathy for his fellow human beings.

Many 221 D 3 and 235 projects have gone down the tubes because the developers and insurance companies involved in these programs proved no more capable of dealing with the problems of the inner-city disadvantaged than the retired merchant landlords they were supposed to replace.

The hostility of the we/they landlord/tenant relationship must be substantially defused through resident and community involvement. There must be adequate funding for the special costs of operating housing for the disadvantaged. Investors and management should be given the incentive of an extra return if they do an outstanding job by operating the project at costs below those budgeted.

Obviously, if the tenants cannot afford to pay for those services, the government subsidies must be increased. There is absolutely no firm rationale for limiting subsidized housing developed by private enterprise to only interest reduction subsidies. Although this might sound harsh, it is better for the government to do nothing than to compound present complex socioeconomic problems by messing around with halfway measures.

I believe that subsidized programs in housing will be needed to insure proper housing in this country. I believe that there should be tax incentives so that the private sector can invest and supply monies for such housing. I believe that this sector will be vital to the housing recovery after the 1974 to 1975 debacle. But it will take a dynamic President who places HUD in the hands of a strong and imaginative leader to make this happen.

Until these changes are made, investors would do well to stay away from subsidized housing. Section 8 is new and can be important to present and new apartment owners.

Outlying Vacant Land

I cannot count the number of friends who have made money buying raw land. Some of them made it easily. One sharp friend said that the problem arises after you buy the land: Someone has to make use of it for you to make money. The longer it takes to get that land into use, the less the last buyer will be able to make on the deal.

Land deals always went well until zoning became a pain and interest rates ate up feasibility (the ability of the finished deal to make money). When interest rates are high, holding costs mount. When there are zoning problems brought about by any of a variety of reasons, holding costs mount even more. This makes the selection of land risky, depending upon its use, the timing, and the profitability.

The rules have also changed because getting land into profitable use is tough as hell. Holding it is more expensive. Sure, there will always be "sleepers," but extreme care as well as expert advice are necessary today in any land purchase.

Value, as we have seen, is tied to use. Only an extremely limited amount of vacant land in outlying areas—areas not already urbanized and not serviced with utilities and municipal services—will be developed in the near future. Where new development does occur, it is likely to be on a large new-community scale that justifies rapid-transit linkages to existing urban modes and which itself provides a complete human environment with residential, commercial, employment, and recreational facilities. The day of small, scattered subdivisions, where a developer could get the right land buy, are disappearing from many cities.

The smart developer today does not speculate with vacant land. He buys only when he is sure that property can be developed and then only with an advance inventory for 2 or 3 years. With everything else going up, developers are exerting a great deal of effort to stay in the markets they would like to serve, by barganing hard on the price of raw land. However, in managed-growth areas, such as the State of California and in areas where the single-family land is in short supply, hard bargaining is impossible. The landowner is literally getting what the traffic will bear. The builder and the lender are outbidding each other for ready-to-go single-family land in these hot areas. The investor who wants to tie up land that can then be zoned and serve as supply to waiting builders will make good money. The risk here is that he may lose deposits on some land in which the land seller is very independent and to which there can be no utility connections.

Even where developers find land in outlying areas at the right price and which could easily be approved for development, purchases are made with extreme caution. The smart investor-developer remembers clearly the chill of fear when traffic fell off in the fringe areas during the gasoline crisis. Beware of and alert to another such crisis.

If anything, all of these forces that undercut the market for outlying land will probably intensify in the future.

Regional and Large Shopping Centers

I believe that large shopping centers belong only to the very smart, experienced, and professional developers, financed by large financial institutions. The regional center is one area that has no room for small or inexperienced investors. It is the one major area where the little guy can get clobbered.

The best way to invest in this highly skilled arena is to own the land that shopping centers want or own the land next to the giant centers. The huge neighbor will render value to your land as his develops. Also, the best place for a shopping center is next to a shopping center as long as it is large enough. The new supercenters (shopping center complexes—malls) do more business than some downtowns.

The regional center is defined as the largest type, generally more than 50 acres. There was a time when they were smaller, 30 to 35 acres, but today they take plenty of land and parking.

They may include recreational amenities such as ice skating, several minitheatres, and even a hotel or two (as in the Galleria in Houston). The regional is an offshoot of run-down, urban downtown shopping centers. They usually have two to four major stores as anchors, such as Sears, Macy's, Neiman-Marcus, and so on. These insure great traffic for the smaller retailers who really pay the rent and make the investment return good.

At the regional centers, shoppers can find anything they want: clothing, jewelry, appliances, sporting goods, garden supplies, pharmacies, food, and so forth.

Inflation and overbuilding have hurt the regional shopping centers. In many cases the reduced revenues and increasing costs have forced some department stores, variety chains, and small clothing independents into becoming bad tenants. Shopping-center owners have had to reduce or even postpone rents. Diminished sales also mean that the center's owners are not getting the overages (the percentage rents paid upon sales above a base amount) to which they have been accustomed. As a result, their tenants' problems and their own increasing operating costs have reduced their rate of return on their investment to unsatisfactory levels, and in some cases have caused negative cash flows.

The problem with many commercially zoned existing pieces of land is that they do not have the economics (demand) to support new shopping centers. The REITs added to this glut by making money available, thereby saturating market areas. This, combined with increased operating costs, forced some centers into bankruptcies and others into heavy rental adjustments, creating problems, especially for smaller retailers upon whom developers really depend for their profitability.

Real problems are being encountered in renting centers developed under the early-1970s' economic conditions. The sharp increase in interest rates resulted in an increase in return expectations on higher-risk equity investments. For many years investors were satisfied with an 8 to 9 percent return on investments from the rentals to the major chains, with an 11 to 13 percent return from the independent satellite stores, and an overall 10 percent return. Now the majors are strongly resisting such rent increases because of their operating problems, and the satellites are likely to be on thin financial ice if they agree to rentals related to current return expectations.

As if this were not bad enough, the new regional centers must also overcome a number of governmental policies and public attitudes. By encouraging more driving with their huge parking lots, the regionals are considered by the Environmental Protection Agency (EPA) to be a major contributor to air pollution in some areas. In cities with hopes for new or continued downtown renewal the EPA ruling has made the large shopping center a menance to completion of the district. Air-pollution standards cannot be met with a daily influx of cars that increases pollutants in the area. The real-estate investor-developer who comes up with a satisfactory solution to this problem will make a bundle.

Where growth has become an issue in the outlying areas, mistaken notions about development patterns abound. City hall argues that shopping centers trigger subdivision development. And subdivisions mean fast and expensive growth (needing new schools, sewers, water systems and so on). This is partially true, in that more shopping centers than ever try to anticipate future growth and become magnets to builders of housing, who use the shopping center as a focal point for their own operations.

I believe that there are enough obstacles in the way of regional shopping centers that few will be built in the near future. Those that are built will have to show that they make economic sense and advance the urban goal of creating effective mixed-use urban cores. Along with high-rise office buildings, mixed-rise residential units, schools, lakes, parks, and community and recreational facilities, the shopping center will always have a place. But such a plan would have to be undertaken with the most experienced participants possible.

The Fashion Island Center developed as part of California's mammoth new town of Irvine, and Bill Zeckendorf's Century City in Los Angeles and Allegheny Plaza in Pittsburgh are significant steps in the right direction. These developments offer complete living/working/playing environments. But even these advanced developments fall short of the ultimate goal, because they were built more with the auto in mind than the human being. People-movers and personalized mass transit will be required to convert them to a pedestrian-scale environment. Also, schools and other essential community facilities within the core will be required to remedy this deficiency and make them truly people oriented.

But until the imaginative investor-developer comes along who can put together the entire community, and fit the regional shopping center into it with minimal environmental impact, these centers remain highly risky.

Resorts and Second Homes

The resort and second-home industry must be watched carefully. The chances for making a pile here are great—but so are the chances for losing it.

There are always two great unknowns facing us: Will the size of our population steady and, perhaps, arrive at zero population growth; and, is the trend to "follow the sun" going to increase, or will people slow down and tend to stay where they are?

The answers to these questions—and others—will have a deep and lasting effect upon recreational America. The answers will determine whether recreational investments will be solid or soft. They might indicate that sunny places will be good investments, or that no-growth and other pressures will make them not good.

In the mid-1970s, the statistics on recreational land and housing were good. There were tens of thousands of people planning to use the piece of land they had bought in the mountains, the valleys, by the oceans.

But the energy crisis has had its impact on secondary housing, too. When gasoline became expensive, more discretion was used by middle-income second-home owners or prospective owners when planning a trip to their investment property, or planning to invest. The cost of escape came high; if that cost continues to rise, it will outprice itself for all but the most wealthy.

There are reasons why you should watch for a possible investment in a resort or recreation area. But first you must determine whether you are going to use the investment (land, condo, home), or plan it as something that you expect to make money on.

If you are expecting to make money, the chances are slim that you will be able to turn over your investment for anything more than break-even. You pay at least a 10 percent commission going in (added to the price of what you are buying), and you pay the same when you sell. These deals do not appreciate fast in tight-money periods. You are lucky indeed if they appreciate 20 percent in 5 years.

If you are expecting your investment to appreciate, the location must be perfect, in an area where there will always be a limited supply of land, housing, and condos. However, most secondary housing is in areas that are heavily exploited by developers and there is no shortage. If anything, there is a surplus of deals.

- Look at the investment first as a pleasure to you and your family and friends. If you make money on it, then you are lucky and will have a double blessing.
- Look at the location carefully. Is it desirable? Will utilities be a problem? Does it have sewers or a septic tank?
- Is there a homeowners association that can levy extra costs on you?
- If the value of your location is based upon water, is the water guaranteed? Does it come from man or mother nature? If there is a dam involved, whose dam is it? When was it last inspected? A dam can mean that it is an unsafe area and the water must be reduced, killing the recreational value of your location.
- If the primary amenity is a golf course, are you a mem-

ber? How much will it cost to become one? Is the amenity in or promised?

• What are the seasonal changes in the area? Does it snow? If so, what is the snow load on construction? Where does the snow run off?

• If it rains buckets in a particular season, where does that rain go? Can your area flood?

• Does the area have sophisticated access or will mother nature wipe out the roads each season? Who pays for their reconstruction?

• What are the tax rates? How stable have they been?

• Can you park a camper or trailer on your land, or do you have to build by a certain time?

One concept that may ease the burden of owning a second home—by increasing the number of people who own a "piece" of it—is that of "time-share." This device could overcome the obstacles to second-home and resort investment for those people who simply want a place to go on vacation, and not a place to turn over for a profit in a short time.

Still, there are strong negatives to buying recreational deals during the 1970s:

• The deal ties you down to a single vacation and a single place to go.

• Second homes costs a lot of money for upkeep, and if special features are not included in the buying price, more money to join them.

• You may spend a lot of time driving to your second home for the limited use you get from it.

• If you rent out your second home, it is often damaged, costing you more bucks to fix it up again.

Time-share options, as discussed in the special chapter on condominiums, help alleviate some of these problems. But for the real-estate investor—as opposed to the second-home buyer looking for a vacation spot—the recreational-home opportunity remains a major risk. The investment, even with the best of attractions, must be well-placed, well-timed, and lucky.

Even so, like apartments and other so-called "losers," the second-home investment offers some aspects of the winner, and will get a gentle plugging in the next chapter. After all, a winner is nothing but a loser in a better location.

12

ELEVEN PROBABLE WINNERS

In our present difficult investment climate, there is as much risk in *picking* good deals as in getting into them. Much care and knowledge is required, especially where the investor is going it alone and is directly involved.

By the mid-1970s there were some obviously hot deals, although some of them had begun to wobble by 1976: picking up REIT packages laying dead in the water; buying existing apartments and office buildings in decent locations; buying condominium developments and converting them into apartments until the market turned; buying land that was immediately usable by builders or which could be rezoned quickly.

The following investments that I'm recommending are seen as consistent performers. Approached with the caution emphasized in this book, with good research and timing, they should do well for you, the investor. The top eleven (not in order of recommendations):

1. Conversion of solid-income properties.
2. Miniwarehouses.
3. Mobile-home parks.
4. Recreational-vehicle parks.
5. Industrial parks.
6. Developable land.
7. Profitable groves.
8. Shopping centers.
9. Ground leases.
10. Real-estate stocks.
11. Apartments—nonsubsidized.

Some of these have also appeared in the chapter on probable losers, but don't get nervous. There are strong differences within certain categories (like shopping centers), and what you pick determines whether you win or lose.

I will indicate in the appropriate sections of this chapter the type of risk each investment entails, and the class of investor for which that investment opportunity is suitable. It is up to each investor, however, to get under the umbrella of solid, independent advice from experts who are paid for what they know—and not for what they peddle.

1. Conversion of Solid-Income Properties. Big money has been made in real estate by converting land or old buildings from one use to another more valuable use. Agricultural land is converted to sites for residential development; land zoned for single-family residences is rezoned for multifamily residential or commercial use. The scope of conversion is almost limitless.

Opportunities still exist for profiting from conversion of vacant land. One major conversion opportunity is emerging where existing income properties (like condominiums) are converted from a sale use to a rental use, or from one rental use to a more profitable one.

The key to this opportunity is that the price of income property is determined by capitalizing income, while the price of sales property is largely based on replacement cost. As we have learned already, some of the problems in apartment and office rental units result from rents that do not increase as costs increase. This spread between rents and costs has the corresponding effect of diminishing a property's value as an income property to below its value as a sales property. Profits made from upgrading the rental income, on the other hand, lead to gain, because more income means greater value on the property, both before and after conversion.

Successful operators like Joe Noble of Los Angeles, who have specialized in the conversion of rental apartments to equity condominiums, have charted the way for others. Joe thinks that the key to conversion is finding an apartment building that people immediately see as a place where they would like to live, and not just rent. Once you determine that a difference between rental and sales value exists, the following factors must be evaluated: location, building condition, and price.

Location is critical. The most desirable location is the quality apartment building in an upper-middle-income area. The next critical factors are the size of the units and condition of the building. People want more and better space when they purchase than when they rent. Ideally, the physical conversion process should be limited to sprucing up exterior and interior, and providing new appliances and fixtures.

The disruption of present tenants should be kept to a minimum. This will help to reduce loss of cash flow during conversion, limit the risk of escalation of construction costs during conversion, and increase the chances of selling units to present residents. The converter should be considerate of present tenants and keep all commitments he makes to them. In this way he can significantly reduce his marketing costs, and provide a group within the homeowners' association that is not anxious to fight him.

Joe Noble also warned investors to stay away from apartments with high vacancies due to poor floor plans, substantial deferred maintenance, or irresponsible tenants. He looks for buyers in the present tenant group, and within the immediate neighborhood of the project. His projects are solid buildings that the neighbors know are good buys.

If a building has a poor reputation, however, no amount of money spent uplifting it can overcome the neighbors' reluctance to live there. Bad buildings also have all kinds of skeletons in them which can unexpectedly appear and cause conversion delays and money. Finally, since renters can stand little increase in housing cost, the more physical work that is required, the fewer the present tenants who will be able to afford the finished units.

To move really fast, conversion units must be priced substantially below single-family homes and slightly below new condominiums aimed at your project's market group. Or, they must be near an amenity such as a park, body of water, mountains, and so forth that justifies a premium price.

The price of finished units controls the acquisition price, and should be the same as that for a development project. The operator decides what price the finished units should sell for, deducts profits, brick and mortar, marketing overhead and financing costs, and arrives at the maximum price that can be paid for the property.

Joe Noble provides the following rule of thumb: To earn a profit of 12 to 15 percent, with brick-and-mortar-conversion costs not exceeding 15 to 20 percent and with financing costs and marketing overhead of 15 percent, the site acquisition price should be 50 to 60 percent of the finished units.

With some imagination and courage, old warehouses and store buildings offer profitable conversion opportunities. The excellent central location and sturdy construction of these older buildings frequently is a real bargain at the prices asked for them. Ghirardelli Square in San Francisco, Trolley Square in Salt Lake City, and the Underground in Atlanta are examples of conversions on a large scale, though at this scale, rehabilitation is not always profitable right away. There are situations where individual buildings involving more moderate investments can be profitably upgraded. Architect Paul Thoryk redesigned a group of Miami, Florida, warehouse buildings as a superb office complex for Eastern Airlines. Similarly, two former discount-store buildings in Los Angeles were converted in 1976 into a fascinating marketplace for stores and restaurants. Architect Dan Salerno's own office is a renovated factory building near city hall in San Diego. And Lance Wyman, who designed the graphics for the 1968 Olympics in Mexico City and the Washington, D.C., Metro in 1976, has his offices for Wyman and Cannon in a renovated 1892 brownstone in New York City.

Most conversions and commercial-building upgrades will require the professional expertise and capital of a syndicate of Silver and Gold Chip Investors. They are developments and must be approached as complex businesses involving the relatively high risks and generous returns associated with development. At the other end of the scale, Green Chip and Silver Chip Investors who are handy and not afraid of hard work on their own have also picked up distressed properties and upgraded them for rental or resale. The market for them, as well, can be good if the basic rules of real-estate investment are followed.

2. *Miniwarehouses.* Most people are extremely short of storage space. Multifamily housing projects lack attics, cellars, garages, and out buildings that once provided storage space for the several generations often living in pre-World War II housing. Now, some families buy or rent homes with an extra bedroom or two to serve as a study for the husband, a sewing and crafts room for the wife, a playroom for the children, or a dumping place for family possessions. Attention is even returning to the attic in new homes, which provides an unfinished room on the upper story.

Without adequate storage space, these rooms and garages fill with equipment, discarded furniture, and the paraphernalia of consumer living. The periodic garage sales become a ritual to permit the commencement of new accumulation cycles.

Office and store owners are also cramped for storage space. Single-story shopping centers have done away with the roomy second- and third-story lofts found in the buildings on Main Street. Rents are too high to permit such nonincome-producing use of modern facilities. On the other hand, the paperwork explosion of our increasingly complex business world has created a further need for more storage.

Where can the homeowner, the businessman, and the store owner find the storage space that is denied them in modern buildings?

One answer—and an investment attraction—is the miniwarehouse. The concept began in Texas and has spread throughout the Southwest and California. The miniwarehouse is usually a one-story structure divided into hundreds of steel cubicles with steel doors and removable partitions to accommodate different users. The buildings are generally between 20 and 30 feet wide, and range from 200 to 1,000 feet in length. The storage rooms may be 50 square feet to 300 square feet or larger. The design allows maximum flexibility and security.

For a monthly rental of about 25¢ per square foot, or $12.50 a month (always well under the local warehouse rental rate), a cramped family or businessman can rent 50 square feet in a miniwarehouse. With reduced rents for the larger spaces—perhaps down to 17¢ per square foot per month—the crowded merchant or professional can find storage space for one-third to one-fifth the cost of his primary space.

Miniwarehouses have a strong investment potential, especially in the growing Sun Belt states. The ease of development and low construction time and costs—coupled with low operating costs—add to the attraction. Concrete block is the most desirable construction, with lightweight concrete roof decking. Fifty percent ground coverage is typical, and an efficient 100,000-square-feet unit can be built on approximately 4 acres.

Most municipalities will go along with a well-designed facility on industrial-zoned land. This may be acquired for $2 per square foot, although that price is rising. Location (again) is a key factor, and miniwarehouses should be near densely developed areas with good highway access and visibility. (See Chart 12–1.)

CHART 12–1 The Miniwarehouse: Sample Pro Forma*

I. ASSUMPTIONS:		
Land	2.1 oc. @ $1.55/sq. ft. = $141,790	
Land Coverage	Approximately 50%	
Building Area	44,000 square feet	
Building Cost	$9/per sq. ft. = $396,000	
Other Development Costs (Paving, etc.)	$3/per sq. ft. = $132,000	
Mortgage Financing for 75% of Cost	20 year term @ 9.5%	
Total Project Costs		
Land	$141,790	
Improvements	528,000	
	669,790	
II. REVENUES:		
44,000 sq. ft. x $.215/per sq. ft./mo. x 12 mo./yr. =		$113,520/Yr.
Less: 800 sq. ft. for Manager		(2,060)/Yr.
		$111,460
Less: 5% Vacancy		(5,680)
Gross Operating Income		$105,780
Less: Direct Operating Expenses @ 19%:		(20,340)
Income Before Depreciation & Income Tax		$ 85,440
Before Taxes, Free & Clear Cash Return		
$85,440 ÷ $669,790		13%
III. MORTGAGE FINANCING:		
Cash Equity	$169,790	
Loan Amount	$500,000	
Debt Service (11.3% constant)		$56,750
Income After Financing		$28,690
Before Tax, After Financing Return on Equity:		
$28,690 ÷ $169,790 =		17%
IV. TAX CALCULATIONS:		
Less Interest (1st Year)	($47,500)	
Less Depreciation @ 3% St. Line	($15,840)	
Taxable Income	$22,100	
Income Tax @ 50%		$11,050
Net Income After Taxes		$17,640
After Tax Cash Return on Equity:		
$17,640 ÷ $169,790 =		10%

Note: Figures will vary depending on geographic location, and specific site and market requirements.

* From *The Mortgage and Real Estate Investor Report*. Published by Warren, Gorham, & Lamont, Inc.

As bare space these projects can be built in a few months for a total development cost of approximately $15 per square foot. Maintenance is minimal, and management and security can be handled by a couple who live in an apartment located over the warehouse facilities or on a corner of the site.

There are several examples of companies who have done well in the miniwarehouse field. Public Storage Inc. (PSI) of El Monte, California, has 57 miniwarehouses under management throughout the country. These range in size from 144 to 723 units. Each warehouse has a manager who lives in a 900-square-foot apartment behind a registration office built into one of the basic buildings. The managers are paid up to $300 a month, plus a bonus depending upon their leasing success.

Topanga, north of Los Angeles, opened in October, 1973, and was fully rented by the next January. Its 404 units range in size from 6 by 6 feet to 14 by 40 feet. Construction is concrete block with concrete floors and metal roll-up doors. Units with inside access through a hall have wooden doors.

After some experimentation, PSI standardized its operations. Sites now run to about 2 acres, with 45 to 47 percent coverage. No more outside storage is provided than zoning requires, because the return on inside storage is better.

The mix usually is 40 percent of units with 5 feet by 10 feet renting for $13 to $17 per month, 30 percent with 10 feet by 10 feet for $21 to $28 per month, 20 percent with 10 feet by 20 feet for $37 to $49 a month and 10 percent with 10 feet by 30 feet for $57 to $68 a month.

All buildings are clear span; partitions, which are dry wall attached to wood or metal studs, are easy to move as needed. All of PSI's buildings are one-story, though 2 stories will be coming.

Rents are standardized by region. Electric service is provided to each unit. Each project has a public restroom and several outside water taps. Heat is not furnished. Because of the importance that tenants attach to security, all projects are fenced and dogs are turned loose in the compound after closing time.

The financial risk in miniwarehouses is minimal. This assumes a good location and limited competitive facilities in your area. The demand for these storage buildings is strong and growing. As mentioned, a major source comes from residents of apartments and condominiums, and from one-family homeowners who suffer from lack of storage areas. Other sources are business enterprises, and owners of boats, mobile homes, and recreational vehicles. In fact, the new miniwarehouses may cater largely to the storage, maintenance, and repair service for recreational vehicles.

The moderate risk of investing in miniwarehouses can be generously compensated by the 15 to 20 percent return on investment. With 75 percent financing, a typical 100,000-square-foot facility will cost $1.5 million and require approximately $300,000 in equity capital.

Miniwarehouses, therefore, are best for the Silver and Gold Chip Investors. Some Gold Chip Investors might also want to take several entire deals themselves.

3. *Mobile-Home Parks.* The mobile home is no longer the last refuge for retirees. Today, almost 10 million Americans live in mobile homes, and more than 65 percent of them are younger than 55, although not the case in warm climates like Southern California, Arizona, and Florida. Better than one out of every five mobile-home household heads has a median income of better than $10,000.

Mobile-home parks, used by the young and rising middle class, offer an excellent opportunity—and a high risk. With the prices of new homes going through the ceiling, mobile homes will become an increasingly attractive buy. This offers an investment opportunity for you.

Traditionally, mobile homes and mobile-home parks were an acceptable housing option for the newly retired and the empty-nester couple. New communities sprung up in the warm climates of Florida, Arizona, and California. They featured social and economic needs for these older Americans, low living costs, and a quieter, less hectic way of life.

Mobile-home parks were holding areas for future use. Land was bought cheap, trailers put on it, and held for future "highest and best use." As the population grew and spread into these areas of inexpensive land, the land became too valuable for the cheap rentals the park was getting. The park owner then had the option of getting the land rezoned and going into apartments or shopping centers, rehabilitating the park into a more expensive mobile-home use, or selling to another buyer.

Several changes in the real estate of mobile-home parks took place during the 1960s and 1970s. For one thing, the condominium and apartment surge occurred, and offered the elderly and the empty-nester couples a very attractive alternative to the mobile-home parks. The prosperity of that period also allowed these people to pay the higher carrying charges of these more solid facilities. And these facilities were more often preferred by city fathers as a higher class of municipal environment. However, mobile homes continued to thrive during this period, largely in retirement communities in warm climates.

But then two things happened: the cost of mobile-home-park space went up sharply; and, the cost of housing and apartments also went up, pricing a large segment of the American population out of the housing market.

The mobile-home-park developer who was paying $6,000 to $7,000 an acre for land with a density of 10 or 12 mobiles per acre found himself in 1976 with land priced at $15,000 to $21,000 an acre, which would take only 6 or 7 of the double-width mobiles.

Secondly, the young middle-income wage earner, who is the base of the single-family market, also found himself priced out in 1976. These families could not afford $200 or more a month rent, nor did they have the down payment for a $30,000 home. The mobile home had filled their needs. But because land and manufacturing costs went up—coupled with zoning changes against mobile-home-park expansion—new spaces and mobile-home deliveries fell. Predictions of 600,000 mobile-home units by mid-decade actually saw sales in 1975 of just 240,000 units with perhaps 300,000 in 1976.

By now you're saying: This is a winner? But wait. Be patient. The guy who is squeezed out of buying a single-family house is still in the market for a mobile home. He needs some place to live to start his family and savings. Mobile-home parks that are carefully chosen, zoned, and well maintained can offer this young family a comparatively inexpensive place to live where there's room for them, a yard for the kids and, perhaps, a little equity building for that larger house.

As the single-family house becomes more elusive to a larger and larger segment of the middle class—and it appeared in 1976 that without government intervention with tax incentives, such would continue to be the case—mobile-home parks (and mobile homes) will become increasingly secure investments. By careful location and timing, the investor can lower the risk of these parks and assure himself of high returns. Conversion of the parks into a "higher and best use" continues to be profitable, and with demand for housing at a major pressure point, mobile-home parks appear to be solid. From an investment standpoint, the opportunity might appeal to some Green Chippers, and certainly to the Gold and Silver Chip Investors who can afford the risks.

4. *Recreational-Vehicle Parks.* "Taking off" has long been an American custom. It still offers an important psychological boost, and a chance to get away, however briefly, from our pressured lives is still keenly sought. This tradition is hard to change. Even with gasoline prices heading upward and the cost of recreational vehicles rising, Americans continued to buy these vehicles and take them all over the country after only a brief downturn during the oil boycott of 1973. It will take more than Arabs turning down the oil flow to get Americans to give up weekends at the beach or in the mountains or at our excellent state and national parks.

The recreational vehicle is the cheapest way for families

to give in to the urge to "take off" and also get back to nature. Americans have shown themselves, during the energy crunch of the mid-1970s, very willing to stretch the family budget to cover the expenses of these regular outings.

It follows, logically, that recreational vehicle parks near places of natural beauty will continue to be winners. More of these parks will be developed near tourist attractions, including cities like Orlando, Florida (Disneyworld), San Diego (beaches and the zoo), Anaheim (Disneyland), Atlantic City (beaches and the famous boardwalk). If the Bicentennial interest holds up through the end of the decade, parks may also be good bets near attractions in Philadelphia and Boston.

The next step in providing this facility will be to create it as part of a total resort complex. This would include everything from campsites for young people to motel facilities for those with higher vacation budgets; restaurants, miniature golf, tennis, and shops would be part of this complex as well, serving all groups. One example already in operation is the delightful mixed-use resort in Estero Beach, near Ensenada, Mexico, and Butterfield on the Irvine Ranch, California.

Silver and Gold Chip Investors may get into this field, probably through development and operating syndicates. The recreational-park action was just starting in the early 1970s, and by the end of the decade should be a strong and lucrative investment. Clearly, the next step is the creation of corporations to own and operate chains of these parks in the same way that chains were formed when the cabin courts graduated into motels. In fact, the recreational vehicle may be a logical expansion route for motel chains, especially where they can expand into land alongside or behind present facilities.

5. *Industrial Parks.* Right after World War II, large industrial plants began searching around for ways to expand. One move was toward the industrial parks in the suburbs. These parks offered more pleasant surroundings than the inner-city, the economies of single-story layout, and ready access to major highways. In cities of the 1960s, urban renewal, crime,

and congestion (not to mention rising taxes) pushed the smaller businesses out after the large industrial plants. Most of their business was in the suburbs, anyway, and the lower costs and shorter commuting times were attractions. Multitenant facilities developed which accommodated both the larger and smaller users.

During the 1970s, industrial complexes for the small and medium-sized user sprung up all over the outer-city. In the cities, however, industrial-space development went forward, and soon got as soft as the office-space market. Everywhere, in fact, too much of a good thing resulted in supply outpacing demand.

Still, I see industrial complexes as being attractive. Location, as I've said many times, is important, and so is timing. But I firmly believe that the last half of the 1970s and the early 1980s will see mixed-use development. This will have as its prime attraction the elimination of the automobile as the vehicle to get people to work, back home, to play, shopping, schools, and other facilities used daily. Smart builders are already designing and developing their industrial complexes as near as possible to public, minibus, or other forms of mass transit.

When economic conditions improve, and the spirit to innovate rises again, I foresee the creation of multi-use vertical developments with residential towers (or, if the land is available, a mix of vertical and townhouses) over industrial and office facilities. These may be vertical or horizontal, but self-contained.

Industrial parks will be the forerunner of such complexes. The smart builder will locate so that industry and residential development can take place close together. Providing that oversupply has not occurred in your investment region, this is a golden opportunity for syndicates of Silver Chip Investors to develop and operate industrial complexes. The total ownership of several industrial parks by Gold Chip Investors also makes sense.

6. *Developable Land.* Land continues to be a sound investment. During the 1970s, however, some of the rules changed, and the wise investor now proceeds carefully. The timing has changed.

Investors buying developable vacant land must be prepared to hold it for up to several years until it is fully usable. Managed growth policies have made new land more difficult to use. A 5-year holding period for property in the inner-city (but outside the central business district) is an even sounder investment horizon. Longer holding periods—of up to 10 years—should be expected for central-business-district property, in order to overcome the glut of office space, lack of adequate mass transit facilities, surrounding ghettos, and other problems that will hold back the desired new wave of redeveloping downtown. Politics haunts urban land use.

The Urban Land Institute (ULI) completed a study in the mid-1970s that foresaw a dramatic shift in urban land prices. Barring a major economic depression, the ULI concluded from its survey of developers, "It appears that the urban land market is facing a new era of developable land scarcity and high land-price levels." The study continued: "Energy shortages and corresponding increases in transportation costs, environmental concerns, and the high public fiscal costs associated with sprawl all suggest a great concentration of future development and a tighter urban land market."

The ULI survey indicated that the price of developable land in Dade County, Florida, had increased 150 to 300 percent since 1970. All land in South Florida has risen an average of 200 percent in the past 4 years. The Minneapolis–St. Paul area reported relatively mild increases of about 44 percent since 1970. Developers in Phoenix told of increases from 50 to 100 percent over the first 4 years of the 1970s, while land prices in the San Diego area jumped 80 to 100 percent during the same period. Buildable land in California, Texas, and Arizona appreciated heavily in 1976.

Between 1950 and 1970, ULI discovered, the average

annual increase in urban land prices was 8 to 10 percent, with a total increase over the 20-year period of 400 to 600 percent. During the same time, general price levels rose 60 percent and median family incomes increased 80 percent.

Rural land is also attractive. Robert A. Danziger, president of Northland Investment Corporation of Massachusetts, surveyed large tract investments in New England recently. This investor found that the energy shortage had created a buyer's market for rural land—at least for those willing to abandon strictly short-term speculation and to hold the land for 5 years or so.

Danziger saw the pendulum swinging in favor of the individual investor who had found himself priced out of the large-tract market during the early 1970s. In many cases, top-quality land continues to be offered at the same price as formerly. For example, woodland tracts in Maine and New Hampshire of between 100 and 1,000 acres were still selling in the mid-1970s at $200 to $500 an acre. Vermont farms with between 100 and 200 acres were going for $75,000 to $150,000. Ocean and lake-front properties still commanded $100 per waterfrontage foot.

But to the land investor, terms are sometimes as important as price, since the investor may sell in a few years, before the mortgage is paid off. This makes even a high-priced property a bargain if only 10 to 20 percent must be put down, and a 10-year purchase-money mortgage can be obtained at 8 percent interest.

Still, just buying at a low price or on good terms is not enough. Raw land must increase in value by 15 to 20 percent a year to justify the carrying costs (mortgage interest and real-estate taxes), loss of return on equity, and risk. What will cause this growth in value?

Continuing Inflation. Raw land speculation is as American as apple pie, and besides it has done very well during inflationary times. Inflation should continue to be from 6 percent to 9 percent for the balance of the 1970s, as long as Americans want to increase their standard of living. Raw land is not part of the Dow Jones average. It is the only resource on which a real-estate deal can happen.

Leisure-Time Activities. There are many billions of dollars being spent on the one-third and more time of the average day that Americans are not sleeping or working. In our unionized society income will continue to grow and the escapist nature of Americans will seek new recreational opportunities, creating more land demands.

Cost of Energy. While the oil boycott of 1973 focused itself as a crisis, it is more a chronic problem. The problem will exist for many years as we convert into more exotic forms of energy supply. One thing is sure, however, that as natural gas and oil become more expensive and less obtainable, people will be spending more time in their primary environment: home. The demand for housing will continue as a sociological, cultural, and psychological occurrence, creating future necessities for land.

An important consideration for the developable land investor is the possibility of creating some sort of income during the holding period. Robert Danziger offers three suggestions:

1. Cutting Timber. In New England, up to $150 per acre can be realized from selectively cutting good quality hardwoods. The woodland itself is generally improved with such selective cutting, which in turn aids appreciation. Christmas trees can also be an excellent source of income if the land is suitable and large urban areas are nearby.

2. Grazing or Haying Rights. If you own land with large fields, the leasing of grazing or haying rights can bring as much as $5 or $10 an acre, more than enough to cover taxes.

3. Selling Off Portions. A large tract may contain an old farmhouse or other structures. Selling off the house for first-home use is an attractive possibility and may earn back most of the cash of your investment.

Well-located, vacant land, therefore, is a good investment for all net-worth builders. Green Chip Investors can pick up individual residence lots, and Silver and Gold Chippers can acquire the larger parcels. By choosing wisely, investors can realize 10 percent annually on a venture with moderate risk.

A wise choice depends upon having an independent expert determine the likely future use of the property, the probable price for that use, the holding period until that use will be justified, and the estimated interim-holding costs.

Independent experts can further help you to structure the acquisition of the property to your lowest level of risk by limiting personal liability, providing for the lowest possible initial-and-holding-period cash outlays to the seller, and (where appropriate) by permitting the partial release for sale of portions of the property.

7. *Profitable Groves.* The avocado is not only delicious and nutritious, but also a very tasty real-estate investment. So are oranges and grapes, and in fact a wide variety of agricultural operations. These operations offer good investments and solid tax shelters. But remember that the investment must make good economic sense first. And the key to an economically sound agricultural investment as in any other business operation is the skill and integrity of the management.

If you and your advisors decide that you should invest in agricultural groves, there are two basic options: To select, buy and manage the property yourself or to invest in a syndicate that is operating such an investment.

In selecting either alternative, a great deal of care must be exercised. If you expect, under the do-it-yourself plan, that the land selected for the agricultural operation will yield a separate gain later by being suitable for development, location becomes vital to the success of your operation. Agricultural land near big cities has a dim prospect for future development if it is distant from an existing urban settlement, or if it lacks amenities, such as a lake or ski resort, nearby.

The best bet for an agriculture now/development later

project is land adjacent to small towns that can become satellite communities for a major city. The worst bet for development is land that is between two urban settlements and separated from them by some distance.

Individual investments in agriculture by Gold and Silver Chip Investors are dynamite. Perhaps the best means to enter the field is through a syndicate that can hire pros to look after the fields. The high risk of agriculture means that this type of investment is best handled within the diversified portfolio of the Silver or Gold Chipper. The investor must further be prepared to put in extra cash to carry the operation when occasional market or natural disasters occur.

Turning over groves to syndicates is an increasingly popular form of investment. One example might be a limited partnership in California avocado groves. Investors could get in for a minimum limited-partnership investment under one plan. Each investor then puts up a specific amount, gets back a lovely tax shelter, and the syndicate handles the overall management. There are tax shelter, cash flow and long-term profits. In 1975, for example, in Southern California alone, Kaiser-Aetna marketed more than 75 groves to investors.

Good management in these situations is absolutely essential. Shortcuts or skimping of any kind can result in economic disaster. An orchard or vineyard must be properly developed to have the potential for high-quality fruit, high yields, and long life. One must be certain that the varieties planted are suited for the region and that there is an attractive market.

Whether you are seeking an investment through a syndicate or going it alone—and possibly wish to retire in 5 to 7 years with an income-producing asset (after enjoying a high tax write-off)—there are some words of caution:

- Deal with an organization that knows the fruit business —grapes, avocadoes, and so forth—that you want to enter.
- Check the broker's track record.
- Look forward to owning or working the grove so that there is a personal involvement. There are many airline pilots

in Southern California with this philosophy. They consider their avocado groves a lifestyle and homelife for their families "away from the rat race." It's a change of pace and a pleasure for them all.

• Select a workable location that can be resold for a profit while producing other tax and cash-flow benefits.

• Don't expect to make a killing. Relax and enjoy your grove.

• Of course, there are tax benefits. Have your accountant look at the tax implications in terms of new legislation affecting tax shelters.

Pricing your avocado grove or vineyard has to do with location; ease of picking the crop, freedom from disease (very important); and the size, age, and plentitude of the trees or vines. Obviously, the more trees or vines, the more you pay; the younger the trees, the less you pay.

• Be sure to check the water supply with the utility district, not just the broker.

• It takes about 5 years to break even with a mature crop. Count on your land taking at least that long.

Agricultural projects are not for everyone. Prices and terms vary according to the cash down and the tax shelter implications. You can get into the groves for between a 20 and 25 percent down payment and have fun besides.

8. *Shopping Centers.* Unlike the regional shopping centers mentioned as no-no's in the last chapter, specialty and convenience-shopping centers are making major gains in selected parts of suburbia. These may be neighborhood shopping centers of half an acre to 12 acres that serve at least 1,000 families. Or, they may be the community shopping centers that occupy 20 to 35 acres and serve about 5,000 families.

The smaller shopping centers have several attractions. They offer the friendliness of the small corner grocer, they are more accessible to the consumer and provide lower overhead costs to the merchant than big centers. Notice how the Seven-Eleven and other minimarkets are popping up all over.

In Del Mar, California, where we have our principal offices, several one- and two-story strip commercial centers have been built. They house specialty merchants selling anything from groceries to flowers to Levi's. They also rent office space to doctors, lawyers, architects, interior decorators, and other professionals.

I think these shopping centers make attractive investments because they offer a significant countertrend to the overwhelmingly large, modern shopping centers. In fact, some builders have started calling the smaller centers shopping villages. Two excellent examples are Stonecroft, 23 miles north of Milwaukee, Wisconsin, and Olde Mistick Village in Mystic, Connecticut.

At Stonecroft, each shopkeeper lives over his shop. Residence and shop, in fact, are sold together as a condominium, and the bylaws require that the owners live in the shopping village. Stonecroft occupied 5 acres of a 70-acre parcel, including parking, and the surrounding land is leased for farming. Sales of the shops-condominiums were instantaneous: the condos sold out at $44,600 to $56,000 each. By 1975, each store was doing an average of $350 a day in business, although the two largest were hitting $1,000.

Olde Mistick Village has 46 shops: stores, banks, and a theater located in 24 buildings on 22 acres. All the buildings are small and were designed to look like a New England village circa 1720. Construction costs were below that of a large center, running between $14 and $15 a square foot, or $18 including land and improvements.

There are many other fine examples of the new shopping villages. One of these is Cheyenne Mountain Ranch, a 3,000-acre new community in Colorado Springs, Colorado, which features a one-story center of brick and wood exterior, with 17 stores and small specialty shops in a little vale surrounded by trees. Neighbors like the low profile.

The design of these shopping villages is extremely important. It serves as the magnet for shopkeepers and customers alike. Many large shopping centers thought they could make it on volume; but the parking lots are scary and they now look too huge and impersonal. Sufficient income and population are always important, but don't forget size, accessibility, and special attractions like design.

Smaller commercial centers require limited equity investments and offer few management problems. They are ideal for Silver and Gold Chip Investors, and their moderate risk makes them suitable for Income Seekers as well.

9. *Ground Leases.* Ground leases are complex but attractive investments. Such a lease is simply an agreement for the use of land only, sometimes secured for the user's improvements to be placed on the land—that is, buildings. This conserves the builder's cash.

Because they are a lease and not a debt, ground leases can provide returns to investors in excess of the returns permitted under the usury law. Moreover, through cost-of-living adjustments of both rents and repurchase options prices, investors can receive inflation protection.

Since the return received by the investor is income, there is not the problem of reinvesting periodic, small principal payments. Ground leases make much more sense for Income Seekers than the second mortgages in which they have typically invested, although the yield may not be as high. Ground leases are also a suitable investment for part of the funds of pension plans and profit trusts. Securities and insurance should be used to provide liquidity and insure the trust's ability to meet its commitments.

To borrowers, ground leases provide essential secondary financing for new projects. Ground leases may be used on existing projects when tax shelter is about to be lost, in order to take cash out of the project and restore debt service (and its interest). Although ground leasing during inflation can be very expensive financing, the provision of repurchase options in the lease permit the borrowers to refinance when lower-cost financing becomes available.

Income Seekers might find ground leases attractive. Silver and Gold Chippers might consider ground leases for college-age children, aged parents, or others for whom they would like to provide a regular income. The creation by those investors of trusts invested in ground leases has the advantage of providing the required funds with a much lower tax bite than would be the case if these trusts were not used.

10. Real-Estate Stocks. What about the stocks of builders? That depends on the company. Let's make clear that publicly owned builders are very different from private entrepreneurs. One can do his thing quickly, while the other is still reporting to a junior vice president. The publicly owned builder has to have profits regularly and they must be climbing.

Some of these outfits make good buys. But I caution you to know about the management of the company before buying its stock. Even in the worst securities market there are good buys. All Net Worth Builders should consider investing part of their portfolio in the securities of underpriced real-estate-industry operations. Look for REITs and limited partnerships that: (a) own equities in solid-income properties, (b) are generating a good return on investment, (c) have had limited portfolio write-offs, (d) have assets with a book value in excess of their share of market value, and (e) above all, have solid real-estate-industry management.

A careful analysis of the industry will uncover home builder and other real-estate stocks of value. Some of the manufacturers of mobile homes and recreational vehicles also have good price-earnings ratios, and offer solid opportunities. These should be watched carefully, and if they fit your needs, acted upon.

13

TWO PROBABLE LONG-TERM WINNERS

There are three areas where investors have traditionally put their money: homes, apartments, and condominiums. The condos, of course, are comparatively new to the real-estate market, but are now solidly entrenched. All 3 areas offer the investor a certain amount of risk. In one case—apartments—I am actually arguing out of both sides of my mouth: apartments offer opportunity, but may also be a lousy investment.

By 1976, there were major changes taking place that affected all three of these top investments. These changes should be clear to you, and you should keep up with them as you approach real-estate deals:

• Rents are going up. In 1974, HUD reported that rents averaged $200 a month. By 1975, they had jumped to $213. In 1976, they jumped again. And this trend will continue as long as housing remains expensive and people slow down their traditional patterns of moving every 2 or 3 years.

• Hikes in utility costs and other operating expenses are far higher than projections made them. The all-electric home may be a thing of the past. Solar energy units in individual homes are slowly rising in demand in New England and the Southwest, and may be the utility of the future.

• Home prices are continuing to rise, largely because of increased land costs. And as home prices rise, more and more Americans are being priced out of the home-buying market.

• Yet, demands for detached housing and its land are climbing, and prices are rising rapidly, too.

• The inventory of completed condominiums, which saw a market glut in 1974, was cut down through discount auctions, financing, and lender closeouts, as well as demand. Some condo owners rented, willing to wait for the market to rise again.

• New condos, surprisingly, will not come down in price because of higher land prices and costs of construction.

• Land prices will not drop, though density allowances will.

• Getting land upon which to build is becoming more difficult because of delays in planning and government red tape.

• Financing for builders of housing and apartments became very expensive in 1972, and has remained relatively so into the second half of the decade. The cost of money has impacted in the 1970s. It will remain high on apartments.

Apartments

As I said in Chapter Eleven, apartments are the best of deals, and the worst.

Apartments were the downfall of some of the big merchant builders of the early 1970s. Wall Street was so hungry for profits from the publicly owned building companies that they pushed single-family builders into becoming the tycoons of the apartment world. The need for profits joined with the need for tax shelters and created a surge of multi-family construction. A builder had only to announce an apartment project, and it was syndicated, or sold to a syndicate, or sold on a private placement.

Between 1974 and 1975, about 1,250,000 *fewer* apartments were built than in the previous 2 years. By the end of 1975, only about 224,000 apartments were being built; in 1972 to 1973, some 1,961,000 apartments had been built. That meant that in 2 years, the bottom had fallen out of the apartment-building industry. By the end of the first quarter of 1976, only 27,000 multifamily units had been started in the entire country, although 1976 ended up slightly.

The reasons were easy to find: higher costs, lenders unhappy with making apartment loans, the high interest on money for new construction. Lenders had gotten into trouble by making too many loans for condos, apartments, and office buildings during the 1972 to 1973 boom. The easy money and the boom flooded the market with multifamily units, and created vacancies. Those who waited didn't lose much: By mid-decade, this oversupply was beginning to stabilize and the vacancies were filling, largely due to cutbacks in production and the continuing growth of population.

The alert real-estate investor will watch this trend carefully. He will look for good apartment deals in excellent locations. He will know who the builder is, and exactly what his track record has been. He will know who is going to manage the project, and whether or not the builder is going to waltz away after completion. He will also be alert to syndicates earning commissions, front end loads, or builders handling the deal internally.

I believe that new-apartment development belongs only to the pro. There are too many risks for the inexperienced. That doesn't mean that good profits can't be made by careful selection of location and good timing. I think apartments have been overbuilt due to the tax law changes during 1966 to 1969, syndicators and others getting rid of money, and builders and developers going wild with naive investors. It is tougher to make a good case for building, today, except in isolated cases.

Of course, costs are too high. The rents required to cover costs are creating heavy forces dedicated to rent controls. Rent controls are already in effect in many cities. It has become a very serious impediment to lenders investing in new apartments.

But while I'm not enthusiastic at this moment for *building* apartments, I do like the attraction of established units. I buy units that are 5 to 10 years old, those that have been foreclosed a few times. I have been able to buy apartment buildings for the amount of the original loan on the property that was made several years earlier. I don't buy new buildings. I look for older buildings with a track record. I buy the used buildings, improve them up to my standards, and then either keep them, refinance them, or sell them.

I don't believe the public will allow rents to get out of control, particularly people on fixed incomes. I see rents going up 10 to 15 percent and giving decent returns to the investor. But, if property taxes continue to spiral, and you can't increase rents, we will see the day when a lot of buildings will be owned by the city, county, or state. In New York City, for example, these buildings get demolished because nobody will maintain them.

Buildings that are now 10 years old seem to pass through cycles. They have gone through low occupancy, rents dropping, and then they work their way back up to viable occupancies making them much better than they were the first years. I believe that increased demand will fill the vacancies in these old buildings. People won't be moving as much as before, and will stay in rentals for 3 or 4 years, especially older people. Buildings located where people can walk to work and to shopping areas will be increasingly attractive; there's a direct savings in getting people out of their automobiles.

On the positive side, therefore, I see demand getting stronger during the second half of the 1970s and rents increasing. Older buildings offer the investor a good opportunity now, and if the demand-rent spiral described holds, newer buildings will be increasingly attractive.

There are four basic reasons for purchasing any investment property such as apartment buildings:

- Tax shelter.
- Cash flow.
- Estate building (equity build-up and appreciation).
- A place to live (not a basic reason except for smaller units).

The most common reason for owning an apartment building is that it offers tax shelter. By taking deductions for expenses, interest charges, and depreciation, you may show a tax loss on your building that can be used to offset your other income. These losses can be substantial, and the tax shelter great.

Cash flow, or spendable income, is another desirable aspect of owning apartments. The spendable income is left after all the expenses have been paid. This money may supplement an income, or offer income for retired or semiretired people.

Estate building should not be overlooked, and yet it is one factor that most investors fail to consider. Using care and skill, an investor can turn a small amount of capital into a substantial estate in 15 to 20 years. The method also provides a certain amount of tax shelter along the way.

Investing in an apartment building—as in other real estate—means getting into something with a down payment which you can manage financially. The more cash you have, the more units you can buy. But don't overextend yourself, especially in this market. You may require some money to fall back on; you should have investment security—that is, protection against losing your entire investment.

The question is often asked: "Shall I make a bigger down payment if the seller will reduce the price of the apartment, home, condo, or whatever?" My feeling is that it is governed by the following:

a. Do not strap yourself is always the first rule.

b. However, if you can get a significant reduction because of the seller's need for cash, then it usually is a sound move to give more cash in the front end.

c. Paying a little more for the building or unit, with a smaller cash down, is all right if there is any chance for the building to appreciate, as is so often the case.

Smart investors, with high incomes, are looking for buildings they can leverage with small cash at the front so as to take advantage of the great chance for appreciation in real estate. In this case they are simply trying to gain control of the real-estate item, making larger monthly payments. They then take whatever tax shelter possible and sell the building within the coming 24 months with a good gain of from 10 percent to 35 percent or more, in equity, plus cash flow and shelter, if they have chosen the real-estate area with care.

You should decide how many units will satisfy your needs. Can you manage that many units yourself? If not, you will have to hire a management firm.

If you decide upon an apartment with fewer than 16 units, you should seriously consider whether or not it makes sense. Expenses and time involved in maintaining the building may be too great. To some extent, the economy of scale plays a role here: The more units you have, the easier it is to operate the facility. The age is very important also.

Risk in buying apartment buildings can be diminished. One cardinal rule of real estate is: The higher the risk, the higher the return. You should pick an area that best satisfies your needs, and be certain that the building you select is financially structured for your own real-estate objectives. The age of the property and the condition may be of great importance; older property will require more maintenance and may not have the amenities of newer buildings. Your analysis of the property should include: the type of units, whether unfurnished or furnished, rent per unit, size of units, competition from surrounding buildings.

Check Out the Deal

• If the seller is asking more than 8 times gross income, make sure he proves that you can make money on your investment. Some apartments in 1976 were going for 11 to 15 times gross income, which essentially means that the investor will never make money on them unless the rents become astronomical or the investment appreciates drastically.

• Look at all expenses carefully. Make certain that they represent this year's expenses, and not last year's. Look at fire insurance (which can be canceled after a year or raised after a year, even if written for 3 years); miscellaneous supplies (which seldom show up on projections); maintenance (especially if a family apartment); pest control; gardener; pool maintenance; payroll taxes; advertising; and professional-management fees of 3 to 5 percent.

• Look at lease and rental rolls to make sure that a raise didn't just occur. That would make it difficult for you to raise your rents to keep pace with rising utility and other expenses. Most rentals have been going up too slowly since 1971. In the end of the 1970s, their movement will accelerate from 12 to 20 percent at least.

Also make sure that present leases do not have a month or two free rent at the end of the lease. That surprised many REITs.

• Look at the building's age. Get the roof, wiring, and plumbing checked (it's worth paying for). Examine the landscaping, the age of the appliances, who will manage the apartments. Management is now a profession, and it frequently makes the difference in renter turnover.

Since I consider the apartment-buying business risky, here is a detailed apartment-marketing procedure for you to follow. Finding your building, filling it and keeping it filled is the name of the game. Here are 8 major things to consider:

1. Number of Units. If your apartment building is under 8 units, it will be difficult to get good returns. Expenses will run too high per unit. If it is 8 to 16 units, some will make very good investments; watch, especially, the area and the cost per unit. Up to 30 units, these buildings make excellent investments for 1 or 2 investors, and if operated properly should give a solid return. Between 31 and 60 units, you'll need professional help and management, and over 60 offers excellent returns for 3 to 8 investors with a very knowledgeable operating partner.

2. *Price.* Price alone isn't the most important item; you can overpay for the property if you get good terms. You shouldn't pay a premium for properties purchased through a trade or exchange. All apartment buildings you consider should be priced at under 8 times gross income, unless it's a super situation. Furnished buildings should go for under 7 times gross income in any area, and less, if utilities are included in the rent.

3. *Down Payment.* If you are asked for 30 percent or more, the building must offer a large cash flow or some other special attraction (that is, assuming a 6 percent loan with a fast equity build-up). For 20 to 30 percent down, you should get prime location and a rock-bottom price with outstanding financing (owner carries financing at an interest rate 2 or 3 percent below the market). For 15 to 20 percent down, the transaction should be sound and offer security. Below this, the transaction is average in a good area with some tax considerations; 10 percent down is the maximum you should pay for marginal areas.

4. *Financing.* Total loan payments of the first and second trust deed (T.D.), generally, should be under 55 percent of gross income. The first T.D. should be in the range of 65 to 75 percent of the selling price. The terms are important (that is, interest rate, pay-back rate, prepayment penalties, late charges, loan assumability).

Call several financial institutions to get the range of interest rates and loan fees. Get the facts on existing loans (holder, interest rate, approximate balance, can it be assumed, original amount, due date).

The second T.D., if their is one, should be due in 10 to 12 years at a reasonable interest rate, and payments structured for a sound transaction. Avoid an acceleration clause in the second T.D. Monthly payments should be interest only or a maximum of three-quarters of 1 percent of original amount.

Avoid 2 to 5 year "balloon payments" on T.D.s or even an additional down payment in a short period of time.

5. *Fixed Expenses.* Check the taxes—verify with a tax bill—and check assessed values for land and improvement ratio.

Get the cost of insurance and exactly what it covers. Make sure that the insurance is adequate for the property.

Who pays the utilities? This is a vital point!

Get costs for gardener, pool, trash collection, and the number of pickups and difficulties of getting a pickup container. Go through the seller's canceled checks.

How much is the manager paid and what are his responsibilities?

Make sure that the seller warrants taxes, insurance, and utilities. The fixed expenses should usually not be higher than 28 to 30 percent of gross income.

6. *Variable Expenses.* Maintenance repairs are about 5 percent of gross income but vary with the age of the building, condition, and location.

The vacancy/turnover rate should be about 5 to 8 percent, and this also depends upon location, condition, and rent per unit. This also includes a factor for noncollection of rent from skippers.

As a rule of thumb, the expenses on most buildings should be 40 to 45 percent of gross income, including vacancy and maintenance. (Rules of thumb are only checking devices.)

7. *Rent Schedule.* Popular rents for good investments in the mid-1970s would range in this manner:

- 3 bedrooms, 2 baths: $200 to $350 a month (unfurnished)
- 2 bedrooms, 2 baths: $175 to $250 " "
- 2 bedrooms, 1 bath: $160 to $225 " "
- 1 bedroom, 1 bath: $140 to $200 " "
- Efficiency, 1 bath: $125 to $175 (furnished)

In some urban areas, in excellent locations, the rents will reach $500 a month or more for 2 bedrooms, 1 bath. Obviously, rents will vary *widely* with size of the apartment, location, furnished or unfurnished, floor, and age!

8. *Returns—Ranges.* For cash flow, return may reach 5 to 8 percent of the cash down payment, fully tax sheltered and using realistic expense figures.

For equity build, return may be 6 to 10 percent of the cash down payment. This depends upon interest rates of loans.

For tax shelter, and every property should give this, make sure you get a fair return on your invested money.

Don't estimate appreciation as part of your return. It depends on too many factors you can't control. If you get appreciation when you sell, take it as a bonus!

Before buying, you should know and understand the following points:

- What are the strong and weak points of the owner's complex?
- Get a profile of the competition and the community.
- Put together information to create tenant instructions and orientation when you take over.
- Make certain you don't trap yourself with utilities. Their costs can throw all other projections off!

In the Addenda you will find a complete listing of what you should look for before buying an existing apartment building. There are some 18 areas of the building which you should carefully examine before putting down any money.

Homes

For home builders, 1974 to 1975 was a disastrous period, the worst in 3 decades. To me, that means everything from here on is gravy. James E. Carlson, housing expert for Merrill Lynch, Pierce, Fenner & Smith, thinks that the decline was the largest since the war, that it was cyclical, and that the housing market should bounce back quickly. It has for builders of single-family housing.

In 1973, housing starts totaled more than two million units. In 1975, the rate of beginning housing construction passed below 1.2 million. Inflation, the moratorium on Federal housing programs, and localized overexpansion contributed to the drop. Carlson thought that both single family and multifamily housing starts would show strong improvement by 1977. For one thing, the inflow of funds to the savings and loan institutions surged to some $35 billion in 1976. Mortgage rates also dropped to around 9 percent, and some optimists saw them dropping to 8.5. The number of new single family homes should be more constant than multifamily, having stayed between 810,000 to 1.3 million starts since 1967, each year. They should continue to run between 900,000 and 1.1 million for the next few years.

There are, to be sure, problems facing the housing market and investor. On the bright side, housing is the one area every investor can reach. A home is a good inflation hedge (you pay off the mortgage with cheaper dollars as the home appreciates), and it is a place in which you may live and gain pleasure. The home offers you flexibility, which is a good criterion for investing. You can live in it, rent it, lease it, resell it, or trade it.

The home has tax benefits: You can deduct mortgage interest and property taxes. If you sell the home at a profit, the profit is deferred from taxes as long as the revenues from the sale of your home are reinvested in a new home within 12 months. (Seniors are getting better benefits.)

The home as an investment is also one of the few areas that has outperformed inflation. The sale price of single-family homes has increased 84 percent since 1963. Further, homes are always in demand. There are cycles: the young couple start their housing as apartment renters until they have children. Then they move into housing, and after the children are grown, back into apartments, condominiums, or retirement homes (which can include mobile homes). These factors cause more than 20 percent of all U.S. families to move every year. The move-ins and move-outs, obviously, are not completely synchronized, and 2 to 4 percent of all housing is vacant at any one time due to mobility.

All of this is good news, if you already own a home with a low interest rate on its mortgage. It is bad news indeed if you are in the market or investing or building. Prices for new homes have soared to such heights that the majority of the housing-consumer market is now financially frozen out.

A recent Library of Congress study reported that in 1973 some 21.5 percent of the nation's families earned enough to afford a median-priced $37,100 home with the usual 10 percent down payment. In 1974, however, this percentage of families had dropped to 15 percent; the price of the same home had risen to $41,300 and to $45,000 in 1975.

The Congressional Joint Economic Committee looked at the problem from another point of view. Its 1975 report on housing revealed that an annual income of $23,300 was required for the purchase of a new home. But the median income for an American family of 4 is just $12,840. That means that about 85 percent of all American families cannot afford the median-priced homes now being built. Increasing property taxes should be watched carefully in your investments.

This has resulted in a situation where the majority of builders are now building in a price range that most of the market cannot afford. Even among those who can afford new homes in the higher price ranges, fewer and fewer of them are being enticed to buy because the land cost bears such a high relationship to the total price of the home that a very poor value is reflected, but speculators and affluents are buying.

Worse, some builders have increased their prices in order to offer more space. In many cases they risk the danger of overbuilding and overpricing their product, depending on location.

The trend is toward only the rich or the subsidized poor being able to buy houses. This will drive up the prices of resales, as well as apartments. These evils of inflation, I believe, are creating excellent reasons to invest in new homes or condominiums. The market is not weak—but it is changing significantly and the home-building industry and home investors must change with it. The opportunities are good, but they must be keenly ferreted out. Location . . . location . . . location!

The single dwelling, detached from its neighbor, is still king in the consumer's mind. It is still a winner. Unlike other investments, houses are actually lived in. People's personal tastes for beauty and environment color their judgment. Yet, when all is said and done, a home investment should be looked at without passion. It will be a better deal for you. Here are ten checkpoints to consider when you appraise a home as an investment:

1. Does the house look attractive from the street?
2. Is the landscaping neat?
3. Is it in good repair? Can the house be made to look good without spending your life's savings?
4. Is the walkway or approach in good repair? Is the land stable?
5. Is the front door in good shape with good hardware?
6. Is the roof in long-lasting condition? This is a troublesome area and should be checked carefully.
7. How is rain and snow runoff handled?
8. Is the driveway in good shape?
9. Are the homes on either side of your investment in attractive condition? Or, do they kill your opportunity?

10. Is there an empty lot next to the home, across from it? If so, check the zoning at the tax assessor's office. Another kind of zoning can tip your neighborhood from residential to commercial. You will be surprised—and dismayed—by what can be built on a small lot in many cities.

There is another area of home investing to be examined: the consumer. Because of the factors discussed in this and other chapters, a new consumer has entered the market. If you are a builder-developer, or a home buyer, you should know this breed and study him or her.

This is a generation of smart, skeptical shoppers who have been forged in the recession. They are looking for good and fair price, value, and efficiency. These are the watchwords of the future.

This breed of consumer is quickly affecting the housing market. The new buyer is seeking smaller size, energy efficiency, fewer frills. The buyer has a sharper intelligence. Merchandising, interior-model decoration, and floor-plan design will have to change to meet the needs and expectations of this consumer.

Daniel Yankelovitch, the consumer-attitude pollster, says that middle-class shoppers are developing "a subtle, yet decidedly different relationship with their money and the way they perceive the things they buy." The trend is toward a "new functionalism" in purchases. The same trend is expressed in people baking their own bread, favoring grass-fed beef, planting their own gardens, and insisting on "naturalness" in their foods.

By 1980, 40 cents out of every dollar will be spent on homes where the head of the family has had at least some college education. Energy efficiency and ecological considerations will be increasingly important, with a greater impact on a wider range of purchasing decisions.

What kind of housing will be in demand? Smaller, more energy-efficient housing, with strong interior detailing and opportunity for personalized expression.

Where will the demand for housing increase? My research at "mid-decade" indicates the estimated housing demand for the top 10 U.S. markets, 1975 to 1980, to be:

Rank	*Metro Area*	*Annual Housing Demand, in Units*
1.	New York	80,000 to 90,000
2.	Miami–Ft. Lauderdale	70,000 to 80,000
3.	Washington–Baltimore	50,000 to 60,000
4.	Chicago	50,000 to 60,000
5.	Los Angeles	40,000 to 45,000
6.	Tampa–St. Petersburg	35,000 to 40,000
7.	San Diego	25,000 to 30,000
8.	Orange County, Calif.	25,000 to 30,000
9.	San Francisco–Oakland	25,000 to 30,000
10.	Phoenix	25,000 to 30,000

These are theoretical demands, depending a great deal on the availability and cost of money and land.

Beware of lotteries and overspeculation. All markets go through overbuilt periods. Pay market (current) prices for your home. Speculation is O.K. if the supply of homes is below the demand, and when new buildable land is in short supply for the future.

Homes and apartments bought at probate or foreclosure should go through a good, experienced attorney. You can get bargains if you are wise, patient, and have excellent counsel.

14

A THIRD LONG-TERM WINNER

The condominium is very misunderstood. People feel that because it suffered adverse publicity and overbuilding in the early 1970s it is not here to stay. I very strongly disagree with this shortsightedness. The condo is another form of HOME suffering a ridiculous name, "condominium," and some poor architectural/design, which we'll discuss later in this chapter.

What is a condominium? Buyers often ask. I always reply that it's a deal whose time is fast approaching.

In fact, a condominium is a form of ownership whereby each resident of a project has fee title to his or her own apartment and joint ownership of the "common" areas. A condo is purchased in much the same way that one buys a home: A deposit is made, an agreement to purchase is signed, credit is approved, and a unit selected. Condos are now financed with a loan either from a savings and loan association or a commercial bank or other type of financial institution.

The down payment on a condominium varies from 5 percent to 20 percent of the purchase price, depending upon the sale price of the condominium unit, your credit rating, and your ability to make the appropriate monthly payments. Loans of 95 percent are available to qualified buyers, but only for units generally selling for between $25,000 and $35,000.

As with any home purchase, you can pay more in cash than the required 10 percent down payment. You may also have to pay charges for items that have been paid for in advance by the seller, like real-estate taxes, insurances, and so on.

As with a home, condominium owners pay real-estate taxes. You will get an individual tax assessment based on the value of your unit. A tax estimate should be provided with the sales information on a condo. In most cases, the lender will pay the taxes out of your escrow funds and monthly payments, which include 1/12 of the estimated annual real-estate tax anticipated for that year. Both mortgage payments and real-estate taxes are deductible from your taxable income, although the exact tax savings may vary from one buyer to another.

Condo buyers often ask: Who owns the land, lobby, halls, elevators, and other public places? These are the common elements, and are owned by all of the condominium unit owners jointly. The cost of operating these common elements is carried by each condominium owner, based on the proportion of space you actually own (that is, each condo unit represents a percentage of the total units).

Your monthly charge includes heat, light, and other utilities; repair and maintenance of all the common elements; payroll and management fees; fees for the elevators, exterminators, boiler and air conditioning, and so forth; landscape, snow removal, swimming-pool operation, lobby furnishings, carpet replacement, and other costs relating to the operation of the common elements. That charge does not include any interior repairs to your own unit or insurance covering your individual possessions.

The management of the condominium usually hires and supervises, as part of its duties, managerial people who are responsible for maintaining the air conditioning, swimming pool, and so on. Interior and exterior maintenance of the common areas is also the responsibility of the managing agent. You, of course, pay a fee for this, which is included in your monthly charge.

Who controls the condominium? Usually, there is a board of directors (which may be known by another title) chosen by each owner. Each owner usually votes, in proportion to his ownership interest in the condominium, for the election of the board of directors. The lenders making loans on the various condo units may also be allowed to designate a member to the board.

This elected board transacts the business of the condominium. It makes all policy decisions, selects and deals with the management agent, and establishes policies for hiring and firing condominium workers. It is governed by a declaration and by-laws, which have usually been set up by the condo owners.

You sell your condo in the same way that you would sell your home or any other real estate you own. You can also make any interior nonstructural changes that you wish, so long as those changes do not affect your neighbors. Structural changes would require approval from the board of directors.

In sum, a condominium isn't really substantially different from owning a home. You pay a monthly fee which covers costs of your condo, mortgage payments, taxes, etcetera. Part of this charge is tax deductible, depending upon the size and cost of your unit. The condo management will notify you about what this amount is, for your tax records. In exchange for your fee, you get a fantastic place to live, maintenance on your property, and amenities that come with your condo.

Condo Deals

There are several varieties of condominium deals that the real-estate investor can get into. In Puerto Rico and Latin

America, many office buildings are owned as condominiums. That hasn't really caught on here yet; most office condos are limited to health-service professionals who have stable space needs once their practices are established. But even those have not gone well in the U.S., so far.

With the commercial condo market still uncertain, I would not recommend the real-estate investor pioneering the office-condo idea. By the 1980s, however, I believe the condo market may pick up, because professionals will recognize condos as a means of protecting themselves against varying space needs. With a condominium, they can purchase additional space, and rent it out until it is needed. They can also lease or sell space when it is no longer needed. Further, a businessman could, as his needs change, trade up his equity in the same way home-owners parley their gain into better facilities.

Office condos must have an edge over rented office space. For health-service condos, especially, location is crucial. Doctors desire facilities near hospitals and near residential areas. Moreover, there is a clear pattern in medical offices: as more emphasis is placed on Federally approved laboratories (for Medicare and Medicaid patients), doctors' offices will have to be located within areas serviced by these approved labs.

Medical-Dental Condos. Syndicates of Silver Chip Investors can get in on the medical-dental condo act. The market risk of these syndicates can be hedged by including in the syndicate many of the health-care professionals who will buy the units. There should be, of course, real-estate pros with bottom-line participation in both the development and management ends of these syndicates.

Medical-dental condominiums offer several advantages to the doctor: tax shelters, some office-space flexibility* (and therefore practice flexibility), special medical or dental services that individual doctors could not offer, amenities for the comfort and convenience of doctor, patient, and visitor to the building.

* This should be planned at the beginning of the sales period.

Doctors may be better off forming a limited partnership around the condominium venture. This offers tax-shelter advantages, and reduced liability to the doctor's estate.

Two important aspects of your condominium will attract doctors: its flexibility for adding office space and services, and its location.

• Flexibility: Condominium ownership assumes a sharing of the basic building: the main entrance, lobby, corridor, elevators, and stairways are usually owned by all and shared by all. Services such as building maintenance, trash removal, security and paging systems, mail distribution, and receptionists are often also shared.

Inside the medical-dental condo, there can also be other equipment-and-service sharing. While it is unlikely, it is possible that two or more separate medical practices might share their instruments, examination rooms, consultation offices, or even nursing staff.

There are several services and specialties that could be integrated into a medical condominium for the convenience of physician and patient. A laboratory in the condominium could be set up to provide all hematology, urinalysis, bacteriology, chemistry, neurological, and audiological examinations. Recording and reporting results could be efficient; the service would be convenient to both patient and doctor alike. Further, if the combined number of referrals from all physicians within the condominium is sufficient, an in-house radiology suite might make sense. Standard radiographic and fluoroscopic examinations would be done easily.

The flexibility of the medical condo might also allow the doctors to install an "emergency" room where routine examinations and minor surgery could be performed. There, the physician could see his patients on weekends or after normal business hours. Without opening up the entire building, an examination and diagnosis could be made, and the patient treated if possible—thus avoiding the emergency room of a hospital.

Other features that might be shared in the medical-dental condominium could be: a pharmacy, an optician's shop, a child-care area, a food service. The flexibility of the basic idea makes it very attractive to both investor and buyer.

• Location: The developer of condominiums must base the decision of location on several specific factors. First, he must be aware that the movement of doctors to the suburbs has come to a halt. This is largely because of the government's changed attitude toward medical care. The tremendous costs of laboratory and testing facilities usually paid for by Medicare and Medicaid and other government funds are dictating the location of these labs, and, therefore, the doctors who use them. Since most of these labs, in the coming decade, will be located at or around large medical-school complexes, which are usually in or near urban areas, the exodus of doctors to the suburbs will soon be a thing of the past.

As a condominium developer or investor, consider the following factors:

• The proximity of the condo to major hospitals. The distance of your medical-dental condo from hospitals will determine its attraction to doctors. Consider, also, whether these hospitals are private or public, how well (and how much) they serve the surrounding community, and what their laboratory facilities are and where located.

• The distance of the condo from the doctors' homes. If the doctors using your condo can walk or take short rides to their office and the hospital, you may be sitting on unpanned gold.

• The accessibility of the condo to the doctors' patients. This would include parking and the interior amenities.

The best location is next to or near a major hospital, and in a central location convenient to doctor and patient. Without such good fortune, however, the final site will probably involve compromises between availability and distances. The success of the condominium will depend on how well the three location considerations above are satisfied. In doubt, take convenience over the special needs of the office-space user. Doctors usually base their decisions to purchase space on how convenient the location will be to their patients. If you are uncertain, follow the steps in the questionnaire in Chart 14; this will help you best meet your clients' needs.

Every site has risks. But the risk of location is greatest. Never go forward with a condominium development on a specific site without a clear knowledge of the market acceptance. To do so is to increase your risk, and to be in a dangerous situation. There are methods of selecting a good location—when the perfect location is not available—and the questionnaire approach is an excellent method for testing buyer interest for medical-dental condos at a specific site—*before* you put down your money. Such a questionnaire should include the pattern of questions included in Chart 14.

Finding your condo market takes some effort. Location also determines what the market will pay. Families attracted to higher-priced attached housing are motivated primarily by location. They purchase condominiums in a desirable area where good single-family homes are beyond their economic abilities. Unlike doctors, who also buy for location, these condo purchasers cannot afford something else. Location offers status, and the freedom from maintenance; it is better than renting and better than a small, overpriced home in the same area.

Doctors and families differ in their attraction to condos. Doctors like the idea of space control, tax advantages, convenience. Families like the feeling of environment, recreation possibilities, design. All condominium purchasers have the following interests in common: price and financing, equity build-up, location, freedom from maintenance, security. Put broadly, the condo-buyer family ultimately decides whether to buy or not, if they feel that the condo will improve their total life-

CHART 14

- Name (partner(s))
- Business address
- Specialty
- What hospitals do you practice in?
- Would you prefer having your office close to a hospital, and if so, which one?
- Do you own or rent your present office space?
- Do you share an office with other doctors?
- If the answer to the above question is yes, with how many other doctors?
- What is the size of your present office space?
- Is it sufficient? If not, how much more space do you need?
- What is your present rental rate per month?
- Does this rate include janitorial service and utilities? If not, how much do you presently pay for the services?
- What services would you like in the building? Coffee shop? Pharmacy? Lab? Radiologist? Etc.?
- What amenities would you like included in the building? Gym facilities? Spa facilities? Etc.?
- What special features would you like incorporated into your office which you do not now have?
- Would you be interested in owning a medical condominium suite in a medical-office condominium in a good location?
- List five general locations you feel would be desirable to build a medical office condominium: (Ask respondent to rate in order of desirability allowing five or more spaces for answers.)

As visualized from a reading of the sample questionnaire, a host of information can be accumulated regarding desirability of purchasing, site location, amenities, size of office

Additional Considerations

Other considerations that should be explored and which influence site selection include:

- Feasibility projections related to economics of the cost of land in certain locations and the profitability of the development.
- Zoning density restrictions as they relate to the economics of the project.
- Cost of utilities and services.
- Tax costs and assessment practices.
- Adequate room for parking facilities and other amenities.
- Proximity to public transportation systems and major highway access.
- Existing and future plans of immediate area.
- Existing and future medical office condominium developments in the general area.

- What size office space would you need?
- What special equipment do you need in your office? Electrical outlets? Compressed air? Lavatory? Etc.?
- Would you prefer a regular as opposed to a hospital-size elevator?
- What are your parking needs for yourself, partners, and patients?

space, and commercial facilities. This method has proven to be a very effective way of determining site advisability and market acceptance for medical office condominiums.

- Existing and future rental office space in general area.
- Community attitudes.

By weighing these factors with the basic location considerations the developer of medical office condominiums will be in a better position to reduce the risks in condominium developments of this nature.

* From *Condominium World* magazine. Published by Warren, Gorham, & Lamont, Inc.

style. The professional, the doctor condo-buyer, is looking at the finances and the space/location options; can he treat his patients easier?

Financing a Condominium

Let's walk through a typical condominium transaction. Potential investors in condos will want to know how their money is risked.

A common pattern of financing a new condominium may go as follows:

- Standby Commitment. The developer obtains a standby commitment to take out the construction lender if the project is converted to rental or if the developer is left with a large number of condo units unsold.
- Construction Loan. The developer obtains this from a REIT or commercial bank equal to 90 percent of total cost (including land, construction, interest, and overhead).
- End (Permanent) Loans. When the units are sold, the purchasers will obtain long-term loans from a savings association or insurance company.

For the investor, there is some risk in construction cost overruns that forces the lender to choose between putting up more money or seeing the loan in default. To insure against this, the construction loan balance must always be equal to the balance of the construction cost. Moreover, cost estimates should continually be updated during construction. If there is any slowdown in the project, this is often a warning signal.

Condominium Check List

- Location. The project must be feasible for the area and be harmonious with existing or proposed development. Check neighborhood trends and growth patterns, and the availability of services, like shopping and commuting.

• Site Evaluation. An analysis should be made of the topography of the land, soil condition, and the location of the various improvements on the site. The local zoning and planning boards and the building department should be contacted to be sure that there are no violations. For added insight, talk to local appraisers and brokers.

• Competition. Study the competition in your area and what their sale prices might be. Analyze sale prices on a square-foot basis. You might actually try to purchase a unit from a competitor to see if deals can be made at the asking price. Extras offered as inducements to buy will force adjustments in your sale prices.

• Layout. You should compute the area of each building, with and without balconies, and list all amenities that will be offered.

• Carrying Costs. What is the maximum financing available? Compute the constant payment that will be required under the end loans. Talk with the tax assessor and compare taxes on recently completed condos; estimate the real-estate taxes. Utility costs should be estimated for water, sewer, electricity, and fuel. Insurance, common-area maintenance, and other expenses should be factored in. The result will be total carrying costs. The portion that is tax deductible should be identified.

• Physical Analysis. Your condo should have less density, larger units, garages or covered parking, storage facilities, and higher-quality fixtures and finishing work than your competitor or comparable rental units.

• Presale Requirement. If the unit's marketability seems questionable, presale commitment should be required with end-loan commitments to the purchasers confirmed.

• Local Condo Regulations. Condo sales are affected by a variety of local laws. These cover the need for disclosures, escrow deposits (and the conditions under which these are returnable to the purchaser), recreational leases, and management contracts.

• The Borrower. Don't become involved with a beginner. Check and double-check his cost projections. Be especially sure that the builder can carry the project if there are cost overruns or if the project gets delayed by a strike, shortage of materials, or slow sales.

• Guarantees. The builder should not be doing several projects at one time. Further, both the completion of the project and the mortgage must be guaranteed. An irrevocable letter of credit is an excellent backup for this guarantee.

Protection for the Lender

The construction lender may want some or all of the following protection:

• Evidence that all equipment and fixtures will be ready for installation (many are in short supply).

• Sales deposits and funds held in escrow with the lender.

• The mortgage should cover the recreational facilities and any contiguous land owned by the builder.

• An agreed percentage of the first section must be completed before the builder begins work on the second.

Limited Partnership

There are other approaches to condominiums, and International Housing Systems, Inc. in Fort Lauderdale, Florida, suggests the limited partnership.

Many real-estate investors are finding that conversion of existing buildings to condominium usage is better than starting from scratch. Long-term construction problems, such as rising costs, shortages, strikes, and other risks are eliminated. Financing and marketing are simplified. There may already be existing financing on your structure. As mentioned in previous chapters, converting an existing building may give you a built-in group of prospective purchasers. The building and the neighborhood are known quantities. Best of all, with a little bit of luck, you can be in and out of the conversion with good profits in a short time.

International Housing's president, James W. Winans, suggests a solid financing approach to conversion. Here's how his operation works out a typical purchase:

- IHS lines up interim financing for 80 percent of the purchase price of the existing buildings plus the conversion cost.
- IHS raises the remaining 20 percent through the sale of limited partnership interests.

IHS has found that the limited partnership offers a variety of attractions. The firm does not have to rely upon internally generated funds for growth. Another benefit is that higher equity usually brings lower interest rates on debt financing. Carefully selected limited partners may also bring in interim and permanent lenders, or lead to additional properties for conversion and management assistance. Limited partners may also become a source of continuing financing.

IHS, without any investment, is usually compensated with an incentive marketing fee. This may run to 50 percent of the profits.

Limited partnerships are attractive, IHS believes, because high profits can be achieved on a short-term investment, through high leverage and resale prices. It is not unusual to sell the condominiums at an aggregate price of 50 percent over the purchase price of the property.

Limited partnerships allow tailoring of the investment vehicle to the needs and requirements of the investors. Any partnership may be limited to one project, two or more specific projects, or may be open-ended. The partnerships may also be structured so that investors interested in tax deferral can be given expense deductions, while investors interested in current income will show profits.

In purchasing an existing building, IHS tries to obtain whatever benefits it can from the existing financing. There are, however, three principal problems:

- The existing mortgagee will probably raise objections to releasing his lien unit by unit for condominium sales.
- Some states require that the lender approve condominium plans before the state permits sales.
- The existing financing will usually be inadequate.

Sometimes, the additional financing required to handle the purchase and conversion costs can be a wraparound mortgage. The new mortgagee pays off the old at a fixed or determinable time. No additional financing may be required, however, when the existing financing represents a high portion of the purchase price and the mortgagee goes along with the condominium conversion.

IHS, in the process of a conversion, sometimes carves out a land or recreational lease, and sells condominium units subject to the lease. IHS may use these leases to trade for the seller's equity in other property that it wishes to acquire. Such a trade may be structured as a tax-free exchange. This may permit acquisition at a lower price, and that may be passed along to the partners on the subsequent sale of the acquired property to a limited partnership.

The use of leases, if properly structured, can be an extremely useful financing tool. There can, however, be tax problems, since the IRS has taken the position that the capitalized value of the lease is taxable.

Advantages of a Condominium

As a potential investor in condominiums, you should understand the major advantages of this type of real estate. Condominiums are far better than renting because:

• You can't get bumped out of your office space if your lease is not renewed.

• Your office space is designed to serve your needs, not merely to fit the available space.

• You build equity in a condominium, which can be sold or rented to realize a return on your investment.

• Inflation works for you. Your condominium appreciates in value with the years, while your monthly principal and interest payments remain the same.

There are also major tax benefits from owning a condominium:

• Your condo may be depreciated at 150 percent of straight line.

• Other components of the property such as air conditioning, heating units, cabinets, light fixtures, carpeting, and landscaping may be depreciated over short periods. This can be equal to or greater than 200 percent of straight line.

• Investment credit may be taken from certain components of the property. This is deducted directly from your income tax liability.

• You can deduct real-estate taxes, interest on mortgage, utilities, and other maintenance costs.

If you are incorporated, other advantages in owning a condominium accrue to you:

• You can buy the condominium and rent it back to the corporation. The corporation gets a deduction for the rent. While the rent is taxable income to you, you can deduct depreciation, real-estate taxes and interest on the mortgage. The corporation pays for the utilities and maintenance, which are also tax deductible.

• If you have a pension plan or profit-sharing plan, the trust could buy the land and lease it to the corporation. The corporation would own the building, and the following advantages might result:

a. The pension or profit-sharing trust gets a better-than-average return than would be available from investment in securities.

b. Land appreciation offers an additional benefit to the trust.

c. The corporation gets a deduction for rent paid, deduction of accelerated depreciation, real-estate taxes on the building, interest on the mortgage, and operating expenses.

Let's say that you like the idea of condominiums. You've found a good location, and are either going to build or convert an existing building. During the early 1970s, when condominiums looked like the hottest real estate going, unscrupulous builders mislead buyers. As the market cooled, these buyers set up a hue and cry that turned other, potential buyers off. As a result—both of poor marketing and bad consumer relations—the condo business dropped sharply.

I firmly believe that the condominium—whether for professional-office space, homes, or recreational second-homes—is a strong real-estate investment. Changing lifestyles, environmental concerns with use of space (indoors and out), and the simple economics of land have made condos workable and valuable.

To avoid the acrimony of the past, there are some guidelines that should be followed between condo investor-builder and condo buyer:

- There must be full disclosure before the sale is completed.
- The buyers should understand that condos and homes are approximately the same in price. Condos are not cheap housing, and as densities are pushed lower and costs rise, this will continue to be the case.
- The cost of management, and who the manager will be, must be made very clear to the buyer. Professional management should be part of the condo deal.

• The crooked builder must be exposed and thrown out of all building associations. All ads must include the builder's name (not his made-up name for the development). His track record should be easily (and readily) available.

• The builder and the homeowners association should work closely together. Communication will alleviate 95 percent of the problems.

• Buyers should know that they are not buying into a country club but a residential community. Builder and buyer both have responsibilities, which must be clearly spelled out on paper.

Crazy—Like a Fox—Condo Ideas

The condominium market keeps changing, and several new ideas are worth passing along. One of my favorites involves Wesley Box, who recycles old buildings. In 1972, Wes bought The Chalet at Estes Park, Colorado. It was a run-down, but charming, 1910 hotel with holes in the walls and water pipes that froze in November and thawed in April. He paid $275,000 and they tossed in 35 acres.

Wes Box spent $29,000 moving the pipes, another $35,000 for electric heat, and another $45,000 for a year-round water supply (after shrewdly buying all the water rights). Then he spent another $141,000 refurbishing the rooms and putting in a modern dining area and lounge.

What is Wesley Box up to? He's developed the idea of the "condotel"—the condominium hotel. He's selling off the refurbished rooms of The Chalet. The rooms started at $3,000 for a single and went up to $13,000 plus, depending upon amenities, for a suite. "It's no fun going to the mountains and going to a Holiday Inn," said Tina Fike, who, with her husband, Larry, bought the 103rd of the hotel's 160 rooms. "We're old hotel buffs—you know, the Peabody in Memphis and the Biltmore in L.A.—and we couldn't resist a place like this in the mountains. And it didn't cost $35,000."

Wes Box expected to clear $250,000 profit with his idea of converting an old, worn-out hotel into a condominium. It was a brilliant idea, with excellent timing, superb pricing, and outstanding location.

A second crazy-like-a-fox idea for condominium investors and owners is called time-sharing. So many variations of the time-sharing concept have been created by innovative developers that there are now a wide range of options.

Known as time-sharing, interval ownership or vacation licenses, these programs all start at a common point: greatly lowering the cost of a resort condo by gearing ownership or use to a specific time period. This period may be 1 to 4 weeks per year, and it determines the amount the condo buyer puts up. Time-sharing, as it's widely called, broadens the resort condominium market enormously. One successful program in this field, for example, offers a 2-week annual occupancy of a studio condominium in Hawaii on a 40-year lease basis. You pay $1,500—at terms of $200 down, $35 a month for 4½ years (9.5 percent interest rate). Other variations at the same Hawaii condominium offer 2-week occupancy for a 2-bedroom condo for $3,500—25 percent down. Obviously, prices like these make resort condominiums within reach of a broad stratum of middle- and upper-middle-income people.

The theory here is that since people do not usually need a vacation home for more than 2 or 4 weeks every year, why not relate the purchase to the period of use? Moreover, the cost of interval ownership or use works out to be considerably lower than the comparable vacation without the condominium. The resort condo, moreover, with its amenities tends to be as plush or more so than the typical resort hotel or motel room.

There are several methods of handling this form of condominium:

- Rental Arrangement. The condominium purchaser retains title to his unit at all times. Management, however, leases his unit under a variety of arrangements. The owner reserves the option to use his unit (or a similar one) at specific times or after notifying the management.

• Time-Sharing. This is the time-slice ownership mentioned above. In this form, the purchaser buys fee-simple ownership of a specified time period (usually 2 weeks to a month) of the condo unit. This includes an undivided interest in the common facilities. Time-sharing is like the basic condo ownership, except that fees, use, and obligations cover a specific calendar period of the year. Pricing may also vary according to the time of year: highest during the resort's peak season and lowest in the off-season. The right to permit others to occupy the condo during your time-sharing period may not be granted in some condo resorts. That is, under the "time-slice" the condo owners may not be able to treat their time-slice as an investment.

• Vacation License. This entitles long-term use privileges, but does not involve an interest in real estate. One Florida operation, with condos also in San Juan and St. Croix, sells a "license" to occupy a specified unit for 1 week annually for the estimated life of the project. That generally lasts 40 to 60 years. Prices have ranged from $2,000 for a lower-floor studio to $6,000 for a penthouse suite. Terms are 10 percent down and 4 years to pay. The Florida group, the Caribbean International Corporation, sets up its condo "vacation licenses" for a specific period and specific unit, and then allows its members to switch to similar accommodations at any of the company's locations at a different time, if desired. This flexibility has attracted more than 6,000 purchasers of vacation licenses.

• Recreation Club. Under this program, the club creates a limited partnership which owns the property. The purchaser of a limited-partnership interest receives a membership that gives him a pro rata right to use the property according to club regulations.

A variation of this occurs where the club creates a network of condo space by acquiring blocks of units in various resort locations. Individual investors may use the various properties. The club retains ownership, and the members do not have an interest in any real estate.

The club avoids the problems and risks of actually developing its own condos. Instead, it buys a number of units in an existing project—enough to meet the needs of its members and to warrant getting a price deal from the developer. Such clubs have not been started yet, but several are on the drawing boards.

One sponsor envisions beginning with a national network of prime condos in a first-class resort development where the use membership would be aimed at upper-middle-income families. Later, another network of lower-cost condos would be created for middle-income families. Membership might be as low as $1,000.

Aside from the rather substantial front-end financing requirements, the trick to this kind of operation seems to be in selecting locations keyed to the desires of members, and acquiring the units on favorable terms. Among the markets for this kind of club approach are labor and teacher unions, and professional groups.

As yet, there have not been any big multiple-ownership or time-sharing programs in the continental United States. Time-sharing operations have been very successful in Europe. If the primary interest is a good vacation plan that is substantially cheaper than other available options, this condo program is for you. A good bet for the late 1970s is time-sharing with an investment feature: use relates directly to need, and equity build-up is maintained.

Whatever form of condominium you select as either an investor or buyer, there are so many variations on the market that the right one in the right place is likely to exist for you.

15

TEN KEY RULES TO REAL ESTATE INVESTING

Most people get hurt in real estate when they allow themselves to get trapped by unreal expectations. Remember, the basic rule is: Be cautious. No one makes a killing overnight. The following ten key rules may not make you a lot of money. But they will insure that there is less chance that you lose your investment because you didn't think about what you were getting into. Briefly, the ten key rules are:

1. Know the lay of the land.
2. Pick the favorites and avoid the long shots.
3. Know the principals in your deal.
4. Know the principles of your deal.
5. Buy quality deals, dealers, and advice.
6. Consider tax benefits the icing on the economic cake.
7. Look out for too much leverage.
8. Be patient and don't look for a killing.
9. Beware of the deal that is over the head of the dealer.
10. Look before you leap.

1. Know the Lay of the Land

Value relates to use, and valuable use is often tied to a good location. Use in turn is controlled by the consumer preference and economic-growth patterns of the area where a piece of property is located. In every community there is a right side and a wrong side of the tracks. Many commercial streets have a right side where businesses prosper, and a wrong side with revolving-door ownership. Some suburbs blossom and others wither.

The profit potential of a good location can be lost if it is developed with the wrong product or at the wrong time. Three years may spell the difference between disaster and success in the case of a high-rise building built in a suburban center. In some areas a brick finish is essential to sell a home and in other areas it is a risky luxury.

Thus, the right location, product, and timing are all local matters, and vital to the success of your real-estate investment. There is no substitute for knowledge of the locality in which a real-estate investment is made. If the investor does not know, he should buy the services of someone who does.

2. Pick the Favorites and Avoid the Long Shots

Pioneers get the headaches, and those who follow them get the profits. A revolutionary new product in any field is dangerous; in real estate, where people expect solidly established values, it is almost always suicidal.

For example, a long time has been taken to win customer acceptance for light-weight aggregate, which has many times more strength and many times less weight than regular concrete (which therefore makes it cheaper to work with). But for many years builders took one look at it and said: "It doesn't *look* as strong as regular concrete."

So, let the promoter who is ready to astound the world with his new construction technique or to build the first high-rise in town, prove it first, before you invest. Real estate is basically a conservative game.

There are few sleepers today in real estate. The property touted as an underpriced bargain is likely to turn out to be a dog with some bones of trouble buried beneath the surface. Remember, the higher the return, the higher the risk. Save your betting on long shots for the race track, and look at real estate for the short odds. Mathematically, the favorites will bring you out further ahead in the long run. The expected value of an 80 percent probability of making a 25 percent return is 20 percent; the expected value of a 30 percent probability of making a 50 percent return is only the mathematical equivalent of a 15 percent return.

3. Know the Principals in Your Deal

Throughout this book I have emphasized that the dealer is the key to the deal. First, you must be certain of his integrity and ability. Second, he should have a real economic stake in the deal by making his compensation dependent upon the results of the deal, and even better, by having some of his own cash in the deal. Third, the dealer should have financial resources available to throw into the deal to pull it out if trouble occurs.

The best way of checking out the dealer is to meet him. You'd be surprised how many people plunge into real-estate investments without seeing the property or meeting the dealer. Question him thoroughly about his background, motives, and knowledge of the deal. Will he achieve what he proposes?

If you cannot meet the dealer himself because it is a public deal, then you should have a thorough analysis made of the deal itself. This should be done by a knowledgeable, independent expert who works for a fee and not a commission.

However, of primary importance is the impression that you and your expert form regarding the degree to which the person representing the deal has personally checked it out.

Don't rely, however, merely on your impressions of the dealer or his representative. Ask for and check the references of people with whom he has done business: customers, banks, creditors, and others. It is surprising the number of people who accept someone at face value and do not check below the surface! Con men frequently rely upon the laziness of people by furnishing nonexistent references. One call to the right reference can spell the difference between avoiding a clear loser and having the sense of confidence that you have a probable winner.

4. Know the Principles of Your Deal

If seeing the person is the first step in evaluating the dealer, seeing the property is the first step in evaluating the deal. Go look at the site and walk or drive through the area surrounding it. If you see signs for the sale or rent of property similar to that proposed for your deal, stop in or telephone and get the relevant information on rent, available space, and other pertinent factors.

You will be surprised how often you get a gratuitous comment that will be very helpful to you in making a decision on the deal. Furthermore, as you get experienced you will get a strong intuitional feeling about whether or not the location is good or the proposed use makes sense.

Another crucial principle is having the right expectations about the deal. You should critically determine the risks—of fluctuating income, of loss of capital, of getting cash out quickly, and the probable benefits—how much cash flow, capital appreciation, and tax shelter. Once you can see the deal with your eyes wide open, you then can decide whether it will give you the kind of benefits you want, and whether the likely benefits are fair compensation for the projected risks.

Analyze the deal three ways like the pros do: What is the worst that can happen? What is the best that can happen? And what will probably happen? Then, seriously question yourself as to whether you will be happy with the probable outcome or how badly you actually will be hurt. How much sleep will you lose if the worst comes to pass? Never go into any deal that can seriously damage you financially or psychologically.

In any deal, you should have fail-safe sales indicators (if you are selling homes, condos, or so on), which will help you sell the product, or take other drastic action to cut losses. That is, if the fail-safe indicator shows something wrong in the first phase of a multiphase deal, you may be able to take action to cut your losses. This process of redefining future action on the basis of the effectiveness of past action is the feedback process that lies at the heart of a good-systems approach to management.

5. Buy Quality Deals, Dealers, and Advice

A quality dealer will want a healthy chunk of the action. His value as a profit producer will have been clearly established in past deals, checked out by you, and agreed upon by your other experts. He will not work cheap. The prospect of a substantial contingent payoff induces him to work as hard as he does. He will line his pocket at the same time that he is lining yours.

The novice in real estate frequently ends up with second-rate locations in his search for bargain deals. No location at all is better than a second-rate location. Real estate is a big-ticket item, and the public looks for quality sites and quality products on those sites. The investor who thinks that he is saving money when he provides insufficient elevator service or parking for his project is being penny wise and dollar foolish. He quickly finds out how wrong he is when he has to dig into his pockets to keep the project afloat until he can find enough fools like himself to rent or buy his units.

Always buy quality advisors. Recently, I saw some legal documents, drafted by an inexperienced lawyer that, in effect, made the same deal both a sale and a lease. The lawyer's client, the buyer, could have ended up with the transaction being considered a lease for tax purposes, with a consequent loss of depreciation tax shelter; a sale for financing purposes, with the result that an expensive refinancing of the indebtedness would be required; and a lease as far as the seller was concerned, which could have let him wipe out the buyer in the case of a default.

That investor's cheap legal advice could have put him in a very expensive bind. Similarly, the difference in the sale price and the rate of sale on a project designed by a hack architect and on one designed by a knowledgeable architect can be light years apart. So, too, the work of good or bad accountants, financial advisors, and so on.

Perhaps the most important advice of all is that obtained from the independent expert who helps the investor make his ultimate "go" or "no-go" decision. Former developers and bankers, astute real-estate brokers, down-to-earth market researchers, solid attorneys and accountants, and the other real-estate pros are a rare breed. When you can get what the security industry calls "due diligence," you should not quibble about the price. On the bad deals the investor avoids, he should consider the experts' fees the same as an insurance premium, which represents a small, certain loss incurred to avoid a probable greater loss. The solid advisor also is likely, on a good deal, to give the investor some suggestions that will make the deal even better.

6. Consider Tax Benefits the Icing on the Economic Cake

Income-property buyers usually set a minimum required return on investment as the basic prerequisite for putting their money into something. Only then do they—or should they—consider tax shelter as a distinct additional benefit. If the probability is minimal that the investors will receive little more than front-end write off, they might better donate the same amount to charity and avoid the grief of seeing their investment lost.

The current Congressional sentiment toward cutting down tax preferences makes reliance on the tax effect of an investment especially dangerous. Without economic substance in his investment, the investor faces the possibility of being caught as unprotected as the emperor with the invisible clothes. Especially foolhardy is the expectation that deductions from the investment will shelter other income.

7. Look Out for Too Much Leverage

Leverage increases down-side risk as well as up-side return. In uncertain times, the investor should reduce the capital he borrows and increase his equity investment. A solid equity will mean that the investor will have lower break-even requirements and can ride out occasional adverse fluctuations in income.

An alternative to substantial equities in some investments is to establish an appropriate reserve to be held in a savings account or in monetary or government securities as the down-side buffer for an entire portfolio of investments. On the contrary, the pyramiding often used by sophisticated investors —borrowing against equities to buy more equities, which in turn can be borrowed against to buy still more equities—should be avoided.

In addition to avoiding leverage to protect capital, the investor sometimes finds that high interest rates make it hard to get any income leverage from borrowed capital. If money actually costs 12 to 15 percent, an attempt to make up that money in rents charged to the user is likely to be acceptable only to the marginal tenant who flakes out at the least appropriate moment.

A sound alternative to borrowing from the institutional investor (and to make it easier to find financing) is to bring in the investor for a piece of the equity action. The ability of an institutional partner to dig into his pocket when the going gets rough reduces the possibility of having your investment rocked out from under you.

8. Be Patient and Don't Look for a Killing

For the short term, I don't see any basic improvement in the economic conditions. Income property investors, therefore, should look to capital appreciation as their primary benefit during any recovery period. Appreciation will come from rent increases made to reflect current development and operating costs as vacancy rates drop because of reduced building activity.

On the other hand, developers should look for "in and out" deals that yield moderate returns, keep them in the market, and keep their capital turning. Big profits on double escrows are definitely a thing of the past.

With real-estate investment back where it should be—as an intermediate and short-term investment—and with the higher risks associated with increased uncertainty, portfolio diversification becomes very important. Investors should put only part of their eggs in the long-term real-estate basket, and should put some of their investment capital in short-term, high-yield monetary and governmental securities. That diversification also establishes the reserves that I urged in rule 7 on the dangers of too much leverage.

9. Beware of the Deal That Is Over the Head of the Dealer

The smaller the deal, the better.

Even if you are cautious of how much you invest in a deal, if the dealer is not equally cautious you can have trouble. Everything said about the appropriate uses of leverage, reserves, and diversification applies even more to the dealer than to the individual investor. An injudicious investor causes a ripple in the financial pond when he goes under; when a big dealer goes broke, he can cause a tidal wave.

Small size minimizes risk by increasing the diversification potential of a given amount of capital, and by reducing the time required to dispose of the investment. The investment may be disposed either as an ordinary course of business sale of a development investment, or as the liquidation of an income-property investment. Size also reduces the overhead required to service the investment.

Especially to be avoided are investments in large-scale development deals with enormous front-end and carrying costs, unless a financial institution or major corporation is involved to carry the land as an equity partner.

10. Look Before You Leap

Beware the deal where the dealer wants your investment yesterday.

The fact that the dealer failed to foresee the amount and timing of his capital requirements does not speak well for his management ability. Sometimes the urgency is artificially created by a hustler to prevent his "mark" from seeing all of the dimensions of the deal. No deal is the last deal. Deals, like beautiful women, keep coming along the road, and as long as you are in the game, the deals will keep coming your way. You are better off passing up a few "good" ones in order to avoid getting hooked by a negligent or high pressure operator.

On the other hand, procrastination is a thief of time (and money). Once you have the information you really need, you should fish or go on to the next stream. The failure to say "yes" or "no" is a decision itself that deprives you of the value of the time you have spent in investigating the deal. Unless there is some specific reason for waiting (say, financing is not available), a short additional wait is unlikely to change the market and other basic conditions upon which the soundness of the deal depends. Rather, a long wait is likely to change enough material factors to create an entirely new ball game.

A sound decision-making process involves three steps: (1) your gut or intuitional feel about the soundness of the deal and the dealer when it is first presented; (2) a thorough investigation of all of the relevant factors that affect the deal; (3) the identification and evaluation of a few critical factors central to the success of the deal. Frequently, the gut feel deals with the marketability, the thorough analysis, projected profits, and cash flows in relation to investment, and the acid test of whether the deal can be financed.

A word of caution is in order. The fact that a reputable financial institution will commit money to a deal is important, but it is not conclusive that the deal is good—or we would never find financial institutions eating the deals that they do.

Have the good sense to get the right information before you decide, including the opinions of independent experts. Then have the guts to recognize that unless a gun is held to your head or you are defrauded, you are the one who ultimately writes out the check.

Men learn from their experiences; little boys cry, and then go out and make the same mistakes again and again. If you are not prepared to take the occasional licking and admit that you did, then you are unrealistically overlooking the inherent risk in real estate. Investment realism means that you have made reasonable efforts to evaluate the risk in a particular investment, and the return associated with that risk. The question comes down to whether or not you want to undertake that level of risk in exchange for that expected return. I hope this book helps you to make that crucial decision, and to avoid the wheeler-dealer who claims, "Have I got a deal for you!"

APPENDIX A

Marketing Development Check List

1. Market feasibility study.
2. Profit feasibility study.
3. Equity capital financing.
4. Timetable for development package.
5. Zoning analysis.
6. Site planning.
7. Joint-venture financing.
8. Architectural-design supervision.
9. Environmental-impact reports.
10. Landscape-planning supervision.
11. Engineering planning.
12. Tentative map processing and approval.
13. Final map processing and approval.
14. Lenders loan package.
15. Construction bidding—onsite and offsite.
16. Construction and supervision—responsibilities.
17. Department of real-estate approval.
18. Interim and take-out financing commitments.

19. Preselling analysis.
20. Marketing budgeting.
21. Time-sharing feasibility.

Merchandising Check List

1. Site management.
2. Seminar sales training.
3. Establish sales procedures.
4. Shop salespeople.
5. Hiring and firing of personnel.
6. Sales newsletters.
7. Establish sales aids.
8. Establish sales kits.
9. Establish traffic control.
10. Traffic-to-sales ratios.
11. Work assignment control.
12. Set up internal communications.
13. Establish lead follow-up control.
14. Establish construction-sales liaison list.
15. Create sales incentives and contests.
16. Instruct closing techniques.
17. Establish formal site tours.
18. Price inventory.
19. Instruct on telephone prospecting.
20. Set up phone rooms.
21. Training in use of T.O. (take-over) procedure.*
22. Broker co-op program.
23. Prospect generation.
24. Escrow processing.
25. Set up on- and off-site signing program.
26. Execution and creation of collateral material.
27. In-person solicitation for prospects.
28. Sales motivation.
29. Sales management.
30. On-site activity promotions.
31. Vendor co-operation promotions.

* A trained manager who "takes over" from the salesperson to *close* the deal.

32. Escrow-reinforcement programs.
33. Establish and set up homeowners associations.
34. Office-efficiency studies.
35. Move-in kits.
36. Area appreciation table comparables.
37. Welcome guide to the area.
38. On-site group bus tours.
39. Move-in coordinations.
40. Cost per lead reports.
41. Absorption rate studies.
42. Economic trend studies.
43. Establish rental program.
44. Competitive project comparison studies.
45. Sales meetings.
46. Direct mailings creation and coordination.
47. Model decorating.
48. Buyer demographics studies.
49. Lease-back financing.
50. Lease to purchase program.
51. Lease option program.
52. Trade-in program.
53. Buyer-profile advertising.
54. Referral program.
55. Sales walk-in lead report.
56. Budget reports.
57. Land-use studies.
58. Gourmet client catering.
59. Media services.
60. Legal services.
61. Plant-care services.
62. Cleaning services.
63. Furniture-rental services.
64. Graphic services.

APPENDIX B

Definitions of Market Segments

1. *Singles:* Unmarried, active, mobile, many interests, entertain informally.

Design Implications: Emphasis living room area and master bedroom suite.

2. *Potential First Home Buyer:* Young couple, working wife, entertain informally, amateur gardeners planning on a large family.

Design Implications: Emphasize kitchen, informal dining area, master bedroom area, smaller secondary bedrooms.

3. *Compact Family—Young Married #2:* Discretionary income available. Active, entertain informally and often, some formal entertaining, independent, dual-income household, do-it-yourself buffs, sports car.

Design Implications: Emphasize entry, living room/dining room combo, master bedroom suite, den; emphasize usable space, dramatic, decoratable.

4. *Compact Family—Move-Down:* No maintenance, informal living, some formal entertainment, away from home often, occa-

sional visits from family or guests, some separate bedrooms, focused active and passive recreation.

Design Implications: Quality not quantity, emphasis in living room and master bedroom area, large secondary bedrooms, den, breakfast nook or informal eating area, privacy.

5. *Compact Family—Divorcees:* Family-oriented activity, limited entertainment, informal lifestyle. Limited maintenance.

Design Implications: Emphasis on family room, separation of master bedroom suite, informal dining, treat family size of 2.8 as an average household size of 3.8.

6. *Family Move-Up:* The monthly payment group, family activities, casual and informal, unemployed female "the housewife," numerous interests, mostly child oriented. Amateur gardeners, transitional.

Design Implications: Space house, large family room, yard, zoning or separation of living and sleeping areas extremely important, number of bedrooms as important as size of bedrooms.

7. *Established Family:* "Making monthly payments comfortably," some discretionary income, approaching the peak of their economic and social lifestyle curve, some formal entertaining, older children: teen-agers, many interests, three-car family, limited maintenance.

Design Implications: Separate formal living and dining areas, den or formal family room, separate master bedroom suite, large secondary bedrooms, formal exterior yard area.

8. *Luxury Families:* Have arrived, tremendous discretionary income, very formal house, don't entertain often, but when they do it's formal, teen-agers (maybe a mistake—a 5 year old), less active athletic-wise, one or two formal sport affiliations, dine out often, no maintenance, privacy mandatory.

Design Implications: Formal entry, living room and separate dining, den, master bedroom plus retreat, guest room or maid's room, privacy and security important, possibly separate master bedroom suites.

9. *Empty Nester:* No debt, older couple, often away from home, occasional visit from family, focus on catching last "act of life," privacy, limited maintenance, limited investment in house costs, mobile in attitude, but permanent in residence, near grandchildren, many

hobbies, one child in college, one or two married, self-sufficient couple.

Design Implications: No maintenance, compact unit, all useful space, very informal, low-priced, living space designed as a large kitchen-family room combo, small intimate patio/deck.

10. *Active Retired:* Still working maybe two or three days per week, active either socially or politically in community affairs, self-sufficient, many hours away from home, don't entertain often, but when they do it is semi-formal.

Design Implications: Formal orientation of house, quality as opposed to quantity, functional house, secondary bedrooms used for hobbies, informal dining area.

11. *Retired:* Dependent, limited activities, outside of community, passive recreation, privacy important.

Design Implications: Separate master bedrooms, informal eating accommodations, one-car garage.

APPENDIX C

Project Analysis

The following chart, filled in by you for potential investments, will be helpful in seeing how your property might pencil out. Use it; it could save you from making a bad deal.

NET CASH RETURN

Gross income	$__________
Less expenses and vacancies	__________
Less ground rent	__________
Net income before financing	$__________
Less principal and interest 1st mortgage	__________
Less principal and interest 2nd mortgage	__________
Less payments on land-sale leaseback	__________
Less overrides on financing	__________
Net cash return	$__________

PROJECT COSTS

Land	$________
Sitework	$________
Personality (personal estate or property)	$________
Carrying charges—financing	$________
Fees	$________
Direct construction	$________
Marketing costs—advertising and/or sales	$________
Total project costs	$________

PROJECT FINANCING

Total project cost		$________
Less:		
1st mortgage	________	
2nd mortgage	________	
Land sale leaseback	________	
Total financing		________
Equity capital required		$________

ANALYSIS OF INCOME

Cash return	$________
Plus amortization on loans	________
Taxable revenue before depreciation	________
Less depreciation	________
Taxable income (loss)	________
Taxes paid (saved) (tax rate____%)	________
Cash return	$________
Plus (less) taxes saved (paid)	$________
after tax cash return	
Plus amortization	________
After tax total return	$________

RETURN ON INVESTMENT

Cash return/equity	$________
After tax cash return/equity	$________
After tax total return/equity	$________

APPENDIX D

Format of Covering Letter to Lenders

The following sample letter outline should help you to cover all the bases needed when corresponding to a potential lender.

Dear Mr. ____________:

In accordance with our phone conversation, I enclose the following information on the ____________ project. As we discussed on the phone, this project will be (is) (description). In order to acquaint you with the project, we enclose the following items:

1. A descriptive memorandum giving information on:
   (a) The project itself.
   (b) The builder/developer.
   (c) The location.
   (d) The property-purchase agreement.
   (e) Timing.

(f) Estimated costs and revenues, and a preliminary cash flow.
(g) An estimate of the value of the property when completed.
(h) The market for the project.

2. Additional exhibits including:
(a) An MAI appraisal of the property being acquired.
(b) A legal description of the property.
(c) Summary plans for the site.
(d) Summary plans for the physical assets.
(e) Financial statements of the builder/developer (borrower).
(f) Agreement with general contractor (if any).

We are seeking (amount) of (interim, permanent, other) financing to (carry out the project or do something else related to the project). These funds will be borrowed over ____________ months beginning ____________ and ending ____________, and repayment of this amount should be from (a take-out loan of ____________ arranged with ____________ or amortization over ____________ years or some other means).

After you have had an opportunity to review this material, please phone and we will endeavor to get you whatever additional information you need to determine the nature of your interest in our proposal and the terms of the financing you can make available to us.

Yours very truly,

APPENDIX E

Land Purchase and Development Check List

Before you run out and buy that fantastic property, this check list should be used. It will help you be sure that the location, use, terms, and so on are the best you can get.

Property (Name of Seller) ______________________
Date ______________________
Division ______________________
Division Pres. Signature ______________________

I. PROPERTY DESCRIPTION AND NEIGHBORHOOD CHARACTERISTICS

A. Location

1. Legal Description/Address ______________________
2. City ____________ County ________ State ________

B. Size and Zoning

1. Total Acres ____; Total Potential Units ____; Density Per Gross Acre ____
2. Net Usable Acres ____; Density Per Net Usable Acre ____
3. Present Zoning ____
4. (Optimal) Desired Zoning ____
5. Realistic Potential Zoning ____
6. Parking Spaces Per Unit ____

C. Suggested Development Program

Type of Unit	*No. of Units*	*No. of Acres*	*Units/ Acre*	*Proposed Price Range*	*Estimated Finished Land Cost Per Unit*
Detached	____	____	____	____	____
Townhouse	____	____	____	____	____
Quad	____	____	____	____	____
Apartment	____	____	____	____	____
Non-usable (schools, parks, shops, etc.)	____	____	____	____	____
Other____	____	____	____	____	____
Total	____	____	____	____	____

This suggested development program can be undertaken with present zoning: Yes __ No __

D. Site Characteristics

1. Property Terrain: Flat ( ); Gentle Slope ( ); Steep Slope ( ).
2. Physical Attributes: Trees ( ); Views ( ); Creeks ( ); Lake/Pond ( ).
3. Type of Soil: Rock ( ); Sand ( ); Loam ( ); Clay ( ); Existing Fill ( ).
4. Drainage Condition: Good ( ); Fair ( ); Bad ( ); Erosion ( ); Flood ( ).
5. Existing Roads: ____ Access Problems: ____
6. Structures to Be Removed: ____
7. Approach to Property: Good ( ); Fair ( ); Bad ( ).
8. Visibility: Good ( ); Fair ( ); Bad ( ).

9. Noise Problems: Airplanes ( ); Traffic ( ); Industrial ( ).
10. FHA-VA Financing Available: ____________
11. Remarks: ____________

____

E. Neighborhood Analysis

1. Schools

	Transportation			Sessions (Single or Double)	New School(s) Under Construction
	School District	Can Walk	Need Bus		
a. Elementary	____	____	____	____	____
b. Jr. High	____	____	____	____	____
c. Sr. High	____	____	____	____	____

2. Walking Time in Minutes To:
   a. Public Transportation ____
   b. Rec. and Playground ____
   c. Neighborhood Shopping ____

   Driving Time in Minutes To:
   a. Regional Shopping Center ____
   b. Major Employers ____
   c. College or University ____
   d. Churches ____

II. FINANCIAL

A. Terms of Purchase

1. Price: $____ Total: $____/Acre: $____/sf.; $____/Unit
2. Terms: $____ Down Payment
   $____ Balance @ ___% Due in Payments of $____ Every ______ Mo./Yr.
   $__________ Commission
   $__________ Title and Legal Fees
3. Other Information: (Releases) ____________

____

____

____

____

____

B. Comparables

Unimproved and/or Improved Land

#____ Contains ____ Acres, Sold @ $_______ acre on ______
#____ Contains ____ Acres, Sold @ $_______ acre on ______
#____ Contains ____ Acres, Sold @ $_______ acre on ______
#____ Contains ____ Acres, Sold @ $_______ acre on ______
#____ Contains ____ Acres, Sold @ $_______ acre on ______
#____ Contains ____ Acres, Sold @ $_______ acre on ______

C. State of Division Interest and Timing

1. Division Interest
   - ____ Owned
   - ____ In escrow (if so, closing date ______)
   - ____ Offer accepted (if so, ending date ______)
   - ____ Offer made, but not accepted
   - ____ No offer made yet

2. Timing

   (If applicable), date free look ends ______

   Timing of nonrefundable deposits ________________

   ____

D. Titles

1. Is Property Title in Order: ________________
2. Is Boundary Survey Necessary: ________________
3. Existing Easements: ____________________
4. Mineral Rights: ______________________
5. Remarks: __________________________

III. UTILITIES AND DEVELOPMENT

A. State of Land Improvement

____ Raw ____ Semifinished (partially developed) ____ Finished

B. Utilities and Improvements

	Type	*Cost*	*Who Installs*	*Who Pays*	*Avail. to Site Yes/No*
1.	Sewer	$______	______	______	______
2.	Water	______	______	______	______
3.	Storm Drain	______	______	______	______
4.		______	______	______	______
5.		______	______	______	______

C. Estimated Developed Land Costs

1. Raw Land $______
2. Improvements ______
3. Total w/out
   Carry, Landscape
   or Rec. Facilities ______ $______/Unit $______/Ac.

D. Status of Environmental Impact Report

1. Is it needed? ( ) Yes ( ) No (call local agency)
2. Has adjacent land required an EIR? ( ) Yes ( ) No
3. Can you get a waiver? ( ) Yes ( ) No

E. Status of Potential Moratoriums

Briefly describe present condition and your best estimate of future: (example—none or none imminent)

1. Schools ______________________________

   ____

2. Sewer ______________________________

   ____

3. Water ______________________________

   ____

4. Gas and Natural Power ____________________

   ____

F. Explanation of Other Applicable Items or Additional Narrative On A and B Above ______________________________
____
____
____
____
____
____

G. State of Land Plan

_______ No map filed.
_______ Tentative map submitted but unapproved.
_______ Tentative map submitted and approved.
_______ Final map submitted but unapproved.
_______ Final map submitted and approved.

H. Engineering Study to Determine Land-Improvement Costs

_______ Has been completed.
_______ Has been authorized and will be completed by _______.
_______ Has been neither authorized nor completed.

IV. DOCUMENTATION

The Following Have Been Obtained:

_____ Plot Map	_____ Assessor's Map	_____ Title Report
_____ Topo Map	_____ Zoning Map	_______________
_____ Soil Report	_____ Zoning Regulations	_______________

APPENDIX F

Check List for Buying an Office Building

A good check list is a valuable tool for the real-estate investor. It gives him most of the key questions to ask. Answers will come from the seller, the broker, and some may involve retaining the services of an engineer, real-estate consultant, or other specialist. Here, then, are some major considerations in buying an office building:

(I) ECONOMIC POTENTIAL

- (1) Is city growing or declining?
- (2) Is area progressing or declining?
- (3) Is building proper for the area?
- (4) Is building modern or obsolete?
  - (a) Cost to modernize?
  - (b) Does it offer potential rent increase by change of tenancy, modernizing?
  - (c) Investigate zoning of area.

(5) Is building fully rented? Why not?

(6) Are rents in line with rents of other buildings?

(7) Type of tenant:
  (a) Financial responsibility.
  (b) Percentage of building occupied.
  (c) Length of leases.

(8) Management of building:
  (a) Is it progressive?
  By owner or agency management?
  (b) Is building clean, well maintained, with satisfied tenancy?

(II) PHYSICAL CONDITION OF BUILDING

(1) Date when constructed:
  (a) Modern or obsolete?
  (b) Obtain a copy of certificate of occupancy.

(2) Exterior:
  (a) Are walls, roof, and sash watertight?
  (b) Is basement watertight?
  (c) Does exterior have eye appeal, or is steam cleaning and metal maintenance necessary?
  (d) Sidewalk—are repairs necessary?
  (e) Is there a sidewalk vault? Has fee been paid to city?

(3) Entrance:

Is lobby attractive and properly maintained or does it need modernization or improvement by new lighting, redecoration, new cabs, new elevator doors, and new entrance enclosures?

(4) Elevators—what is the condition of:
  (a) Hoisting machinery, motors, gears, controllers, cables, and sheaves?
  (b) Shafts?
  (c) Cabs—flooring, lighting, and car gates and trim?
  (d) Signal system, hall lanterns, and main lobby panel?
  (e) Consider cost of conversion to automatic elevators.

(5) Floors:

(a) Does layout permit the most efficient use of rentable space? Are column and window spacings suitable for intensive subdivision?

(b) Are toilet facilities adequate and attractive?

(c) Condition of floors, walls, and ceilings.

(d) Do surrounding buildings block out light and air?

(e) Will construction of adjoining buildings close off lot-line windows through which light and air are presently enjoyed?

(6) Electrical:

(a) Is present service adequate for present needs and for future demand for air conditioning, improved lighting, and tenants' increasing demands for new office machines and the like?

(b) Are fixtures in lobby, corridors, and tenant areas modern and attractive?

(c) Are there sufficient convenience outlets for tenant and building use?

(d) Are electrical risers, service switches, distribution boards, and floor circuits adequate and in good condition?

(7) Plumbing:

(a) Age and condition of pipes.

(b) Are risers sufficient for air conditioning needs?

(c) Condition of water pumps, tanks, sump pumps, and ejectors.

(d) Are washrooms modern?

1. Toilets and urinals.
2. Wash basins.
3. Walls, ceilings, and floors.
4. Is proper ventilation provided?

(8) Heating facilities for building and hot water:

(a) Oil, coal, or electrical steam service?

(b) Conditions of boilers, tubes, stack, burners or grates, tanks, pumps, risers, returns, and radiators?

(c) Is system sufficient to heat building, and is there a

reserve in case of breakdown? Are there sufficient radiators in all areas? Condition of traps and valves?

(9) Air conditioning:
- (a) Central plant.
- (b) Window or package units?
- (c) Is system adequate for building?
- (d) Determine operating hours and conditions required by leases.

(10) Building services:
- (a) What services are performed for tenants? Who pays?
  1. Office cleaning.
  2. Washroom cleaning and towels and soap.
  3. Window cleaning. Investigate personnel engaged in cleaning buildings as to work area assigned and quality of work, whether by contract building force.
  4. Exterminating.
  5. Rubbish removal.
  6. Replacement of bulbs.
  7. Repairs.
- (b) Charges for hot and cold water.
- (c) Electricity—metered, rent inclusion, or direct? If rent inclusion, investigate charges included.
- (d) Air conditioning—cost of operation. Are tenants being billed for any overtime service at proper rates?

(11) Personnel:
- (a) Is building adequately staffed with competent employees?
- (b) Does payroll reflect labor cost of all services required to operate building?
  1. Services performed by own personnel.
  2. Is building signatory to any labor agreement? If not, are wages comparable with union agreements?

(12) Alterations and repairs:
  (a) Does building require extensive repairs because of age and deferred maintenance?
  (b) Does building require extensive alterations because of obsolescence, faulty design, or to prepare premises for tenants' use?

(13) Operating costs:
  (a) Do costs indicated provide for all operations necessary to provide the required services?
  (b) Are costs in line with costs of other buildings?

(14) Legal requirements:
  (a) Does building design and equipment meet state and local laws and regulations?
  (b) Is present use in conformity with certificate of occupancy?
  (c) Are any violations recorded against the building?
  (d) Are fire department regulations for building complied with?
  (e) Are there encroachments that must be removed or for which an annual fee must be paid to the city?

(15) Insurance:
  (a) Is fire-insurance coverage adequate and is coverage to 80 percent of replacement value?
  (b) Are alterations or repairs needed to meet insurance requirements, or secure a lower rate?
  (c) Obtain makeup of fire rate to see if reduction can be effected or if part of premium can be charged to tenant because of extra hazardous occupancy.
  (d) Does building have adequate public liability insurance of bodily injury and property damage?
  (e) Are there unusual risks in building, neighborhood, tenancy, city, etc., which would require extra coverage?
  (f) What are premiums on Workmen's Compensation Insurance, and are employees properly classified?
  (g) Are boilers and machinery covered?
  (h) Is plate glass insured, and do leases provide for store tenants to carry policies?
  (i) Should rent insurance be carried?

(16) Real-estate taxes and assessments:
- (a) Real-estate taxes. (Past trend and prospect for future.)
- (b) Water rates—sewer charges.
- (c) Assessments for special improvements.

APPENDIX G

Check List for Buying an Apartment Building

As with buying an office building, buying an apartment building should be done with check list in hand. Here, your cynical eye—and that of a structural engineer—is your best guide. There are twelve areas you should examine on the outside, and six on the inside.

1. PAINT

a. Consider the color and condition and any chipping or cracking. The color can give you an idea of the general age of some properties.

b. Check the trim for color, peeling, fading, and cracking.

c. Sometimes by painting the trim and cleaning up the grounds, you can improve the appearance tremendously.

2. WINDOWS

a. Are they clean?
b. Do they contain any cracks?
c. Are any broken?
d. What types of windows and glass are used?
e. Some types can be more costly to replace.
f. Are the windows a common size?

3. SCREENS

a. Use the same check list as for windows.

4. STUCCO

a. Look for cracks, chips, sagging, rust spots, and water stains.
b. Carefully inspect around the doors and windows, near the roof line and the ground level.

5. GARAGE AREA

a. Look at the type and condition of the structure.
b. Look for oil spots, broken or dented poles, cracked cement and holes in the wall.

6. TRASH AREA

a. Check the type, condition, size, and number of bins, as well as their proximity to trash pick-up and to the apartments.
b. Check the condition of the general trash area.

7. GROUNDS

a. Little things like trees, grass, and bushes can make a building better or worse than the competition.
b. Is the lawn taken care of?
c. Are trees trimmed?
d. Are sidewalks and decks clean?
e. Look for cracks in the sidewalk and decking.

8. POOL

a. Make certain the pool is clean and all equipment is well maintained and working properly.

b. Note the condition of the general pool area and pool furniture.

9. ROOF

a. Check the type, age, condition, and drainage pattern.
b. Look for any holes or tears.

10. DRIVEWAY

a. Check the type of driveway.
b. Look for cracks or holes, tire damage, water damage, sinking, or oil and gas spots.

11. UTILITY METERS

a. Where are they located and how are they protected?
b. What is their general condition?

12. MISCELLANEOUS ITEMS

a. Always check location and condition of mail boxes and magazine racks.
b. Make certain the entrance is clean and the doors, if any, work properly.
c. Make certain the hand rails are properly maintained and strong.
d. Steps should be clean and without major chips, holes, or cracks.
e. The decks and fences should be checked for general conditions.

If properly done, the detailed exterior inspection tells you a great deal about the seller, tenants, and general area. It also tells you what has to be completed to put the building in good condition. Remember: don't pay top dollar for a property with much deferred maintenance.

An inspection of the interior will help verify information obtained from the exterior inspection. Be certain to inspect each unit for the following:

1. PAINT

a. Check the color of the walls and ceiling.

b. Look for black marks near the vents, chips, cracks, and any water marks or stains.

c. What type of paint was used—flat or enamel—and where was it used?

d. Note the general condition of walls and ceilings.

2. CABINETS AND COUNTER SPACE

a. "The female's touch." Look at design, location, size, type, condition.

b. Are there any burns or chips?

3. SIZE OF ROOMS AND AMENITIES

a. *Kitchen*—Very important. Is there a dishwasher, garbage disposal, stove, working area?

b. *Bathroom*—Number, size, location.

c. *Living Room*—Size and layout.

d. Consider these items in all units:

1. Tile or linoleum.
2. Size of sinks.
3. Type of heating and air conditioning.
4. Size and location of closets, mirrors and light fixtures.

4. CARPETS AND DRAPES

a. Type of material.

b. Color.

c. Condition.

d. Rips or tears, stains, holes.

e. Water marks.

f. Type of padding and type of curtain rods.

5. PLUMBING

a. Types of pipe—copper, steel, galvanized.

b. Color of the water.

c. Condition of pipes under sinks.

d. Check toilets for pressure and leaks. Check for condition of tanks and plunger.

e. Water pressure from sinks and showers.
f. Working conditions of garbage disposals.
g. Condition and working order of the showers and tubs.
h. Size, age, and condition of water heater.

6. GENERAL OR MISCELLANEOUS

a. Squeaks in sub-flooring.
b. Water marks on carpets or ceilings.
c. Windows and screens.
d. Conditions of doors, locks, and handles.

APPENDIX H

Glossary of Real-Estate Terms and Phrases

The field of real estate has developed a complicated list of terms, some of which we hear every day, and some of which are very esoteric. Knowing what each term means, however, is important to your real-estate investing and your deal. We are indebted to Kenneth Leventhal & Company, certified public accountants, for this most excellent glossary.

A

ABSTRACT OF TITLE—A summary or digest of the conveyances, transfers, and any other facts relied on as evidence of title, together with any other elements of record which may impair the title. (See—TITLE INSURANCE.)

ACCELERATION CLAUSE—Clause in trust deed or mortgage giving lender right to call all sums owing him to be immediately due and payable upon the happening of a certain event. Synonyms: due on sale clause; alienation clause.

ACCESS RIGHT—The right of an owner to have ingress and egress to and from his property.

ACCOMMODATION PARTY—A person who, without receiving any consideration, signs a note on behalf of another. (See—SURETY.)

ACRE—A measure of land equaling 160 square rods, or 4,840 square yards, or 43,560 square feet, or a tract about 208.71 feet square.

AD VALOREM—According to the value, as with ad valorem taxes on real property.

ADVANCE BILLINGS—Synonym for progress billings. (See—RETENTIONS.)

AFTER COMPLETION COSTS—The costs incurred for the development of real property after the regular construction has been completed.

AGREEMENT OF SALE—A written agreement or contract between seller and purchaser stating the terms and conditions of the sale. Synonym: purchase agreement. (See—SALES DEPOSIT RECEIPT.)

A.I.T.D.—All-Inclusive Trust Deed. A trust deed which is subordinate to, but includes the encumbrances to which it is subordinated (the underlying loans). A device used, similar to a sales contract, to preserve the favorable terms of underlying loans and to provide other financial and tax advantages to the parties concerned. The difference between the all-inclusive loan and the underlying loan is sometimes referred to as an "effective second lien." For example, a person sells real property which is encumbered by a first lien of $400,000 for a price of $500,000. The seller retains his liability on the first lien (the underlying loan) and takes back an A.I.T.D. from the buyer for $450,000 and cash of $50,000. The buyer makes payments to the seller on the A.I.T.D. and the seller in turn continues making payments on the $400,000 underlying loan. The $50,000 difference between the first lien and the underlying loan is the amount of the effective second lien. Synonyms: all-inclusive loan; hold-harmless trust deed; over-riding trust deed mortgage or trust deed. (See—ALL-INCLUSIVE MORTGAGE.)

ALIENATION—Transferring of property to another; the transfer of property and possession of lands, or other things, from one person to another.

ALIENATION CLAUSE—(See—ACCELERATION CLAUSE.)

ALL-INCLUSIVE MORTGAGE—Essentially the same as an all-inclusive trust deed, except that the mortgage instrument is used. (See—A.I.T.D.)

A.L.T.A.—A policy of title insurance originally created by the American Land Title Association. An extended coverage form of title insurance usually requiring the physical inspection of the subject property and survey—opposed to a standard coverage policy.

AMENITIES—Attractive features of a property; these might be the position of a building on its lot or the existence of a swimming pool, sauna, golf course, etc.

AMORTIZATION—The systematic extinguishment of the cost of some asset or the extinguishment of some liability. For example, the write-down of prepaid interest to extinguishment by periodic charges to expense, or the principal reduction of a note payable over its life. (See—BURN-OFF; DEPRECIATION.)

ANTICIPATION—The economic principle that value is created by anticipated benefits to be derived in the future. In real estate this is the theory that the worst house in a given neighborhood will benefit by the greater value of those houses around it. Opposite of regression. Synonym: progression.

APARTMENT—A dwelling unit of one or more rooms providing complete living facilities for one or more persons.

APPRAISAL—An opinion as to the market value, estimated in terms of money, of a specific property, as of a specific date, supported by factual and relevant data. (See—M.A.I.; S.R.A.)

APPRAISER—One qualified by education, training and experience who is hired to estimate the value of real and personal property based on experience, judgment, facts, and use of formal appraisal processes. (See—M.A.I.; S.R.A.)

APPRECIATION—A rise in value as opposed to depreciation.

APPURTENANCE—Something annexed to another thing which may be transferred incident to it. That which belongs to another thing as a barn, dwelling, garage, or orchard is incident to the land to which it is attached. (See FIXTURE; TRADE FIXTURE.)

ARCHITECT'S PUNCH LIST—A list of discrepancies in building plans or other construction flaws written by the original architect during his final inspection of the structure.

ASSESSED VALUE—Value placed on property as a basis for taxation.

ASSESSMENT—Value of property for purposes of applying

taxation—often refers to the value assigned for such purpose. It does not imply true value. May also be "Special Assessment," which is a specific levy for a definite purpose (e.g., sewer, etc.). Also used in co-op apartments and condominiums as a special payment for a purpose or cost not usually funded through regular maintenance charge.

ASSIGNMENT—A transfer or making over to another of the whole of any property, real or personal, in possession or in action, or of any estate or right therein.

ASSISTED HOUSING—Housing, the construction, finance, or purchase of which is being assisted by the government. (See—B.S.P.R.A.; FHA; LOCAL HOUSING AUTHORITY.)

ASSUMPTION AGREEMENT—An undertaking or adoption of a debt or obligation primarily resting upon another person. The assumer becomes primarily liable and the original debtor becomes secondarily liable. (See—ASSUMPTION FEE; ASSUMPTION OF MORTGAGE; SUBJECT TO MORTGAGE.)

ASSUMPTION FEE—The fee paid to a lender (usually by the grantee) resulting from the assumption of a mortgage. (See—ASSUMPTION AGREEMENT; ASSUMPTION OF MORTGAGE.)

ASSUMPTION OF MORTGAGE—The taking of title to property by a grantee, wherein he assumes liability for payment of an existing note secured by a mortgage or deed of trust against the property; becoming a co-guarantor for the payment of a mortgage or deed of trust note. (See—ASSUMPTION AGREEMENT; ASSUMPTION FEE; SUBJECT TO MORTGAGE; SUBSTITUTION OF LIABILITY.)

ATTACHMENT—Seizure of property by court order, usually done to have it available in event a judgment is obtained in a pending suit.

B

BALLOON PAYMENT—A term generally used where the final installment payment on a note is greater than the preceding installment payments and it pays the note in full. The term may also be applied to an extraordinarily large interim payment.

BASE AND MERIDIAN—Imaginary lines used by surveyors to find and describe the location of private or public lands.

BENCH MARKS—A location indicated on a durable marker by surveyors.

BENEFICIARY—(1) One entitled to the benefit of a trust; (2) One who receives profit from an estate, the title to which is vested in a trustee; (3) The lender on the security of a note and deed of trust. (See—MORTGAGEE.)

BETTERMENT—An improvement upon property which increases the property value as distinguished from repairs or replacements, where the original character or cost is unchanged.

BLANKET MORTGAGE—A lien on more than one parcel or unit of land—frequently incurred by subdividers or developers who have purchased a single tract of land for the purpose of dividing it into smaller parcels for sale or development. Synonym: blanket trust deed. (See—MORTGAGE RELEASE PRICE.)

BLANKET TRUST DEED—(See—BLANKET MORTGAGE.)

BLIGHTED AREA—A declining area in which real property values are seriously affected by destructive economic forces, such as encroaching, inharmonious property usages, infiltration of lower social and economic classes of inhabitants, and/or rapidly depreciating buildings.

BONA FIDE—In good faith; without fraud.

BOOK COST—Total actual recorded cost including added capital improvements and before any charge for depreciation but with credit for partial liquidations.

BOOK VALUE—Amount at which an asset is carried on personal, partnership or corporate books; computed as cost less depreciation, plus improvements and additions. This value is the basis for computing profits (or losses) derived from a sale.

B.S.P.R.A.—Builder/Sponsor Profit and Risk Allowance—the developer's remuneration for assuming the risks involved in building low-income housing; e.g., FHA Section 236 housing; an amount regulated by the government. (See—ASSISTED HOUSING; FHA.)

BUDGET—A formal estimate of the most probable total costs of operation for a future period including allowance for expenses and capital outlays. Cash budget is forecast of disbursements in a coming period.

BUILDING EFFICIENCY—The ratio of net rentable area to total building area. Net rentable area will include areas such as conference rooms and other spaces (excepting halls, stairwells, etc.) available for private or occasional private use.

BUILT-INS—Cabinets or similar features built as part of the house.

BUNDLE OF RIGHTS—Beneficial interests or rights; e.g., access rights, the right to sell, rent, give away, etc.

BURN-OFF—Usually the amortization of front-end prepayments, e.g., prepaid interest. (See—AMORTIZATION.)

BUYER'S CLOSING COSTS—Escrow costs to the buyer, including his share of prorates, the cost of a policy of title insurance, etc. (See—SELLER'S CLOSING COSTS.)

BUYER'S COMMITMENT—The cash or other valuable consideration given by the buyer in a transaction either as a part of his initial investment (downpayment, prepaid interest, etc.), or his continuing commitment. This consideration may take the form of letters of credit, payment to third parties to reduce previously existing debt, or even labor performed by the buyer on the subject property without compensation. (See—CONTINUING COMMITMENT.)

BUYERS' EXTRAS—(See—CUSTOMERS' EXTRAS.)

BUY-OUT ESTIMATE—The projected cost of a structure based upon the price of jobs for which contracts have been completely let.

C

CAPITAL GAINS—In real estate, the difference between book value and selling price; used in compilation of tax liability.

CAPITALIZATION—The process of converting into present value a series of anticipated future annual installments of income by discounting them into a present worth at a specific rate of interest.

CARRYING CHARGES—Costs incurred by a developer, principally interest on land and construction loans and property taxes, to carry the property.

CASH FLOW—The net cash remaining after all operating and fixed charges including interest and principal payments, but excluding depreciation and income tax charges.

CASH-ON-CASH RETURN—The rate of return on an investment measured by the cash returned to the investor without regard to any tax savings.

C. C. & R.'s—Covenants, Conditions and Restrictions. (See CONDITION; COVENANT; RESTRICTION.)

CERTIFICATE OF OCCUPANCY—Written authorization given by a local municipality (e.g., a city's department of building and safety) allowing a newly completed, or substantially completed structure to be inhabited.

CERTIFICATE OF REASONABLE VALUE—A document required for federally insured (FHA), or guaranteed (VA) loans which evidences the physical inspection of a property by a federal employee to determine the loan-to-value ratio. Synonym: C.R.V. (See—FHA; VA LOAN.)

CHAIN OF TITLE—A history of conveyances and encumbrances affecting the title from the time the original patent was granted, or as far back as records are available.

CHANGE ORDER—A change in the original plan of construction by the owner or general contractor. Opposed to customers' extras.

CHATTEL MORTGAGE—A personal property mortgage. (See—SECURITY AGREEMENT; SECURITY INTEREST.)

CHATTEL REAL—An estate related to real estate, such as a lease on real property.

CHATTELS—(See—PERSONAL PROPERTY.)

CLOSING—(See—FORMAL CLOSING; PRECLOSING.)

CLOSING COSTS—(See—ESCROW COSTS.)

CLOUD ON TITLE—Any conditions revealed by a title search which affect the title to property; usually relatively unimportant items but which cannot be removed without a quit-claim deed or court action.

COMMERCIAL ACRE—A term applied to the remainder of an acre of newly subdivided land after the area devoted to streets, sidewalks and curbs, etc., has been deducted from the acre.

COMMISSION—Compensation paid to an independent contractor for service rendered on a customary or established percentage of the amount of principal involved in a transaction.

COMMITMENT FEE—The fee paid by a potential borrower to a potential lender for the lender's promise to lend in the future. The fee is usually a percentage of the expected loan. (See—LOAN COMMITMENT; STANDBY COMMITMENT.)

COMMON AREAS—Land or improvements existing for the benefit of all tenants, property owners, etc. For example, shopping center parking lots, and residential parks and playgrounds are common areas. Synonyms: green belts; median strips. (See—PLANNED-DEVELOPMENT PROJECT.)

COMMUNITY APARTMENT PROJECT—A subdivision where operation, maintenance, and control are usually exercised by a governing board elected by the owners of the fractional interests. An undivided interest in the property is conveyed, coupled with the right to occupy a certain unit or apartment. Synonym: cooperatives. (See—CONDOMINIUM.)

COMMUNITY PROPERTY—A form of ownership of property, different in characteristics from joint tenancy or tenancy in common. In certain states, such as California, property acquired during a marriage is presumed to be community property when not acquired as a separate property of either spouse.

COMPARABLES—Properties which have been recently sold, which have characteristics similar to property under consideration, thereby indicating the approximate fair market value of the subject property.

COMPENSATING BALANCE—(See—LINK FINANCING.)

COMPLETED CONTRACT METHOD—A method of recording income from construction contracts where income is recorded upon completion of the project. Opposed to percentage-of-completion method.

CONDEMNATION—The act of taking private property for public use by a political subdivision; declaration that a structure is unfit for use.

CONDITION—A qualification annexed to an estate, upon the happening of which the estate is enlarged or defeated. In a deed, a condition may give the grantor the power to terminate the interest conveyed in the event a violation of the condition occurs. (See—C.C. & R'S.)

CONDITIONAL COMMITMENT—A commitment of a definite loan amount for some future unknown purchaser of satisfactory credit standing.

CONDITIONAL SALES CONTRACT—(See—SALES CONTRACT.)

CONDOMINIUM—A system of individual fee ownership of units in a multifamily structure, combined with joint ownership of common areas of the structure and the land. Sometimes referred to as a vertical subdivision. (See—COMMUNITY APARTMENT PROJECT.)

CONSTRUCTION COSTS—Direct costs to improve raw land. Opposed to land, finance, and sales costs. (See—OFF-SITE COSTS; ON-SITE COSTS.)

CONSTRUCTION LOAN—Financing arranged for the development of real property. Opposed to land loan, or permanent loan. Synonyms: interim loan; intermediate financing.

CONSTRUCTION LOAN DRAW—A partial funding of the construction loan. Synonym: draw.

CONSTRUCTIVE NOTICE—Notice given by the public records.

CONTINUING COMMITMENT—The consideration given by a buyer in a transaction after his initial investment. This would generally take the form of regular level payments which fully amortize the debt instrument held by the seller over a reasonable period. (See—BUYER'S COMMITMENT.)

CONTRACT OF SALE—(See—SALES CONTRACT.)

CONTRACTOR—(See—GENERAL CONTRACTOR; SUBCONTRACTOR.)

CONTRACT RENT—Rent as called for in the rental or lease agreement. Opposed to economic rent.

CONVENTIONAL LOANS—Loans made by private institutions (conventional lenders) which are *not* insured by a government agency. (See—GOVERNMENT LOANS; GUARANTEED LOANS; INSURED LOANS.)

CONVEYANCE—The transfer of the title of land from one to another. It denotes an instrument which carries from one person to another an interest in land.

CO-OPERATIVES—A facility in which ownership purchases participation to the extent of value; title is by proprietary lease. (See—STOCK COOPERATIVE PROJECT.)

CORPORATION—An artificial personality created by law for the conduct of business or other legal activities. Liability is limited to extent of its capital.

COST CERTIFICATION—Term generally applied to the independently audited statement of FHA insured housing projects as required by Section 227 of the National Housing Act, and FHA regulations. (See—FHA.)

COST-PLUS CONTRACT—A type of construction contract where the contract price is equal to the cost of construction plus a profit allowance to the builder. Opposed to fixed price contract.

COVENANT—An agreement contained in a deed or other instrument for the performance or nonperformance of a certain act, or the use or nonuse of property in a certain manner. (See—C.C. & R.'S.)

CREDIT REPORT—A report to a prospective lender on the credit standing of the prospective borrower—often requested by the lender/seller concerning the borrower/buyer in conjunction with the escrow.

C.R.V.—Certificate of Reasonable Value.

CURTAIL SCHEDULE—A listing of the amounts by which the principal sum of an obligation is to be reduced by partial payments and of the dates when each payment will become payable. Synonym: mortgage amortization schedule.

CUSTOMERS' EXTRAS—Improvements not included in original plans, but requested by the buyer. Synonym: buyers' extras.

D

DEBT SERVICE—The sum of principal and interest portions of the payment necessary to amortize a loan—the total loan payment.

DEDICATION—An appropriation of land by its owner for some public use accepted for such use by authorized public officials on behalf of the public.

DEED—Written instrument which, when properly executed and delivered, conveys title.

DEED IN LIEU—A deed given by an owner/debtor in lieu of foreclosure by the lender/mortgagee. (See—FORECLOSURE.)

DEED OF TRUST—(See—TRUST DEED.)

DEFAULT—Failure to fulfill a duty or promise or to discharge an obligation; omission or failure to perform any act of foreclosure by the lender/mortgagee.

DEFEASANCE CLAUSE—The clause in a mortgage that gives the mortgagor the right to redeem his property upon the payment of his obligations to the mortgagee.

DEFERRED PAYMENT SALE—A sale where the proceeds are to be received in more than one payment.

DEFICIENCY JUDGMENT—A judgment given when the security pledged for a loan does not satisfy the debt upon its default. (See—EXCULPATORY PROVISION; PURCHASE MONEY MORTGAGE OR TRUST DEED.)

DEPRECIATION—In valuation, a deduction from the upper limits of value caused by deterioration and obsolescence and location. In *taxation*, an allowance for recapture of investment, deductible from income derived from the investment, not attributable to land. *Accelerated:* Depreciation methods other than straight line (i.e., 125 percent, 150 percent, 200 percent declining balance methods and sum-of-the-digits method). *Curable physical:* Is synonymous with deferred maintenance. It is a reduction in value resulting from neglect or deferment of regular maintenance and repair. *125 percent:* An accounting method in which the percentage annual charge is 1 to 114 times the applicable straight line recapture; percentage charged reduces basis or improvement value before calculating the present year by the amount deducted in the previous fiscal period. There is no salvage value. (See applicable tax laws). *150 percent:* Same as 125 percent except the annual percentage charge is at 1½ times the straight line allowance. (See applicable tax laws.) *200 percent:* Same as 125 percent except that the percentage annual charge is twice the straight line percentage. Available only to a "first used." *Straight Line:* Accounting method based on total remaining economic life of improvements, in which an equal annual percentage charge is made so the entire established improvement value will be reduced to salvage value at the end of the estimated economic life (salvage value is deducted—if appropriate). *Sum-of-Years Digits:* The Digits (1, 2, 3, 4 . . .) for all years of estimated economic life are totaled and become the denominator of the depreciation fraction with the numerator being the number of years remaining economic life at the beginning of the depreciation year. The fraction is multiplied by the building value to determine the depreciation charge. Available only to a "first user." Salvage value is deducted, if appropriate. (See tax laws.) (See—AMORTIZATION.)

DEPRECIATION, FUTURE—The loss in value which will probably occur in the future.

DEPRECIATION, INCURABLE PHYSICAL—A reduction in value resulting from wear and tear, use or deterioration, the repair of which cannot be economically justified.

DEPRECIATION, PAST—Loss in value which has already taken place resulting from any cause.

DETERIORATION—Impairment of condition. One of the causes of depreciation and reflecting the loss in value brought about by wear and tear, disintegration, use in service, and the action of the elements.

DIRECTIONAL GROWTH—The location or direction toward which the residential sections of a city are destined or determined to grow.

DISCOUNT POINTS—(See—LOAN FEE.)

DRAW—(See—CONSTRUCTION LOAN DRAW.)

DUE ON SALE CLAUSE—(See—ACCELERATION CLAUSE.)

E

EARNEST MONEY—Something of value given as a portion of the price of property, usually in a contract's preliminary stages, which evidences the good faith of the buyer. (See—SALES DEPOSIT RECEIPT.)

EASEMENT—A right, privilege or interest which one party has in the land of another. (Example: right of way.)

ECONOMIC RENT—Optimum rent that a dwelling unit might bring if currently rented in the open market—the fair rental value of a dwelling unit. Opposed to contract rent.

EFFECTIVE GROSS INCOME—The gross possible income attributable to a property after allowance for vacancy and collection losses. Referred to as E.G.I.

EFFECTIVE SECOND LIEN—(See—A.I.T.D.)

EMINENT DOMAIN—The right of the government to acquire property for necessary public or quasi-public use by condemnation; the owner must be fairly compensated.

ENCUMBRANCE—Anything which affects or limits the fee simple title to property, such as mortgages, easements or restrictions of any kind. Liens are special encumbrances which make the property security for the payment of a debt or obligation such as mortgages and taxes.

EQUITY—The interest or value which an owner has in real estate over and above the liens against it.

EQUITY KICKER—A term usually applied to the income participation (equity participation) given to a lender, broker, syndicator, etc., as part of the consideration for his service.

EQUITY OF REDEMPTION—The right to redeem property during the foreclosure period, such as a mortgagor's right to redeem within a year after foreclosure sale. (See—MORTGAGE; REDEMPTION.)

ESCALATOR CLAUSE—A clause in a contract providing for the upward or downward adjustment of certain items to cover specified contingencies; e.g., the provision in a lease to cover increased property taxes and operating costs.

ESCHEAT—The reverting of property to the State when heirs capable of inheriting are lacking.

ESCROW—The deposit of instruments and funds with instructions to a third neutral party to carry out the provisions of an agreement or contract; when everything is deposited to enable carrying out the instructions, it is called a complete or perfect escrow.

ESCROW CLOSING—(See—FORMAL CLOSING.)

ESCROW COMPANY—(See—ESCROW HOLDER.)

ESCROW COSTS—All the costs to the buyer and seller individually which are associated with the purchase/sale or financing of real property. These include prorates, the cost of title insurance policies, the cost of credit reports, recording fees, escrow fees, etc. Synonyms: closing costs; settlement costs. (See—ESCROW FEES; PRORATES; RECORDING FEE.)

ESCROW DEPOSITORY—(See—ESCROW HOLDER.)

ESCROW FEES—Fees charged by the escrow holder for his services. (See—ESCROW COSTS.)

ESCROW HOLDER—The person or organization having a fiduciary responsibility to both buyer and seller (or lender and borrower) to see that the terms of the purchase/sale (or loan) are carried out. Synonyms: escrow company; escrow depository. (See—ESCROW INSTRUCTIONS; ESCROW STATEMENT.)

ESCROW INSTRUCTIONS—Instructions to the escrow holder given, for example, by the buyer and seller as to the terms of the purchase/sale, which may, but do not necessarily, supercede the terms of the deposit receipt. Escrow instructions may constitute a valid contract of sale. (See—ESCROW HOLDER; ESCROW STATEMENT; SALES DEPOSIT RECEIPT.)

ESCROW SETTLEMENT SHEET—(See—ESCROW STATEMENT.)

ESCROW STATEMENT—Document given, for example, to buyer and seller at the escrow closing itemizing the terms and associated costs of the sale. A statement of the escrow transaction. Synonym: escrow settlement sheet. (See—ESCROW INSTRUCTIONS; ESCROW HOLDER; PRORATES.)

ESTATE—As applied to the real-estate practice, the term signifies the quantity of interest, share, right, equity, of which riches or fortune may consist, in real property. The degree, quantity, nature, and extent of interest which a person has in real property.

ESTATE FOR YEARS—An interest in lands by virtue of a contract for the possession of them for a definite and limited period of time. A lease is an estate for years.

EXCLUSIVE AGENCY LISTING—A written instrument giving one agent the right to sell property for a specified time but reserving the right of the owner to sell the property himself without the payment of a commission.

EXCLUSIVE-RIGHT-TO-SELL LISTING—A written agreement between owner and agent giving agent the right to collect a commission if the property is sold by anyone during the term of his agreement.

EXCULPATORY PROVISION—The provision in an agreement holding one party harmless in the event of some default, etc. For example, the provision in a note that the debtor will not be held personally liable in the event of a default. (See—DEFICIENCY JUDGMENT; NONRECOURSE NOTE; PURCHASE MONEY MORTGAGE OR TRUST DEED.)

EXIT PENALTY—(See—WALK-AWAY RISK.)

F

FAIR MARKET PRICE—(See—FAIR MARKET VALUE.)

FAIR MARKET VALUE—The price a given property will bring if exposed for sale in the open market allowing a reasonable time to find a buyer who buys with knowledge of all the uses to which it is adapted and to which it is capable of being adapted. Synonyms: fair market price; F.M.V.; market price; market value.

FANNY MAY—(See—F.N.M.A.)

FEDERAL INSURED LOANS—(See—FHA; INSURED LOANS.)

FEE—Ownership of real property which is not limited as to duration, disposition or descendability, as opposed to a life estate or an estate for a term of years (leasehold). In modern usage, the terms "Fee" and "Fee Title" are equivalent.

FEE TITLE—(See—FEE.)

FEASIBILITY STUDY—Application of the principles of an analytic program of study to a proposed project with analysis of attainable income, probable expenses and most advantageous uses and design.

FHA—Federal Housing Administration. A division of HUD which administers the provisions of the National Housing Act. In its operations, the FHA does not make loans; it insures loans made by supervised financial institutions. It has the authority to : (1) insure loans made to the homeowner for the repair, alteration and improvement of his property; and (2) insure lending institutions against loss from mortgage loans made on one- to four-family houses and large rental projects. Some of the more frequently encountered sections of the National Housing Act are:

Section 203—This section provides for financing the construction or purchase of one to four family dwellings, single-family dwellings for victims of major disaster and low-cost single-family homes in suburban and outlying areas.

Section 207—This section is designed for seasonal homes, trailer parks, and more deluxe apartment units with market rate rents and market rate interest on 40-year mortgage loans equal to 90 percent of the replacement cost of the projects.

Section 221 (d) (3)—This section is similar to Section 236 except that the interest rate on the 40-year mortgage loan may be at the market rate or below the market rate with rent supplement subsidies available in either case.

Section 234—This section provides for financing the purchase or construction of multifamily structures where the individual purchases the unit and is given deed to same along with undivided interest in common areas and facilities. This section is commonly known as the Condominium Housing Program.

Section 235(i)—The Section 235(i) single-family home-ownership program provides mortgage insurance and monthly interest subsidy payments to mortgage lenders for the benefit of low-income purchasers, similar to Section 236 assistance payments.

Section 236—The Section 236 program provides for federal insurance of private 40-year mortgages of up to 90 percent of the FHA-certified replacement cost of multifamily housing. The program also provides for monthly interest reduction payments from the government to the mortgage lender, which are passed on to the residents in the form of lower rents. Rent supplement assistance is also available in this program. (See—ASSISTED HOUSING; B.S.P.R.A.; CERTIFICATE OF OCCUPANCY; COST CERTIFICATE; FEDERAL INSURED LOANS.)

FILL-UP PERIOD—(See—RENT-UP PERIOD.)

FINANCE COSTS—Costs (principally interest and loan fees) incurred to finance construction of a project. (See—LOAN FEE.)

FIRST USER—Any owner who develops or acquires property new and wherein no benefits from the improvements thereon have been received by anyone prior to acquisition.

FIXED DISBURSEMENT SCHEDULE—A disbursement system on a construction loan where the lender and borrower have agreed on the number of payments which will be made during the construction period and at which stages these payments will be made. Opposed to the voucher system.

FIXED PRICE CONTRACT—A type of construction contract where the contract price is a specific sum, agreed to before construction begins. Opposed to cost-plus contract.

FIXTURES—Appurtenances attached to the land or improvements, which usually cannot be removed without agreement as they become real property. (See—APPURTENANCE.)

FMV—Fair Market Value.

FNMA—Federal National Mortgage Association. A private corporation designed to operate in the secondary mortgage market. Synonym: Fanny May. (See—GNMA.)

FORECLOSURE—Procedure whereby property pledged as security for a debt is sold to pay the debt in event of default in payments or terms. (See—DEED IN LIEU; NOTICE OF DEFAULT.)

FORFEITURE—Loss of money or anything of value, due to failure to perform.

FORMAL CLOSING—Legal transfer of title, e.g., from seller to buyer. Synonyms: closing; escrow closing; legal closing. (See—PRECLOSING.)

FRONTAGE—The front boundary line of a lot facing the street.

FRONT-END MONEY—Capital required, costs incurred, or money paid at the beginning of a project, transaction, etc. Sometimes synonymous with start-up costs or seed money.

FRONT FOOT—A measure of lot size related to the width of the lot at the street. Generally used in valuing commercial properties.

G

GAP FINANCING—A loan given to fulfill a temporary need of the borrower until a permanent loan can be received. For example, a permanent lender may require a minimum occupancy level in a new apartment building before he will make the permanent loan. To fill the "gap" between the construction and permanent loans, the developer needs gap financing. (See—STANDBY COMMITMENT.)

GAP LOAN—Usually in the form of a second mortgage to finance a difference between the first mortgage and added project costs. Also applies to commercial property occupancy achievement where a portion of the first mortgage may be "held back" until sufficient occupancy is attained.

GENERAL CONTRACTOR—A person who performs or supervises the construction or development of some property pursuant to the terms of a primary contract between himself and the owner. The general contractor may use his own employees for this work and/or the services of other contractors (subcontractors). Synonym: contractor.

GIFT DEED—A deed for which the consideration is love and affection and where there is no material consideration.

GINNIE MAY—(See—GNMA.)

GNMA—Government National Mortgage Association. Under the Housing and Urban Development Act of 1968, the existing FNMA was divided into two separate, noncompeting corporations, GNMA assuming the federal agency responsibilities once held by FNMA alone. GNMA provides a secondary market for housing mortgages and special assistance to housing mortgages financing housing under certain FHA mortgage-insurance programs. Synonym: Ginnie May. (See—TANDEM PLAN.)

GNMA MORTGAGE-BACKED SECURITIES—Securities (backed by FHA, VA or Farmers Home Administration mortgages) which are guaranteed by GNMA. The security holder is assured of timely payment of principal and interest by the "full faith and credit of the U.S. Treasury" behind the GNMA guarantee. (See—MORTGAGE-BACKED SECURITIES.)

GOVERNMENT LOANS—Loans made directly by a government agency; e.g., Cal-Vet loans, which are government loans made directly to qualifying veterans by the California State Department of Veterans' Affairs. Under the terms of this plan, title to the veteran's property remains in the hands of the State, thus making the transaction similar to a sales contract. (See—CONVENTIONAL LOANS.)

GRADUATE LEASE—Lease which provides for a varying

rental rate, often based upon future determination; sometimes rent is based upon result of periodical appraisals; used largely in long-term leases.

GRANT—A technical term made use of in deeds of conveyance of lands to import a transfer.

GRANT DEED—Under a grant deed, the grantor warrants that *he* has not previously conveyed or encumbered the property; is it *not* a warranty that he is the owner of the property, or that it is not encumbered. A grant deed also conveys any after-acquired title of the grantor, unless a different intent is expressed. (See—QUITCLAIM DEED; WARRATY DEED.)

GREEN BELTS—(See—COMMON AREAS.)

GROSS MONTHLY MULTIPLIER—(See—GROSS RENT MULTIPLE.)

GROSS MULTIPLIER—(See—GROSS RENT MULTIPLE.)

GROSS RENT MULTIPLE—A figure used to compare rental properties, giving the relationship between the rental value and the sales price. Synonyms: gross monthly multiplier; gross multiplier.

GROUND LEASE—An agreement for the use of the land only, sometimes secured by improvements placed on the land by the user. Synonym: land lease.

GROUND RENT—Payment for the use of land based on its market value after the allocation of value to the improvements.

GUARANTEED LOANS—Loans guaranteed by a government agency or any other interested party; e.g., VA loans. (See—CONVENTIONAL LOANS.)

H

HARD DOLLARS—(See—HARD MONEY.)

HARD MONEY—Money given in exchange for an improved equity or ownership position in a transaction; e.g., cash down (down payment), and the principal portion of debt service. Money paid which is *not* tax deductible by the payor. Opposite of soft money. Synonym: hard dollars. (See—HARD MONEY EQUIVALENTS.)

HARD MONEY EQUIVALENTS—The sum of hard money and a portion of soft money equal to the amount the payor would *not* receive back in tax savings; e.g., if the payor is in a 30 percent tax bracket, his equivalent hard money payment would equal hard money plus 70 percent of soft money. (See—HARD MONEY.)

HIGHEST AND BEST USE—Use which, at a specific time, is

most likely to produce the greatest net return to the land and/or building over a given period of time. Synonym: most profitable use.

HOLD-HARMLESS TRUST DEED—(See—A.I.T.D.)

HOUSE COSTS—(See—ON-SITE COSTS.)

HUD—Housing and Urban Development Agency—An agency of the federal government, established by the Housing and Urban Development Act of 1965. FHA is a division of HUD.

HYPOTHECATE—To give a thing as security without the necessity of giving up possession of it.

I

IMPOUNDS—Payments made to a fiduciary (usually a lender) in addition to principal and interest portions of loan amortization, for the purpose of paying property taxes, assessments, insurance, etc. Impounds offer additional security to the lender that no tax liens, etc., will be imposed against the property on which he has made a loan.

IMPROVED LAND—Land on which onsite and/or offsite work has been performed. Opposed to unimproved or raw land.

IMPUTATION OF INTEREST—The use of present value measurements to re-evaluate a note when the face amount and the stated interest rate do not reasonably represent the present value of the consideration given or received in the exchange. This circumstance may arise if the note is non-interest bearing or has a stated interest rate which is different from the rate of interest appropriate for the debt at the date of the transaction.

INCOME, EFFECTIVE STABILIZED GROSS—The appraiser's or manager's estimate of stabilized gross income. (See—INCOME, STABILIZED GROSS; INCOME, STABILIZED NET OPERATING.)

INCOME, GROSS POTENTIAL—Sometimes referred to as stabilized gross income. Total periodic income collectable from the operation of a property on the basis of current economic rent (not necessarily existing rents or contract rents); without deducting vacancy. (See—INCOME, STABILIZED GROSS.)

INCOME, NET OPERATION—Net income after all current income and expenses including real-estate taxes, but before income taxes or depreciation.

INCOME, OTHER—Income from coin-operated laundry or other vending machines, etc., and not rent.

INCOME STABILIZED GROSS—The appraiser or manager's estimate of gross potential income from all sources based on past performance, definitive trends, and an analysis of competitive rentals for similar facilities in the area, for the foreseeable future. (See —INCOME, EFFECTIVE STABILIZED GROSS; INCOME, GROSS POTENTIAL; INCOME, STABILIZED NET OPERATING.)

INCOME, STABILIZED NET OPERATING—The remainder after deduction of expenses of operation from effective stabilized gross income (expenses of operation include all operational expenses, but not depreciation or mortgage requirements). (See—INCOME, EFFECTIVE STABILIZED GROSS.)

INCUBATION PERIOD—(See—RENT-UP PERIOD.)

INJUNCTION—A writ or order issued under the seal of a court to restrain one or more parties to a suit or proceeding from doing an act which is deemed to be inequitable or unjust in regard to the rights of some other party or parties in the suit or proceeding.

IN REM NOTE—(See—NONRECOURSE NOTE; PURCHASE MONEY MORTGAGE OR TRUST DEED.)

INSTALLMENT NOTE—A note which provides that payments of a certain sum or amount be paid on the dates specified in the instrument.

INSURED LOANS—Loans insured by a government agency; e.g., FHA loans. (See—CONVENTIONAL LOANS; FEDERAL INSURANCE LOANS.)

INTEREST—Money paid for the use of money; may be at a constant rate or fixed percentage or: a) add-on of a constant rate for the entire amount; or b) as a discount deducted from the face amount in advance.

INTERIM FINANCING—Temporary loan to be repaid from proceeds of a committed term loan.

INTERIM LOAN—(See—CONSTRUCTION LOAN.)

INTERMEDIATE FINANCING—(See—CONSTRUCTION LOAN.)

INVESTMENT TAX CREDIT—7 percent of the original cost for certain specified improvements (elevators, boilers, heavy machinery, etc.), which sum is directly deductible from the calculated income tax only during the year of such improvements. (Consult applicable tax regulations).

INVOLUNTARY LIEN—A lien imposed against property without consent of an owner; example: taxes, special assessments, federal income tax liens, judgment liens, etc. (See—VOLUNTARY LIEN.)

J

JOINT NOTE—A note signed by two or more persons who have equal liability for payment.

JOINT TENANCY—Joint ownership by two or more persons with right of survivorship; all joint tenants own equal interest and have equal rights in the property. (See—RIGHT OF SURVIVORSHIP; TENANCY IN COMMON.)

JUNIOR LIEN—A subordinate lien. (See—SUBORDINATE.)

L

LABOR AND MATERIAL RELEASE—A document signed by laborers and materialmen, given to the developer, waiving their rights under any mechanic's lien—given upon the completion of their work. Synonym: materials release. (See—RELEASES.)

LAND BANKING—A financing activity similar to making a land loan whereby a land owner deeds over his property to a lending institution in exchange for cash and an option to repurchase the property in the future.

LAND CONTRACT—(See—SALES CONTRACT.)

LAND COST—All the costs associated with the purchase of land; e.g., purchase price plus recording fees, escrow costs, interest on land loans, and property taxes prior to construction.

LAND LOAN—A loan received to finance the purchase of raw land. Land loans are usually subordinated to, or paid off by, the construction loan when the latter is taken out. (See—SUBORDINATE.)

LAND PLANNER—A person or firm whose functions generally include the determination of the appropriateness of the location within the larger community, the integration of the particular development and its facilities with those of the various development standards such as density, community service, functional design, and others which would lead to the visual quality and general livability achieved by the final development. Synonym: site planner. (See—SUBDIVISION.)

LEASE, GROSS—Lease under which the lessor pays all expenses of operation of the property, including capital charges.

LEASE, LAND—A lease of ground which provides that lessee assumes all property charges, including charges against land and improvements to be constructed by the lessee. Synonym: ground lease. (See—SUBORDINATION.)

LEASE, NET—Lease which reimburses owner for all regular operating costs in excess of an agreed sum.

LEASE, NET-NET—Lease under which, in addition to agreed rental, tenant assumes the obligation to pay directly all operating costs excluding only income taxes and mortgage loan service but including repairs and replacements, taxes, maintenance, insurance premiums, utilities, etc.

LEASE, PERCENTAGE—A lease which provides rental shall be based on a percentage of the volume of business done on the premises; usually with guaranteed minimum and occasionally with a maximum rental regardless of the business volume.

LEASE, SUB—Assignment of a lease or subletting of leased premises where the original contract lessee continues responsibility for performance.

LEASEHOLD FINANCING—A loan to a lessee upon the security of his leasehold estate. In some cases, under the terms of the lease the owner of the property is required to "subordinate" to the leasehold; i.e., hypothecate his ownership interest in the property as further security for the loan to the lessee.

LEASEHOLD INTEREST—The rights of the lessee to the benefits obtainable from lease covenants.

LEGAL CLOSING—(See—FORMAL CLOSING.)

LEGAL DESCRIPTION—A description recognized by law; a description by which property can be definitely located by reference to government surveys or approved recorded maps.

LEVERAGE—Term applied to investment benefit created by using a large proportion of borrowed funding; technically refers to the differential between the investment's earned yield and the cost of the borrowed funds.

LHA—Local Housing Authority. (See—ASSISTED HOUSING.)

LIEN—A form of encumbrance which usually makes property security for the payment of a debt or discharge of an obligation. Example: judgments, taxes, mortgages, deeds of trust, etc.

LIMITED PARTNERSHIP—A partnership composed of some partners whose contributions and liabilities are limited.

LINK FINANCING—Additional financing received to cover the amount of a compensating balance. For example, a lender of $50,000 requires a compensating balance of $10,000 to be held in the borrower's checking account—link financing of $10,000 is the additional need of the borrower to give him the $50,000 he requires.

LISTING—An employment contract between principal and agent authorizing the agent to perform services for the principal involving the latter's property; listing contracts are entered into for the purpose of securing persons to buy, lease or rent property. Employment of an agent by a prospective purchaser or lessee to locate property for purchase or lease may be considered a listing.

LOAN COMMITMENT—A written promise by a lender to loan a certain sum at a certain rate of interest. Loan commitments usually are paid for (the commitment fee) and are for a specified length of time. (See—COMMITMENT FEE; STANDBY COMMITMENT.)

LOAN FEE—The fee paid to a lender for his service of making the loan (appraisal and inspection fees, etc.) or an amount paid in addition to interest (points). Loan fees are generally a percentage of the face amount of the loan. Synonyms: discount points; mortgage discount; points. (See—FINANCE COSTS.)

LOAN TO FACILITATE—A loan made, often with particularly favorable terms, to facilitate the purchase of real property from the lender, usually a savings and loan institution, with respect to repossessed property. (See—R.E.O.)

LOCAL HOUSING AUTHORITY—The *local* government organization responsible for low- and middle-income housing.

LOCK-IN PERIOD—Period in which a lender will prohibit the borrower from selling or otherwise transferring the property which secures the note, or from prepaying any or all of the balance of the note. (See—PREPAYMENT PENALTY.)

LOT BOOK—A record maintained by a title company to furnish a ready means of ascertaining what transactions have been recorded by the county recorder affecting a particular parcel of real property; a reflection of every instrument describing real property that has been recorded in the county in which the land lies. (See—TITLE INSURANCE.)

M

M.A.I.—The designation of an appraiser who is a member of the American Institute of Appraisers of the National Association of Real Estate Boards. (See—APPRAISAL; APPRAISER; S.R.A.)

MANAGEMENT SURVEY—Complete analysis of the economic, physical and operating aspects of a property with recommendations as to use, change of use, occupancy and benefits to ownership.

MARGIN OF SECURITY—The difference between the amount of the mortgage loan(s) and the appraised value of the property.

MARGINAL LAND—Land which barely pays the cost of working or using.

MARKET PRICE—The price paid regardless of pressures, motives or intelligence. (See—FAIR MARKET VALUE.)

MARKET RENT—The rental which real estate can command in the open market at any given time for its highest and best use.

MARKET VALUE—(See—FAIR MARKET VALUE.)

MARKETABLE TITLE—Merchantable title; free and clear of objectionable liens or encumbrances.

MASTER PLAN—(See—PLANNING COMMISSION.)

MATERIALS BOND—Insurance to the beneficiary (e.g., a contractor) that the person posting the bond (e.g., a supplier) will provide the materials necessary for the completion of some work. (See—PERFORMANCE BOND.)

MATERIALS RELEASE—(See—LABOR AND MATERIALS RELEASE.)

MECHANICS' LIEN—A lien in favor of persons providing labor, services, or materials in connection with the improvement of property. (See—NOTICE OF COMPLETION.)

MEDIAN STRIPS—(See—COMMON AREAS.)

METES AND BOUNDS—A term used in describing the boundary lines of land, setting forth all the boundary lines together with their terminal points and angles.

M.G.I.C.—Mortgage Guaranty Insurance Corporation. The principal underwriter of FHA mortgage insurance programs. (See—MORTGAGE GUARANTY INSURANCE.)

MINIMUM PROPERTY STANDARDS—Sets forth the overall minimum technical standards acceptable to the FHA.

MODEL FURNISHINGS—Furniture and other improvements located in model homes of a real-estate development.

MORTGAGE—An instrument recognized by law by which property is hypothecated to secure the payment of a debt or obligation; procedure for foreclosure in event of default is established by statute. (See—EQUITY OF REDEMPTION; TRUST DEED.)

MORTGAGE AMORTIZATION SCHEDULE—(See—CURTAIL SCHEDULE.)

MORTGAGE-BACKED SECURITIES—Bond-type investment securities representing an undivided interest in a pool of mortgages or trust deeds. Income from the underlying mortgage is used to pay off the securities. (See—GNMA MORTGAGE-BACKED SECURITIES.)

MORTGAGE BANKER—A firm or individual acting as a principal—committing his own money to a loan, and usually servicing the loan. Opposed to mortgage broker.

MORTGAGE BROKER—A licensed real-estate broker who brings the borrower and lender together, receiving a commission—he does *not* commit his own money. Opposed to mortgage banker.

MORTGAGE DISCOUNT—(See—LOAN FEE.)

MORTGAGE FOR FUTURE ADVANCES—(See—OPEN-END LOANS.)

MORTGAGE GUARANTY INSURANCE—Insurance against financial loss available to mortgage lenders. (See—M.G.I.C.)

MORTGAGE RELEASE PRICE—A prearranged amount repaid to a lender to relinquish his lien on an individual parcel, usually upon its sale. For example, when a completed house within a subdivision is sold, the mortgage release price is paid to the lender (usually of a blanket mortgage) to release his lien on the property. (See—BLANKET MORTGAGE; RELEASE CLAUSE; RELEASES.)

MORTGAGEE—One to whom a mortgagor gives a mortgage to secure a loan or assure performance of an obligation; a lender. (See—BENEFICIARY.)

MORTGAGOR—One who gives a mortgage to secure a loan or assure performance of an obligation; a borrower. (See—TRUSTOR.)

MOST PROFITABLE USE—(See—HIGHEST AND BEST USE.)

MULTIPLE LISTING—A listing, usually an exclusive right to sell, taken by a member of an organization composed of real-estate brokers.

MUTUAL WATER COMPANY—A water company organized by or for water users in a given district with the object of securing an ample water supply at a reasonable rate; stock is issued to users.

N

NEGATIVE CASH FLOW—The stream of cash expenditures in connection with the operation of an income-producing property in excess of the cash receipts generated from the property.

NET AFTER TAXES—Net operating income after all charges, including income taxes. Synonym: stabilized net after taxes.

NET LEASE—In general usage, a lease which includes a provision that the lessee pays for some of the direct expenses associated with the leased property; e.g., property taxes. The term "net-net lease" implies that additional expenses are paid by the lessee, and the term "net-net-net lease" implies that all of the expenses associated with the leased property are paid by the lessee. It should be noted that the specific expenses involved will vary among lease agreements.

NET LISTING—A listing which provides that the agent may retain as compensation for his services all sums received over and above a net price to the owner.

NET REALIZABLE VALUE—Fair market value reduced by the cost to dispose. Synonym: N.R.V.

NONRECOURSE NOTE—A debt instrument whereby the lender has *no* recourse against the borrower personally, but must look solely to the property for repayment. Synonyms: in rem note; purchase money mortgage. (See—EXCULPATORY PROVISION; RECOURSE NOTE.)

NOTE—A signed written instrument acknowledging a debt and promising payment.

NOTICE OF COMPLETION—Notice recorded after completion of construction. Mechanics' liens must be filed within a specified period thereafter, usually 30 to 60 days. (See—MECHANIC'S LIEN.)

NOTICE OF DEFAULT—A notice recorded after the occurrence of a default under a deed of trust. (See—FORECLOSURE.)

NOTICE OF NONRESPONSIBILITY—Notice given by an owner to relieve the land from mechanics' liens under prescribed conditions. The notice generally must be posted upon the property and recorded in the county in which the land is situated.

NOTICE TO QUIT—An eviction notice.

N.R.V.—(See—NET REALIZATION VALUE.)

O

OBSOLESCENCE, CURABLE—Loss in value due to being out of date, or due to functional deficiency (not deterioration) but which can be corrected with economic advantage.

OFF-SITE COSTS—Costs incurred for the improvement of raw

land that are not associated with the construction of buildings. Off-site improvements include curbs, gutters, sidewalks, and streets. Opposed to on-site costs. (See—CONSTRUCTION COSTS.)

ON-SITE COSTS—Costs incurred for the actual construction of buildings. Opposed to off-site costs. Synonym: house costs. (See—CONSTRUCTION COSTS.)

OPEN-END LOANS—Secured loans that provide for sums of money to be lent to the same borrower at various times. In operation, this type of loan actually amounts to a continuing source of credit for the borrower. Synonyms: mortgage for future advances; open-end trust deed.

OPEN-END TRUST DEED—(See—OPEN-END LOANS.)

OPEN LISTING—An authorization given by a property owner to a real-estate agent wherein said agent is given the nonexclusive right to secure a purchaser; open listings may be given to any number of agents without liability to compensate any except the one who first secures a buyer ready, willing and able to meet the terms of the listing, or secures the acceptance by the seller of a satisfactory offer.

OPERATING RATIO—Percentage expressing relationship of stabilized operating expenses to effective gross income.

OPTION—Special right or privilege granted by one contracting party to the other for a valuable consideration and upon terms and conditions agreed to in writing.

OPTION LISTING—A listing agreement in which the broker has an option to purchase the property.

ORIENTATION—Placing a house on its lot with regard to its exposure to the rays of the sun, prevailing winds, privacy from the street and protection from outside noises.

OVERALL-CAPITALIZATION RATE—A single rate which is applied to the net operating income (with provision for interest on and return of the investment), in estimating valuation of the property; i.e., land and improvements thereon.

OVER IMPROVEMENT—An improvement which is not the highest and best use for the side on which it is placed by reason of excess size or cost.

OVERLAPPING DEED OF TRUST—(See—WRAPAROUND MORTGAGE OR TRUST DEED.)

OVERRIDING TRUST DEED—(See—A.I.T.D.)

P

PACKAGING—The activity of performing or arranging the performance of certain initial development activities such as market research, land evaluation, land acquisition, project design and concept, architecture, engineering, zoning and obtaining financing.

PARTICIPATION—A sharing of ownership and/or other benefits by a lender as inducement for making a loan.

PERCENTAGE LEASE—Lease on property, the rental for which is determined by amount of business done by the lessee; usually a percentage of gross receipts from the business with provision for a minimum rental.

PERCENTAGE-OF-COMPLETION METHOD—A method of recording income from construction contracts where income is recorded based on costs incurred to date, to total estimated costs of construction. Opposed to the completed contract method.

PERFORMANCE BOND—Insurance to the beneficiary (e.g., the client) that all the work specified in some contract will be performed by the person posting the bond (e.g., the contractor). (See—MATERIALS BOND.)

PERMANENT LOAN—A loan received to finance the purchase or operation of a completed structure—opposed to land or construction loans. Synonym: take-out loan.

PERSONAL PROPERTY—Any property that is not real property. Synonym: chattels. (See—REAL PROPERTY.)

PER-UNIT ALLOCATION—A method of allocating some cost (e.g., land cost) over the total number of units affected. In the case of a subdivision, units may be lots, acres, square feet, or frontage. Opposed to relative sales value.

PLANNED-DEVELOPMENT PROJECT—A subdivision having lots or areas owned in common and reserved for the use of some or all of the owners of the separately owned lots. Synonyms: planned unit development; residential planned community. (See—COMMON AREAS.)

PLANNED UNIT DEVELOPMENT—(See—PLANNED-DEVELOPMENT PROJECT.)

PLANNING COMMISSION—An organization established under state or local law which, among other things, is responsible for the preparation and adoption of a comprehensive, long-term general plan for the physical development of property in its jurisdiction—the master plan.

POINTS—A synonym for discount points or loan fee. A discount point adds approximately ⅛ percent to the yield on a 30-year mortgage, so charging 4 points means that 4/8 (½) percent is added to the interest rate returned by the loan.

POLICY OF TITLE—(See—TITLE INSURANCE.)

POPULATION DENSITY—The average number of persons permanently residing in a community on a per-square-mile or other basis.

PRECLOSING—A transaction preceding formal closing—often used to distinguish between transactions affecting title to real property where there are events that merely appear to be the formal closing. (See—FORMAL CLOSING.)

PRELIMINARY PUBLIC REPORT—A report usually issued by a state agency upon receipt of the filing fee and a subdivision questionnaire filing which is complete except for some particular requirement. In the event a preliminary public report is issued, the developer may accept a reservation to purchase or lease a lot or parcel in the subdivision provided the buyer has read the report and signed a receipt for it, and the reservation agreement is cancelable by the buyer at any time with full refund of his deposit. (See—PUBLIC REPORT.)

PREPAYMENT PENALTY—Penalty for the payment of a mortgage or trust deed note before it actually becomes due. (See—LOCK-IN PERIOD.)

PRIMARY FINANCING—A loan secured by a first mortgage or trust deed on real property. (See—SECONDARY FINANCING.)

PRIMARY LOAN—A first mortgage loan or deed of trust.

PROGRESS BILLINGS—Synonym for advance billings. (See—RETENTIONS.)

PROGRESSION—(See—ANTICIPATION.)

PRORATES—Prorated expenses in an escrow between buyer and seller; e.g., property taxes and interest are divided among the buyer and seller based on the closing date. (See—ESCROW COSTS; ESCROW STATEMENT.)

PROVISION FOR WARRANTY—A reserve for the possible contingent costs associated with repairing or replacing defective items on new products—usually included in the year of sale as part of cost of sales.

PUBLIC REPORT—A subdivision report usually issued by a state agency before the sale of lots in the subdivision. The report is a factual account of the subdivided property, with emphasis on what might be considered its shortcomings. The report is not issued until the agency is satisfied that the subdivider has put in place promised improvements and facilities or has made satisfactory financial arrangements to assure their completion and back any warranties or representations. (See—PRELIMINARY PROJECT REPORT.)

P.U.D.—Planned Unit Development. (See—PLANNED-DEVELOPMENT PROJECT.)

PURCHASE AGREEMENT—(See—AGREEMENT OF SALE; SALES DEPOSIT RECEIPT.)

PURCHASE MONEY MORTGAGE OR TRUST DEED—A trust deed or mortgage given as part of all of the purchase consideration for property to the seller or in some cases to a lender, who lends to the buyer specifically for the purpose of buying the property. If there is a default on payment by the buyer, in certain jurisdictions (e.g., California) there may be no deficiency judgment. Synonym: nonrecourse note. (See—EXCULPATORY PROVISION; IN REM NOTE.)

Q

QUADROMINIUM—A condominium complex consisting of four units.

QUIET TITLE—A court action brought to establish title; to remove a cloud on title.

QUITCLAIM DEED—Under a quitclaim deed, the grantor transfers only such interest as he may have at the time the conveyance is executed. (See—GRANT DEED; WARRANTY DEED.)

R

RAW LAND—Unimproved land. Land on which no offsite or onsite work has been performed. Opposed to improved land.

REAL ESTATE—The physical land and appurtenances, including structures affixed thereto. In some states, by statute, this term is synonymous with real property.

REAL-ESTATE INVESTMENT TRUST—A business conducted under a trust format which enables investors to transfer beneficial shares of interest similar to corporate stock. A real-estate investment trust which qualifies under specific Internal Revenue requirements incurs income taxes only on its undistributed income. Among other requirements, in order to qualify a trust must be owned by at least 100 shareholders and invest substantially all of its capital in real-estate loans or properties and receive income primarily from such real-estate investments. A qualifying trust reduces taxable income to the extent of cash distributions to shareholders. The distributions are taxable income to the shareholders and must be a minimum of 90 percent of trust taxable income before such distributions. Synonym: R.E.I.T.

REAL-ESTATE SYNDICATION—An organization formed for investment in or gain from an interest in real property. The entity may be in the trust, corporate, general partnership, or limited partnership form. Real-estate syndicates offer to the investor the tax, legal, and practical advantages of real property investment, with a comparatively small capital contribution.

REAL PROPERTY—The interests, benefits, and rights inherent in the ownership of real estate. It is the bundle or rights with which the ownership is endowed. (See—PERSONAL PROPERTY.)

REALTOR—A real-estate broker holding active membership in a real-estate board affiliated with the National Association of Real Estate Boards.

RECONVEYANCE—The transfer of the title of land from one person to the immediate preceding owner. This particular instrument or transfer is commonly used when the performance of debt is satisfied under the terms of a deed of trust, when the trustee conveys the title he has held on condition back to the owner.

RECORDING FEE—Fee charged by the county to record the transfer of title from seller to buyer. (See—ESCROW COSTS.)

RECOURSE NOTE—A debt instrument whereby the lender has recourse against the borrower personally—beyond the repossession of the security or collateral. (See—NONRECOURSE NOTE.)

REDEMPTION—Buying back one's property after a judicial sale. (See—EQUITY OF REDEMPTION.)

REFORMATION—An action to correct a mistake in a deed or other document.

REFUNDABLE UTILITY CONTRACT—A contract between a developer and the local utility company, whereby the latter agrees to reimburse the developer out of its revenues for the costs incurred by the developer to install water mains (water contract) or other utility extensions.

REGRESSION—The economic principle that value is diminished by anticipated disadvantages to be derived in the future. In real estate, this is the theory that the value of the best house in a given neighborhood will be adversely affected by the condition of its inferior neighbors. Opposite of anticipation.

REHABILITATION—Is the restoration to satisfactory condition without changing plan, form or style.

R.E.I.T.—(See—REAL-ESTATE INVESTMENT TRUST.)

RELATIVE SALES VALUE—A method of allocating some cost (e.g., land cost) in proportion to the product's ability to absorb the cost—the ratio of its sales value per unit to the total sales value of all the products. Opposed to per-unit allocation.

RELEASE CLAUSE—This is a stipulation that upon the payment of a specific sum of money to the holder of a trust deed or mortgage, the lien of the small instrument as to a specific described lot or area shall be removed from the blanket lien on the whole area involved. (See—MORTGAGE RELEASE PRICE.)

RELEASES—Used in this unmodified form, the term usually applies to a release clause in a loan agreement. (See—LABOR AND MATERIAL RELEASE; MORTGAGE RELEASE PRICE; RELEASE CLAUSE.)

REMODELING—Is changing the plan, form or style to correct functional or economic deficiencies.

RENDERING—An approximate scale picture of an architect's suggested design (usually in color detail).

RENOVATION—Is the collective changes arising from rehabilitation, modernization and remodeling.

RENT ESCALATORS—Any lease term requiring the lessee to pay monies in excess of the contract rent. (See—ESCALATOR CLAUSE.)

RENTAL CONCESSIONS—Agreements between landlord and tenant to forgive rent in some way; e.g., giving the tenant free rent for the 13th month of his lease, or giving the resident manager free rent, etc. In projecting the expected gross income from a rental property, rental concessions reduce the amount of contract rent specified.

RENT-UP PERIOD—Period after construction during which a rental property is reaching maximum capacity. Synonyms: fill-up period; incubation period; start-up period.

R.E.O.—Real Estate Owned—A term frequently used by lending institutions to describe properties in inventory they have repossessed. (See—LOAN TO FACILITATE.)

REPLACEMENT COST—Cost to produce an item with the same utility using modern material, techniques, etc. Opposed to reproduction cost.

REPLACEMENT RESERVE—A cash reserve for the future replacement of fixed assets.

REPRODUCTION COST—Cost to produce an item with identical materials, characteristics, etc. Opposed to replacement cost.

RESERVATION AGREEMENT—(See—PRELIMINARY PUBLIC REPORT.)

RESERVES—A sum calculated to cover renewals and replacements. The object is to equitably extend renewals over expected operations, since actual renewals occur on an irregular basis.

RESIDENTIAL DENSITY—The number of individual dwelling units for given land area.

RESIDENTIAL PLANNED COMMUNITY—(See PLANNED-DEVELOPMENT PROJECT.)

RESTRICTION—A limitation upon the use of real property. For instance, the requirement in a deed that a lot may be used for the construction of not more than a one-party dwelling, costing not less than ten thousand dollars ($10,000), is termed to be a restriction; also a legislative ordinance affecting all properties in a given area requiring that improvements on property shall not be constructed any closer than 25 feet of the street curb is a restriction by operation of law. (See—C.C. & R'S.)

RETAIL LAND DEVELOPER—A person engaged in development for retail lot sales.

RETAIL LOT SALES—The sale of individual subdivided lots to the ultimate consumer.

RETENTIONS—The amount withheld by the party receiving services out of progress billings (invoices received during construction) to insure the final and satisfactory completion of the job. For example, in an arrangement between contractor and subcontractor, the contractor may hold back 5 percent of every invoice received from the subcontractor for payment until completion of the work, and final approval by the contractor. The subcontractor's invoice may show the 5 percent deduction on its face, with the final invoice including the total retentions during the course of the work. (See—ADVANCE BILLINGS; PROGRESS BILLINGS.)

REVERSIONARY INTEREST—The interest which a person has in lands or other property upon the termination of the preceding estate.

RIGHT OF SURVIVORSHIP—Right to acquire the interest of a deceased joint owner; distinguishing feature of a joint tenancy. (See—TENANCY IN COMMON.)

RIGHT OF WAY—A privilege operating as an easement upon land, whereby the owner does by grant, or by agreement give, to another the right to pass over his land, to construct a roadway, or use as a roadway, a specific part of his land, or the right to construct through and over his land, telephone, telegraph, or electric power lines, or the right to place underground water mains, gas mains, or sewer mains.

S

SALE-LEASEBACK—A transaction in which a seller deeds property to a buyer, and the buyer in turn leases the same property to the seller generally under prearranged terms. This may offer certain financial and tax advantages to the seller (e.g., freeing up his capital investment, and being able to deduct his entire lease payment.)

SALES COMMISSION—The fee paid to the agent or broker arranging for the sale of property—usually a percentage of the sales price. Sales commissions are generally paid by the seller through escrow. (See—SELLER'S CLOSING COSTS.)

SALES CONTRACT—An agreement between buyer and seller as to the terms of the sale. This term is usually used to mean a conditional sales contract, where the seller retains legal title to property until some condition is met—usually complete payment of the sales price. A sales contract may be used similar to an A.I.T.D. except that title does not pass to the buyer. Synonyms: conditional sales contract; contract of sale; land contract.

SALES COSTS—Costs incurred for sales promotion of the entire project—usually charged off ratably over the sales period. Opposed to selling expenses.

SALES DEPOSIT RECEIPT—A form which, in addition to

being an acknowledgment of a deposit, may constitute a contract for the sale and purchase of land, when executed by both buyer and seller. It is used to bind the bargain pending the opening of an escrow. (See—AGREEMENT OF SALE; EARNEST MONEY; ESCROW INSTRUCTIONS; PURCHASE AGREEMENT.)

SALES INCENTIVES—Additional concessions made to the buyer as an inducement to buy; e.g., carpets, additional landscaping.

SALES PRICE LIST—A list of houses or models available in a project with the most recent sales price.

SCHEMATIC PLANS—A very preliminary architectural plan with approximate major dimensions and area but without any details of design or specifications.

SECOND MORTGAGE—A mortgage or deed of trust which is junior to the primary loan.

SECONDARY FINANCING—A loan secured by a second mortgage or trust deed on real property, subordinate to the first lien. (See—PRIMARY FINANCING.)

SECURED PARTY—The party having a security interest. Thus the mortgagee, the conditional seller, the pledgee, etc., are all referred to as the secured party.

SECURITY AGREEMENT—An agreement between the secured party and the debtor which creates the security interest.

SECURITY INTEREST—A term designating the interest of the creditor in the property of the debtor in all types of credit transactions. It thus replaces such terms as the following: chattel mortgage; pledge; trust receipt; chattel trust; equipment trust; conditional sale; inventory lien; etc.

SEED MONEY—Front-end money. In assisted housing, advances to nonprofit sponsors of low- or moderate-income housing for initial costs of planning.

SELLER'S CLOSING COSTS—Escrow costs to the seller, including his share of prorates, the cost of selling commissions, etc. (See—BUYER'S CLOSING COSTS.)

SELLING EXPENSES—Costs incurred for the sale of a particular house—usually expensed in the period the house is sold. Opposed to sale costs.

SEQUENCE SHEET—A list of houses or lots within a project in the order of their development.

SERVICE CONTRACTS—Term applied to contracts which

provide maintenance services to a building; i.e., elevator service, window cleaning, or office and public space cleaning.

SET-BACK ORDINANCE—An ordiance prohibiting the erection of a building or structure between the curb and the setback line.

SETTLEMENT COSTS—(See—ESCROW COSTS.)

SHERIFF'S DEED—Deed given by court order in connection with sale of property to satisfy a judgment.

SHOPPING CENTERS—A coordinated group of retail stores, with parking, under a single controlling management.

SITE PLANNER—(See—LAND PLANNER.)

SOFT DOLLARS—(See—SOFT MONEY.)

SOFT MONEY—Money paid which does *not* improve the equity position of the payor; e.g., prepaid interest, and the interest portion of debt service. Money paid which is tax deductible by the payor. Opposite of hard money. Synonym: soft dollars.

SPECIAL ASSESSMENT—Legal charge against real estate by a public authority to pay cost of public improvements such as: street lights, sidewalks, street improvements, etc.

SPECIFIC PERFORMANCE—An action to compel performance of an agreement; e.g., for the sale of land.

SPLIT RATE OF CAPITALIZATION—A term used in the capitalization process denoting the application of different rates to portions of the total net income.

S.R.A.—An appraiser who is a member of the Society of Real Estate Appraisers. (See—M.A.I.)

STABILIZED—Term applied to income and/or expense; the most probable, considering past performance; definitive trends affecting the foreseeable future.

STABILIZED NET AFTER TAXES—(See—NET AFTER TAXES.)

STANDBY COMMITMENT—A lender's promise to a potential borrower to make a temporary loan if the borrower is unable to get other financing immediately. The commitment is paid for, usually based on a percentage of the desired loan. (See—GAP FINANCING; LOAN COMMITMENT.)

STARTS—Units begun under construction; a term used to show the amount of building activity, usually determined by the number of building permits filed.

START-UP COSTS—Costs incurred at the beginning of a project, usually of a one-time nature. (See—FRONT-END MONEY.)

START-UP PERIOD—(See—RENT-UP PERIOD.)

STOCK COOPERATIVE PROJECT—A corporation that is formed or availed of primarily for the purpose of holding title to improved real property, either in fee simple or for a term of years. All or substantially all of the shareholders of such corporation receive a right of exclusive occupancy of a portion of the real property, title to which is held by the corporation, which right of occupancy is transferrable only concurrently with the transfer of share or shares of stock in the corporation held by the person having such right of occupancy. (See—COOPERATIVES.)

SUBCONTRACTOR—A term used to identify a person or company performing contractual work for a developer or general contractor who may or may not have a contract with the ultimate buyer. Literally defined, he is a person who assumes by secondary contract some of the obligations of an original contractor—such as plumbing, electrical work, etc. In practice, however, this term is applied to companies performing work on new subdivisions, etc., where there is no primary contract.

SUBDIVISION—Improved or unimproved land divided for the purpose of sale, lease, or financing whether immediate or future, into a number of parcels. This applies not only to residential land, but may also include sale or lease of lands used for any purpose including business, industry, recreation and agriculture. (See—LAND PLANNER.)

SUBJECT TO MORTGAGE—A term which applies when a grantee takes title to real property subject to a mortgage, and he is not responsible to the holder of the promissory note for the payment of any portion of the amount due. The most that he can lose in the event of a foreclosure is his equity in the property. The original maker of the note is not released from his responsibility. (See—ASSUMPTION OF MORTGAGE; SUBSTITUTION OF LIABILITY.)

SUBLEASE—A lease executed by a lessee to a third person for a term shorter than the remaining term of the original lease. If the term of the "sublease" is coincident with the remaining term of the original lease, it is the same as an assignment of the lease.

SUBLET—Renting or leasing of all or part of a leased premises by the contract lessee.

SUBMITTAL STATEMENT—Sometimes called a "prospectus" or "property brief." Statement usually provided prospective purchaser of income-producing property to present all the physical and financial data concerning the property; can be simple or complex, to show income tax and/or capital gains benefits.

SUBORDINATION—The act of placing owner's claim for ground rental payments in a position secondary to a first mortgage claim. (See—LEASE, LAND.)

SUBORDINATION CLAUSE—The clause in a junior or a second lien permitting retention or priority for prior liens. A subordination clause may also be used in a first deed of trust permitting it to be subordinated to subsequent liens as, for example, the liens of construction loans.

SUBORDINATE—To make subject to, or junior to. (See—JUNIOR LIEN; LAND LIEN.)

SUBROGATION—The substitution of another person in place of the creditor, to whose rights he succeeds in relation to the debt. The doctrine is used very often where one person agrees to stand surety for the performance of a contract by another person.

SUBSIDY PROGRAMS—(See—FHA.)

SUBSTITUTION OF LIABILTY—The assumption of liability by a grantee on a mortgage or trust deed note, with the concurrent release of the grantor by the mortgagee or beneficiary. A type of novation. (See—ASSUMPTION OF MORTGAGE; SUBJECT TO MORTGAGE.)

SURETY—One who guarantees the performance of another. (See—ACCOMMODATION PARTY.)

SURVEY—The process by which a parcel of land is measured and its area is ascertained.

"SWEAT" EQUITY—An ownership position acquired by services, knowledge or other non-case contributions.

SYNDICATION—Combination of investors, often in the form of a limited partnership. (See also—REAL-ESTATE SYNDICATION.)

T

TAKE-OUT LOAN—(See—PERMANENT LOAN.)

TANDEM PLAN—The purchase by GNMA of certain mortgages at par for subsequent resale at market prices to FNMA.

TAX ESCALATOR—A lease provision providing for additional rent if taxes exceed a certain level.

TAX-LOSS CARRYOVER—Amount computed by deducting

interest paid and depreciation taken from net operating income and such deductible items exceed net operating income; resultant loss balance may be carried back for two years, or forward three years and applied as a deduction against other taxable income. (See appropriate tax laws.)

TAX SALE—The sale of property by the taxing authority to satisfy the payment of delinquent taxes.

TAX SHELTER— One of the advantages of property investment; allows depreciation deductions to be taken from net operating income, thus reducing tax liability. A relief from certain tax liability.

TENANCY IN COMMON—Ownership by two or more persons who hold undivided interest, without right of survivorship; interests need not be equal. (See—JOINT TENANCY; RIGHT OF SURVIVORSHIP.)

TENANT CHANGES—A term used commonly with respect to leased real property, such as a commercial office building, referring to interior work (flooring, partitions, etc.) installed for a tenant's use. In some usages it is similar to customers' extras.

TENTATIVE MAP—A preliminary map of a proposed subdivision which subdividers may be required to submit to the planning commission for study. The approval or disapproval of the planning commission is noted on the map. Thereafter a final map of the tract embodying any changes requested by the planning commission is filed with the planning commission.

TITLE—Evidence that owner of land is in lawful possession thereof; an instrument evidencing such ownership.

TITLE INSURANCE—Insurance written by a title company to protect the property owner against loss if title is imperfect. (See—ABSTRACT OF TITLE; LOT BOOK.)

TOWNHOUSE—Formerly any in-town residence; now applies to row houses.

TRACT—In some states, a unit of subdivided land numbered and recorded with the county recorder's office.

TRACT ADMINISTRATION COSTS—Costs incurred for the administration and supervision of the tract construction—usually charged to construction costs.

TRACT MAP—A map usually prepared by the developer, showing the physical boundaries of lots and tracts under development.

TRADE FIXTURES—Articles of personal property annexed to

real property, but which are necessary to the carrying on of a trade and are removable by the owner. (See—APPURTENANCE; FIXTURES.)

TRAILER PARK—Formal site having facilities for permanent or semipermanent mobile homes. Term implies utilities, streets, car parking, and other amenities.

TRUST DEED—The instrument given by a borrower (trustor) to a trustee vesting title in the trustee as security for the fulfillment of an obligation, which is ordinarily repayment of a loan to a beneficiary. Synonym: deed of trust. (See—A.I.T.D.; MORTGAGE.)

TRUSTEE—A fiduciary who holds property in trust. As used in connection with a security interest in real property, one who holds property in trust for another to secure the performance of an obligation.

TRUSTOR—The grantor of property to a trustee. As used in connection with a security interest in real property, one who deeds his property to a trustee to be held as security until he has performed his obligation to a lender under terms of a deed of trust. (See—MORTGAGOR.)

TURNKEY LEASING—The leasing of housing constructed by private sponsors to a housing authority for use by low-income tenants.

TURNKEY PROJECT—A project where payment by the buyer is usually given at project completion with no further commitment on the part of the seller. Also, housing initially financed and built by private sponsors and purchased by housing authorities for use by low-income families under a public housing program. (See—LOCAL HOUSING AUTHORITY.)

U

UNDERLYING LOAN—The loan or loans covered by an A.I.T.D., or sales contract.

UNEARNED INCREMENT—An increase in value of real estate due to no effort on the part of the owner; often due to increase in population.

UNIMPROVED LAND—(See—RAW LAND.)

URBAN RENEWAL—Conservation, rehabilitation or demolition of property within a designated area in accord with a specific plan adopted by a duly constituted governmental body (usually a municipal government).

V

VA LOAN—A loan by a private institution to a qualifying veteran which is guaranteed by the Veterans Administration.

VACANCY FACTOR—A percentage rate expressing the loss from gross rental income due to vacant rental units.

VOLUNTARY LIEN—Any lien placed on property with consent of, or as a result of, the voluntary act of the owner. (See—INVOLUNTARY LIEN.)

VOUCHER SYSTEM—When used in regard to a construction loan, this term applies to the system of giving subcontractors a voucher in lieu of cash which they may redeem with the maker of the construction loan. Opposed to the fixed disbursement schedule.

W

WALK-AWAY RISK—Deterrents to a party in a contract to default at key points in the life of the project. Synonym: exit penalty.

WAREHOUSING—The activity (usually of a mortgage banker) of holding mortgage or trust deed notes receivable in inventory (the "warehouse") for future sale. The purchase or making of these loans generally is financed by short-term loans which are repaid out of the proceeds from the sale of the notes.

WARRANTY DEED—A deed used to convey real property which contains warranties of title and quiet possession, and the grantor thus agrees to defend the premises against the lawful claims of third persons. It is commonly used in states where the grant deed has not supplanted it. The modern practice of securing title insurance policies has reduced the importance of express and implied warranty in deeds. (See—GRANT DEED; QUITCLAIM DEED.)

WATER CONTRACT—(See—REFUNDABLE UTILITY CONTRACT.)

WRAPAROUND LOAN—A procedure of financing in which a new mortgage is obtained in a secondary position; the entire loan is treated as a single obligation and the secondary mortgagee assumes and pays the obligations on the first mortgage from total payments received.

WRAPAROUND MORTGAGE OR TRUST DEED—A financing arrangement using an all-inclusive trust deed or mortgage to preserve the terms of the underlying loan. Synonym: overlapping deed of trust. (See—A.I.T.D.; SALES CONTRACT.)

Z

ZERO LOT LINE—A term generally used to describe the positioning of a structure on a lot so that one side rests directly on the lot's boundary line. Such construction is usually prohibited by setback ordinances, unless as a part of special space-conserving project.

ZONING—Permitted uses of property in accord with legally established governmental codes and ordinances regulating size, use and height.

INDEX

Acceleration/alienation clause, 97
Accountants and accounting, 21, 22, 24, 61, 68, 69, 70, 76, 85, 88, 91, 106, 111, 112, 118, 175, 184, 214, 258
Advertising, 59, 84, 108, 130, 131, 224, 249
Advisors, 17–22, 61, 65–71, 78
  developer's, 76
  fiduciary, 69–71
  how to select, xi, 68–69
  See also Accountant; Attorney; Real-estate broker
Age grouping, population, 34–35
Agricultural land, 6, 102, 156, 197
  groves, 212–214
  risks in, 163–164
  value of land for, 54
Air-conditioning, 138, 142, 234, 235, 247
Allegheny Plaza (Pittsburgh), 191
Amortization, 13, 119, 124, 125
Analysis of research, 58–59, 69, 83, 96, 162
Apartment buildings, x, 5, 16, 18, 21, 22, 26, 27, 28, 45, 115, 123, 131, 134, 135, 137, 146, 149, 155, 157, 160, 161, 183–184, 196, 204, 205, 218, 229, 230, 232
  acquiring land for, 46–48
  check list for buying, 285–289
  converting to condominiums, 197–199
  demand for, 44
  evaluating deals, 138–140, 224–228
  financing, 93, 99–102, 106, 107, 225–226
  high-rise, 9–10, 27, 54, 163–164
  as investment winners, 145
  as long-term investment, 219–228
  managing, 25, 139, 223–226
  package presentation for, 93–94
  as poor investment, 180–182
  risk in, 163–164, 223
  stress deals in, 86
  trends in, 30, 32
  value of land for, 54
Appraisals and appraisers, 84, 106, 139, 141
Appreciation, 13, 16, 24, 52, 80, 105, 117, 123, 125, 126, 146, 181, 193, 220, 223, 228, 247, 248, 256, 260
Architect, 75, 76, 84, 94, 162, 258

Attorney, 21, 22, 24, 60, 61, 66, 68, 69, 70, 75, 76, 79, 80, 88, 91, 159, 162, 175, 184, 232, 258
Audited financial statements, 83

Back-up capital, 77
Bankruptcies, 190
Banks and bankers, 3, 5, 67, 76, 85, 86, 88, 90, 100–102, 104, 108, 121, 129, 132, 135, 136, 142, 187, 215, 233, 242, 258
  joint ventures with, 80
Berman, Dan, 79, 81
Better Business Bureau, 90
Birth rates, 34–35
Bonds, 3–4, 11–12, 21, 66, 67, 80
Box, Wesley, 249–250
Brownstones, 47, 200
  renovation, 47, 48
Building Industries Association (BIA), 141
Building permits, 56
  moratoria on, 151, 153
Building restrictions, 94, 95

Capital gains, 23, 104, 118, 120, 165
  investing for, 12
  tax on, 12, 104, 123, 125, 150
Caribbean International Corporation, 251
Carlson, Don W., 112, 113
Carlson, James F., 228
Carson, Johnny, 34
Cash flow, 84, 109, 113, 119, 133, 157, 176, 183, 186, 190, 198, 214, 222, 225, 227, 256, 262
  analysis, 84, 95–96
Census, 34, 36, 40, 56, 57, 130
Century City (Los Angeles), 183, 191
Certificates of deposit, 4, 67
Chalet, The (condominium hotel), 249
Chambers of Commerce, 56
Chattel financing, 93
Cheyenne Mountain Ranch (shopping village), 215
Cities, trends in, 42–43
Closing costs, 97
Commercial buildings, 18, 21, 128–130, 146, 183, 188, 197
  evaluating, 136–138, 139–140
  financing, 93, 96, 101
  as investment winners, 145
  package presentation for, 94
Comparable sales approach to market value, 122
Competition, 57, 58, 65, 72, 91, 94, 109, 129, 130–131, 139–140, 223
  analysis of, 96
  in condominium, 243
Condominiums, x, 5, 27, 39, 47, 48, 86, 131, 135, 149, 160, 161, 180, 181, 193, 194, 196, 204, 205, 215, 218, 219, 220, 229, 230, 257
  advantages of, 246–249
  check list for, 242–244
  conversions to, 197–199, 244–246, 249–250
  evaluating deals on, 235–242
  financing, 93, 96, 102, 242, 243, 245, 246, 252
  as investment winners, 144–145, 233–252
  lender protection in, 244
  as limited partnership, 244–246, 251
  medical-dental, 236–242
  new ideas for, 249–252
  office, 28, 236
  overbuilding, 53
  as poor investment, 144
  risks in, 163–164
  trends, 32
Congressional Joint Economic Committee, 229
Consolidated Capital Equities Corporation, 112
Consolidated Capital Realty Investors (CCRI), 108, 112–116
Construction costs, 82, 181, 198, 242
  overruns, 104–105
Construction loans, 97, 99, 101, 136, 242
Conversion of properties, 197–200, 206
  to condominiums, 197–199, 244–246, 249–250
Cost analysis, 95
Cost of living, 18, 119, 216
Cost overruns, 85, 104–105, 135, 242
Credit manipulation, 72
Cross and Brown, 185
Currency devaluations, 80

Danziger, Robert A., 210, 211
Deals, evaluating, 17, 25, 48, 62, 127–148

(*cont'd*)
apartment projects, 138–140, 224–228
commercial property, 136–138, 139–140
condominiums, 235–242
diversification and, 143–144
for feasibility, 134–135
for financeability, 135–136
guidelines for, 127–129
homes, 140–143
for marketability, 133–134
rules for, 143–148
steps to follow, 129–133
Death rate, 34–35
Demand, real-estate, 7–11
Demand, watching for, 44–45, 74, 231–232
Depreciation, 13, 14, 104, 118–119, 122–124, 150, 151, 186, 220, 247, 248, 258
Developers, 71–78, 88, 89, 93, 108, 128, 135, 145, 147, 158, 162, 187, 209, 258
advisors to, 76
entrepreneurial ability, 72–73, 82
evaluating, 71, 73–74
financing arrangement by, 76–77
integrity of, 71–72
investor relations, 77–78
land and project inventory, 74–75
organization, 75–76
Development syndicates, 20, 88–89, 91
Direct investment:
caution about, 179–180
expected benefits, 164
risks of, 163–164
types of deals evaluated, 166–174
Disability insurance, 70
Distress deal, 85–86
Diversification, 21, 28, 68, 104, 106, 108, 109, 143–144, 260, 261
Divorce rate, 8, 38–39
Down payment, 99, 136, 222–223
apartment building, 225, 227
on condominium, 233–234

Eastern Airlines, 200
Electricity, 138, 203, 243
Energy costs and shortages, 9, 43, 51, 141, 155, 192, 206, 207, 209, 210, 211
Engineers and engineering, 45, 48, 53, 61, 84, 95, 106, 136, 138, 142
Entrepreneurial ability, developer's, 72–73, 82
Environmental Protection Agency (EPA), 191
Equity REIT, *see* Property trusts
Equity stomp, 146
Estate planning, 70–71, 222

Fashion Island Center (Irvine, Calif.), 191
Feasibility evaluating, 134–135
Federal Housing Administration (FHA), 84, 185
Fiduciary, 69–71, 97, 112, 151
Financial statements, 83, 94
Financing, xi, 7, 45, 59, 92–116, 125, 129, 133, 142, 143, 145, 146, 199, 259–260, 261, 262
apartment buildings, 93, 99–102, 106, 107, 225–226
condominium, 93, 96, 102, 242, 243, 245, 246, 252
developer's, 76–77
evaluating investment for, 135–136
by joint venture, 50, 59, 69, 78, 79–86, 100, 133, 145, 176
package presentation for, 93–96
property trusts, 104, 105–116
REITS, 23, 100–105, 136, 164–166, 190, 196, 217, 224, 242
sources of, 99–102
syndicates, 20, 23, 50, 78, 86–91, 100, 133, 164–166, 207, 212, 213, 220, 236
terms and conditions, 97–99
Fire departments, 11
Fire insurance, 137–138, 224
First trust deed, 97–98
Fixed expenses, apartment buildings, 226
Foreign investors, 80
Franklin Bank, 103
Free and clear return, 13, 14
Front money, 135–136, 147

Galleria Complex (Houston), 10, 44, 190
Ghirardelli Square (San Francisco), 44, 199
Glossary, 290–331
Gold chip investor, 21–22, 200, 204, 206–208, 212, 213, 216, 217

Golf courses, 109
Goodkin Research Corporation, ix
Government securities, 23, 259
Grant Stores (W.T.), 103
Green chip investor, 18–19, 55, 70, 200, 206, 212
Ground leases, 126, 216–217
Groves, 48, 212–214
Growth, restricting, 51, 149, 151–156, 162, 228

Hancock Building (Chicago), 10
Harvard University, 35, 36
Headship increase, 38
High-rise apartments, 9–10, 27
  risks in, 163–164
  value of land for, 54
High-rise office buildings, 134, 191
  as investment loser, 182–185
  risks in, 163–164
Highway Department, 130
Highways, *see* Roads and highways
Hillsides, 53
Hines, Gerald, 10
Holding costs, 72, 74–75, 157, 188, 212
Homes, *see* Single-family homes
Hotels, 25, 28, 102, 109
  risks in, 163–164
Housing, trends in, 30–43
Housing Act (1949), 43

Immigration, 39
Improved real estate, 6–7, 14
  best locations for, 49–50
  risks in, 163–164
  timing in purchase of, 52
Incentive compensation, 76, 83
Income, family, 57–58
Income approach to market value, 121–122, 123
Income property, 20, 21, 22, 93, 104, 105, 107, 108, 118–120, 123, 197–198, 258, 260
  investing in, 12–13
  management, 106
  syndicates, 89–90, 91
Income seekers, 22–29, 216, 217
Income tax, 118, 182, 247
Indirect investment:
  expected benefits, 165–166
  risks in, 164–165
Industrial associations, 56
Industrial buildings, 9, 28, 100, 114, 122, 146
  financing, 93, 96, 101, 106, 107
  risks in, 163–164
  value of land for, 53
Industrial parks, 28, 207–208
Inflation, 13, 14, 41, 52, 66–67, 85, 91, 102, 126, 143, 180–182, 190, 210–211, 216, 228, 230, 247
  hedge against, x, 3–5, 23, 68, 80, 145, 228, 229
Insurance, 70, 119, 216, 224, 226, 234
  premiums, 137–138
Insurance broker, 138
Insurance companies, 80, 100–102, 104, 129, 136, 184, 187, 242
Integrity, developer's, 71–72
Interest, 3, 25, 50, 52, 66, 67, 77, 97–102, 120, 124–126, 144, 180, 181, 188, 190, 210, 216, 220, 225–226, 228, 247, 248
Interim financing, 93, 136
Internal Rate of Return (IRR), 120
Internal Revenue Service (IRS), 91, 150, 151
International City Management Association (ICMA), 151, 155
International Housing Systems, Inc., 244–246
Inventory, land and project, 74–75
Investment counselors, 66, 69
Investment home, 39
Investor relations, developer's, 77–78
Investors, types of, 16–29
  income seekers, 22–29, 216, 217
  net worth builders, 17–22, 217

Johnstown Properties, 114–116
Joint Center Urban Studies, 35
Joint-venture deals, 50, 59, 69, 78, 79–86, 100, 133, 145, 176
  finding partners, 79–82
  making the offering, 82–83
  new changes in, 85
  package presentation for, 83–84

Kaiser-Aetna, 213
Konweiser, John, 72–73

Land, *see* Vacant land
Land planners, 94–95
Land and project inventory, developers, 74–75

Land values, factors in, 53–54
Land-sale leaseback financing, 93
Landscaping, 95, 132
Land-use plan, 159
Leases, 26, 27, 60, 84, 92, 96, 97, 109, 114, 119, 123, 258
  commissions on, 138
  ground, 126, 216–217
Letters to lenders, format for, 271–272
Leverage, 23, 54, 60, 113, 117, 135, 223, 245, 259–260
Levin, Marvin T., 113–114, 115
Liability insurance, 137–138
Library of Congress, 229
Life insurance, 70
Limited partnerships, 176, 213, 237
  in condominium, 244–246, 251
  risks in, 164–166
Loan brokers, 102
Loans, *see* Financing
Location, 9–10, 49–51, 55, 61–62, 68, 99, 101, 134, 139, 153, 198, 220, 225, 226, 230, 254
  of condominium, 242–243
  describing in financial package, 94
  effect on price, 53–54
  map of, 84
  market research into, 58–59
  of medical-dental condominiums, 238–242
  trends in, 32–33, 35–37
Low-income housing, 42, 182

Macy's, 190
Maintenance costs, 132, 138, 144, 181, 198
  of apartments, 223, 224, 226
  condominium, 243, 247–248
  contracts, 138
  of miniwarehouses, 203
Management, 19, 24, 26, 128, 147, 162, 212, 213, 217, 261
  apartment, 25, 139, 223–226
  condominiums, 234–235, 248, 250–251
  construction, 135
  costs, 87, 132
  of miniwarehouses, 203
  property trusts, 106, 107–116
Marinas, 109
Market research, 55–59, 90, 130, 134, 140, 196, 258
  analysis of, 58–59, 69, 83, 96, 162
  original, 57–58
Market segments, definitions of, 266–268
Market values, approaches in determining, 121–123
Marketability, evaluating, 133–134
Marketing development check list, 263–264
Marriages, 38–40
Mass transit, 51, 209
Massachusetts Institute of Technology (MIT), 35, 36
Medicaid, 238
Medical-dental condominiums, 236–242
Medicare, 238
Menegus, Bill, 187
Merchandising check list, 264–265
Merrill Lynch, Pierce, Fenner & Smith, 228
Middle-income apartments, 180–182
Mini-theaters, 28
Miniwarehouses, 25, 28
  as investment winners, 200–204
  risks in, 163–164
Mixed-rise developments, 10, 51
  risks in, 163–164
Mixed-rise residential units, 191
Mobile home parks, 26–27, 28, 48
  as good investments, 204–205
  risks in, 163–164
  trends in, 30, 32
Mobility, population, 8, 30, 35–37, 56, 229
Moratoria, 149, 151–156, 162, 228
Mortgage brokers, 81, 82, 88, 100–102, 129, 146
Mortgage trusts, 104–105
Mortgages, 13, 52, 56, 82, 84, 85, 150, 179, 210, 228–229, 234, 235, 244, 246, 247, 248
  government-insured, 185, 186
  second, 22–23, 125, 127, 216
Motels, 25, 45, 207
  risks in, 163–164
Motivations for investment, 5–6
Municipal bonds, 4, 21
Municipal services, 11, 50–51, 188

National Association of Home Builders, 141–142
Natural growth, population, 38
Neiman-Marcus, 47, 190
Net worth builders, 17–22, 217
Noble, Joe, 198–199

Nonequity investment options, 125–126
Northland Investment Corporation, 210

Offering to joint ventures, 82–83
Office buildings, x, 7, 10, 25, 26, 45–46, 48, 71, 110, 128, 129, 131, 149, 155, 165, 196, 220
  check list for buying, 279–284
  condominiums, 28, 236
  financing, 100, 106, 107
  as good investment, 145
  high-rise, 134, 163–164, 182–185
  as poor investment, 144, 182–185
  risks in, 163–164
  stress deals in, 86
Olde Mistick Village (shopping center), 215
Operating expenses, analyzing, 137–138
Option agreement, 84
Options, investment, 117–126
  basic, 6–7
  in determining market value, 121–123
  nonequity, 125–126
  related to use, 123
  tax-related, 123–125
  types of returns, 118–121
Organization, developer's, 75–76
Original market research, 57–58
Outdoor advertising companies, 130

Paar, Jack, 34
Package presentations:
  for financing, 93–96
  for joint ventures, 83–84
Parking facilities, 27, 28, 93, 95, 130–132, 160, 189, 215, 216, 243
  maintenance, 138
Partnerships, 6, 69, 128, 147
  limited, 164–166, 176, 213, 237, 244–246, 251
Penn Central Railroad, 103
Pension funds, 22, 23, 66, 68, 101, 136, 216, 247–248
  joint ventures with, 80
Permanent financing, 93, 136, 242
Planning agencies, 51, 60
Plot plan, 95
Plumbing, 48, 138, 139
Police service, 11, 51
Population, 17, 23, 55, 59, 109, 129, 130, 134, 151, 192, 205, 216, 220
  characteristics of, 8
  controls, 156
  mobility in, 8, 30, 35–37, 56, 229
  and trends in housing, 30–43
Portfolios, 65, 66, 67, 68, 109, 111, 112, 217, 259, 260
Prepayment penalty, 97–98, 99
Private individuals, loans from, 100, 101–102
Private syndications, 87–88
Profit trusts, 216
Profit-center managers, 82–83
Profits, x, 7, 14, 23, 27, 33, 43, 52, 68, 69, 72, 73, 75, 76, 86, 93, 97, 143, 149, 151, 176, 188, 190, 194, 214, 219, 228, 254, 262
  from conversion of properties, 197–200
  highest and best use for, 52–54
  joint venture deals, 81
  syndicates, 87, 89, 91
Profit-sharing trusts, 22, 23, 247–248
Project analysis chart, 269–270
Project superintendents, 76
Property taxes, *see* Real-estate taxes
Property trusts, 104, 105–116
Public corporations, 79–80
Public relations, 84
Public Storage Inc. (PSI), 203
Purchase agreements, 84, 94, 110

Rapid transit, 51
Raw land, *see* Vacant land
Reader's Digest, 160
Real Estate Investment Act (1961), 104
Real Estate Investment Trusts (REITS), 23, 100–105, 136, 190, 196, 217, 224, 242
  risks in, 164–166
Real-estate brokers, 18, 21, 22, 69–70, 89, 102, 108, 131, 258
  fees, 87
Real-estate investment:
  advisors, xi, 17–22, 61, 65–71, 78
  condominiums, x, 5, 27, 28, 32, 39, 47, 48, 53, 86, 93, 96, 102, 131, 135, 144–145, 149, 160, 161, 163–164, 180, 181, 193, 194, 196–199, 204, 205, 215, 218, 219, 220, 229, 230, 233–252, 257

(*cont'd*)
- developers, 71–78, 82, 88, 89, 93, 108, 128, 135, 145, 147, 158, 162, 187, 209, 258
- evaluating deals, 17, 25, 48, 62, 127–148, 224–228, 235–242
- financing, xi, 7, 45, 59, 76–77, 92–116, 125, 129, 133, 135–136, 142, 143, 145, 146, 199, 225–226, 242, 243, 245, 246, 252, 259–260, 261, 262
- joint ventures, 50, 59, 69, 78, 79–86, 100, 133, 145, 176
- location, 9–10, 49–51, 53–55, 58–59, 61–62, 68, 84, 94, 99, 101, 134, 139, 153, 198, 220, 225, 226, 230, 238–243, 254
- long-term winners, 218–252
- losers, 179–195
- market research, 55–59, 68, 83, 90, 96, 130, 134, 140, 162, 196, 258
- options in, 6–7, 117–126
- reasons for, 3–15
- risks, ix, 6, 17, 60, 67, 92, 117, 118, 128, 149–176, 210, 212, 223, 228, 239, 256
- rules for, 59–62, 253–262
- syndicates, 20, 23, 50, 78, 86–91, 133, 164–166, 207, 212, 213, 220, 236
- timing, x–xi, 51–52, 55, 58–59, 61, 62, 85, 95, 132, 134, 153, 188, 196, 220, 261
- trends in, 30–48, 59, 74, 109, 220, 231–232
- types of investors, 16–29
- use, 52–54, 55, 58–59, 61–62, 123, 129, 188, 197–200, 205, 212, 254
- winners, 196–252

Real-estate taxes, 137, 181, 210, 228, 229
- on condominiums, 234, 243, 247, 248
- deducting, 124

Recapture, avoiding, 149–151
Recreational facilities, 101, 128, 143, 156, 188
- condominium as, 251–252
- as poor investment, 192–195
- risks in, 163–164

Recreational vehicle parks, 25, 28, 206–207
Recurring income, 118–120
Regional planning agencies, 51
Rehabilitation of older buildings, 47, 48, 128, 130, 132, 183, 205
Rent controls, 182, 221
Rent schedule, apartments, 227
Rent subsidies, 182
Rental properties, 10, 20, 26, 27, 32, 39, 49, 92, 96, 107, 109, 114, 118–120, 122, 131, 132, 158, 164, 186, 190–191, 198, 200, 218
- evaluating income from, 137
- miniwarehouses, 203
- *See also* Apartments

Replacement-cost approach to market value, 122, 123
Repurchase options, 216–217
Research, *see* Market research
Research company, 90, 130
Resorts, 192–195
Retirement, 40, 47, 67, 204
Retirement homes, 229
Retirement income, 5, 22–23, 66, 222
Rezoning, 46 47, 54, 60, 128, 149, 151, 162, 196, 197, 205
- guidelines for, 157–161
- moratoria on, 151

Risks, ix, 6, 17, 60, 67, 92, 117, 118, 128, 149–176, 210, 212, 256
- in apartment buildings, 163–164, 223
- avoiding or salvaging bad deals, 175–176
- of direct investment, 162–164
- of indirect investment, 164–166
- of medical-dental condominium, 239
- minimizing, 162
- moratoria, 149, 151–156, 162, 228
- recapture, 149–151
- rezoning, 157–161
- by types of deals, 166–174

Roads and highways, 56, 129, 130
Robbins, Larry, 97
Rolling land, 53
Rowhouses, 47, 48
Rules for investing in real-estate, 59–62, 253–262

Sale, property held for, 118, 120, 197–198
Salerno, Dan, 200
Savings accounts, 3, 18
Savings and loan association, 97–102, 129, 228, 233, 242
- joint ventures with, 80

Schools, 10, 11, 51, 143, 160, 191, 192
moratoria on, 151
Sears, Roebuck Company, 129, 190
Second homes, 27, 38–40
as poor investment, 144, 192–195
risks in, 163–164
Second mortgages, 22–23, 125, 127, 216
Second trust deed, 98–99, 102
Securities and Exchange Commission (SEC), 91
Sellers, loans from, 100, 102
Septic tanks, 143, 193
Seven-Eleven (minimarkets), 215
Sewers, 11, 95, 138, 143, 191, 193, 243
moratoria on, 151, 153
Shopping Center Institute, 130
Shopping centers, x, 7, 8–9, 10, 25, 26, 52, 71, 110, 130, 134, 155, 157, 197, 200–201, 205
buying land for, 47
demand for, 44
financing, 96, 100, 101, 106
as good investments, 145, 214–216
as investment losers, 189–192
rehabilitation, 28
risks in, 163–164
Silver chip investors, 19–21, 70, 87, 200, 204, 206, 208, 212, 213, 216, 217, 236
Single-family homes, 7, 9–10, 25, 46, 122, 134, 193, 197, 199, 200, 204, 206, 218, 219, 257
demand for, 44
evaluating deals for, 140–143
financing, 93, 99, 100, 101
as long-term investment, 228–232
rising prices of, 219
risks in, 163–164
value of land for, 54, 189
Site preparation, 53
Social Security, 38
Soil engineers, 95
Sonnenblick-Goldman (brokerage), 97
Speculative securities, 21
Sports complexes, 28
Standard Metropolitan Sales Area (SMSA), 130
Standby commitment, 242
Stock market, 3–4, 18, 25, 67, 106, 165
Stockbroker, 18
Stonecroft (shopping center), 215
Store buildings, converting to other uses, 199–200
Streets, 74, 95, 142
Structural engineers, 45, 48
Subcontractors, 84–85
Subdivisions, 134, 191
Subsidized housing, 144, 185–187
Substandard housing, 7–8, 40, 43
Suburbs, 32, 42, 43, 151, 155, 181, 185, 207, 208, 214, 238, 254
shift out of, 36
"Sun Belt" areas, 32–33, 35–36, 201
Suppliers, 72, 84–85
Swamps, 53
Syndicates, 23, 50, 78, 86–91, 133, 207, 212, 213, 220, 236
caution about, 90
development, 20, 88–89, 91
income property, 89–90, 91
organizing, 90–91
private, 87–88
risks in, 164–166

Takeouts, 136
Tax assessors, 186, 231, 243
Tax benefits, 117, 258–259
from condominiums, 247–248
Tax deferral, 245
Tax incentives, 187, 206
Tax shelters, x, 4, 7, 13, 14, 20–22, 24, 60, 66–68, 70, 79, 104, 119, 151, 166, 186, 213, 214, 216, 219, 222, 223, 227, 236, 237, 256, 258
best locations for, 49–50
depreciation as, 123–124, 125
Taxes, 9, 72, 81, 87, 109, 160, 208, 211, 214, 217, 222, 224, 226
capital-gains, 12, 104, 123, 125, 150
deductions, 67, 70, 80, 91, 124, 150, 181, 245, 248
income, 118, 182, 247
investor options, 123–125
real-estate, 124, 137, 181, 210, 228, 229, 234, 243, 247, 248
Termites, 141
Thoryk, Paul, 45, 199
Time-share options, 194
condominiums, 250–252
Timing, x–xi, 51–52, 55, 61, 62, 85, 132, 134, 153, 188, 196, 220, 261
in financial package presentation, 95
market research into, 58–59

Title policy, 84
Topanga Plaza (San Fernando), 44, 203
Topography, 95
Townhouses, 160, 208
  financing, 93
Trends, 30–48, 59, 109, 220
  evaluating for opportunities, 45–48
  in housing, 30–43
  watching consumer demand for, 44–45, 74, 231–232
Trolly Square (Salt Lake City), 199
Trust deed, 97, 225, 226

Underground (Atlanta), 199
Underground malls, 44, 199
Unimproved property, *see* Vacant land
U.S. Congress, 24, 166, 229, 259
U.S. Department of Housing and Urban Development (HUD), 153, 155, 218
  subsidized housing programs, 185–187
U.S. Government securities, 4, 5, 18
U.S. Supreme Court, 42
Urban Land Institute (ULI), 130, 209–210
Use, highest and best, 52–54, 55, 61–62, 129, 188, 205, 212, 254
  conversion to, 197–200
  effect on return, 123
  market research into, 58–59
Utilities, 11, 50, 51, 74, 109, 132, 138, 162, 188, 219, 224, 226, 227, 234, 243, 247
Utility buildings, 95

Vacancy rate, 39
Vacant land, 6, 14, 16, 25, 101, 122, 132, 197
  basic rules for buying, 145–146
  check list for purchase and development, 273–278
  financing, 93
  leasing, 126, 216–217
  as poor investment, 188–189
  risks in, 163–164
  selecting location to buy, 50–51
  as sound investment, 209–212
  timing in purchase of, 51–52
  value as open space, 156
Vacation residences:
  condominiums, 144, 251
  risks in, 163–164
Veterans Administration, 84, 115

Warehouses, 27, 28, 183
  converting to other uses, 199–200
  as investment winners, 145
  See also Miniwarehouses
Water supply, 11, 95, 138, 145, 156, 191, 214, 243, 249
  moratoria on, 151, 153
Winans, James W., 245
Wiring, 48
Women's liberation, 8
Working capital, 82, 84, 89, 121, 123
World War II, 30, 34, 41, 43, 117, 156, 200, 207
Wyman, Lance, 200
Wyman and Cannon, 200

Yankelovitch, Daniel, 231

Zeckendorf, Bill, 191
Zero population growth (ZPG), 192
Zoning, 6, 16, 25, 50, 62, 94, 95, 109, 128, 129, 147, 188, 189, 197, 201, 205, 206, 231, 243
  changes, 46, 47, 54, 60, 128, 149, 151, 157–161, 162, 196, 197, 205